THE URBAN ORIGINS
OF SUBURBAN AUTONOMY

Richardson Dilworth

The Urban Origins
of Suburban Autonomy

HARVARD UNIVERSITY PRESS

Cambridge, Massachusetts, and London, England   2005

Publication of this book has been aided by a generous grant from the New Jersey Historical
Commission.

Library of Congress Cataloging-in-Publication Data

Dilworth, Richardson, 1971–
    The urban origins of suburban autonomy / Richardson Dilworth.
      p.   cm.
    Includes bibliographical references and index.
    ISBN 0-674-01531-2 (alk. paper)
      1. Metropolitan areas—United States—History.   2. Suburbs—United States—History.
    3. Infrastructure (Economics)—United States—History.   4. Annexation (Municipal
    government)—United States—History.   I. Title.
    HT334.U5D55   2004
    307.76'4'0973—dc22   2004054250

To Martha

Contents

Acknowledgments

While I suspect that its origins are locked somewhere deep in my psyche, this book began to take a visible form during my time at Johns Hopkins University, and I am grateful to a number of people at that institution who provided inspiration, support, friendship, and intimidation at various points when it was needed. I owe the biggest debt to Matthew Crenson, who provided knowledge, direction, a willingness to listen seriously, valuable criticism, and incredibly detailed editorial comments. Benjamin Ginsberg, Ronald Walters, Gordon Wolman, and John Boland told me most importantly what they did not like, and this book is better for their criticism.

A number of other people graciously extended me a hand in this project. Jameson Doig and Zane Miller both read an earlier version of the manuscript and made invaluable comments. Heather Miller at Ohio State University Press and Michael Aronson at Harvard University Press provided both comments on the manuscript and confidence that my work was worthy. Also at Harvard University Press, Rebecca Hartshorn ably guided my manuscript through the publication process. John Donohue and Charles Eberline at Westchester Book Services gave the book a final and much-needed polish. Patricia Atkins and Paul Mattingly made comments on early versions of what is now the introduction and Chapter 1. Claire Felbinger gave advice on what became Chapter 2 and has been a general source of inspiration for the study of urban infrastructure. During my year as a visiting instructor at Temple University, Barbara Ferman, Sarah Hill, Joe Schwartz, Dan Hajdo, and Nancy Johnson all listened to a presentation of my work and made important comments. Amy Slaton, Bill Rosenberg, Julie Mostov, Erik Rau, Christian Hunold, and Eric Brose worked me over in a constructive fashion during my job talk at Drexel University. Dan Dougherty and Scott Knowles have also been willing listeners, at least over drinks.

It would have been impossible to write this book without the local documents and newspapers preserved at the public libraries of Newark, Jersey City, Hoboken, Bayonne, Mount Vernon, Yonkers, Brooklyn, Queens, and, of course, the New York Public Library, whose collection of obscure local documents provided constant amazement. Several librarians went out of their way to help me. In Jersey City, Ken French, Charles Markey, Bruce Brandt, and John Norton let me have the run of the local history collection after pointing me in useful directions. I would probably not have found Arnold Steigman's important works on Yonkers if John Favareau of the Yonkers Public Library had not pointed them out to me. At Bayonne, Dipali Sen eagerly shared with me her stash of local history. Vincent Seyfried's heroic work in indexing and transcribing Queens County newspapers (now part of the Long Island collection at the Queens Borough Public Library) was a terrific help. Anyone who has written a work on Newark appreciates the enthusiasm and help of Charles Cummings. Also at Newark, Paul Stellhorn took the time to sit with me and discuss my argument. His own dissertation on that city was an inspiration to me.

Thanks as well to Sage Publications for allowing work previously published in two articles to appear in this book in revised form: "From Sewers to Suburbs: Transforming the Policy-Making Context of American Cities," *Urban Affairs Review* 38 (May 2003): 726–739 (© 2003 Sage Publications); and "Urban Infrastructure Politics and Metropolitan Growth: Lessons from the New York Metropolitan Region," *Public Works Management & Policy* 6 (January 2002): 200–214 (© 2002 Sage Publications).

Outside of libraries and universities, I have been blessed with friends and family who have taught me more about urbanism and city life (among other things) than they will ever know. I was raised in Philadelphia by two realtors, Annabelle and Richardson Dilworth, whose occupation sowed the seeds of an interest in urban affairs. When I moved to New York, I developed a circle of friends—Sam Tyler, Andrew Kist, Doug Tyler, Chris Antista, Charles Kassouf, Enslow Kable, Emma Wilson, Jen Eno, Ted Peck, Doris Lee, and Jen and Archie McAlister—who gave me a passion for their city that provided the emotional foundation for this book. Some of them have left New York, but they always return. Finally, my wife, Martha Lucy, has read and made important comments on several earlier versions of this book. She has also preserved my sanity and made life worth living. This book is dedicated to her.

THE URBAN ORIGINS
OF SUBURBAN AUTONOMY

Introduction: Urbanism, Infrastructure, Politics

The sewer is the conscience of the city.

—Victor Hugo

Throughout the nineteenth century and well into the twentieth, cities in the United States replaced their cesspools, privy vaults, drainage pipes, wells, cisterns, oil lamps, and dirt roads with unified sewerage, water supply, and lighting systems that ran underneath streets newly paved with such things as macadam, "Telford," "Nicholson," and asphalt. I refer to these processes collectively as "infrastructural development" or "public works" and use them to examine the long-term impact of developmental policies on urban politics. Infrastructural development was a classic developmental policy, meaning that it was an important tool that cities used to attract labor and capital.[1] I argue, however, that central city infrastructural development also contributed inadvertently to the establishment of independent suburbs that had the capacity to become rivals to the central city. Cities competed with one another for labor and capital through infrastructural development. At the same time, central city infrastructural development increased intercity competition by contributing to the development of independent, technologically advanced suburbs.

Infrastructural development was a necessary feature of urban growth. As sociologist Louis Wirth noted in his famous 1938 article "Urbanism as a Way of Life," "the living together of large numbers of heterogeneous individuals under dense conditions is not possible without the development of a more or less technological structure."[2] Indeed, without the development of comprehensive infrastructure systems, cities would never have achieved the levels of population and population density that they did. Without water and sewerage systems, disease epidemics and devastating fires would have kept city

1

populations at qualitatively lower levels. As Los Angeles's William Mulholland noted in 1905, "A city quickly finds its level . . . and that level is its water supply."[3]More effective street lighting increased public safety and order, thereby making cities livable environments for a greater range of people. Thus to establish a connection between the public works that sustained the central city and municipal independence in the suburbs is to uncover the urban origins of suburban autonomy—also known as "metropolitan fragmentation" or "polycentricity"—which itself has been a defining element in the political development of metropolitan regions in the United States.

Historians such as Sam Warner and Kenneth Jackson have argued that infrastructural development was an important tool that cities used to expand their jurisdictions. Suburban residents wanted their communities to be annexed to the central city with the expectation that the city's water and sewerage systems would be extended into their streets. Likewise, cities have often held out the promise of water, sewerage, and other "street improvements" as an incentive for the surrounding communities to agree to consolidation.[4] Certainly, infrastructural development provided the means by which central cities could annex some outlying territories, but it also set limits to cities' geographic expansion. Cities' geographic entrapment by the turn of the twentieth century laid the groundwork for the flight of middle-class residents and businesses to the surrounding suburbs, which contributed importantly to cities' economic decline and the various pathologies associated with the post–World War II urban crisis.[5]

Central city infrastructural development provided both the means and the motivation for surrounding suburbs to become (or, in other instances, remain) independent municipalities. An intimate relationship between central city infrastructural development and political corruption generated the motivation for suburban autonomy. New public works projects in cities made millions of dollars available to politicians, who used that money to build their power and enrich themselves through padded contracts, insider real estate deals, and other nefarious practices. For instance, political "bosses" in each of the three central cities examined in this book—William Tweed in New York, William Bumsted in Jersey City, and James Smith Jr. in Newark—put themselves personally in charge of the city agency that had responsibility for public works. One result was that large infrastructure projects in cities were often accompanied by well-publicized political scandals. As cities then attempted to expand their borders by annexing outlying communities, they met resistance from suburbanites who did not want to be taxed at exorbitant levels to support what they viewed as venal political organizations.

Suburban infrastructural development provided the means for suburban autonomy. Central city infrastructural development facilitated suburban infrastructural development, and thus suburban autonomy, in at least two ways. First, engineers and contractors who had been trained on large infrastructure projects in central cities could sell their expertise to suburban communities that wanted infrastructure systems installed. A greater degree of infrastructural development in the city created a larger pool of experienced engineers and contractors and thus more competitive markets for expertise, which subsequently lowered the costs of suburban infrastructural development. Second, large public works projects in cities led to the technological advancement of infrastructure systems that decreased their costs and thus made them available to smaller communities.

Infrastructural development, of course, was not the only cause of suburban autonomy, but the relationship between infrastructural development and suburban autonomy has several important implications for the study of urban history and politics. For instance, in what is still the most comprehensive theoretical treatment of urban developmental policies, political scientist Paul Peterson argued in his book *City Limits* (1981) that cities are constrained to pursue policies that either enhance or at least do not harm the benefit-tax ratio of their largest taxpayers (that is, developmental or "allocational" policies) because they exist in a context of greater competition for resources (labor and capital) than do states or nations, which are more able to pursue redistributive policies.[6] Yet I will argue in this book that a classic developmental policy had the effect of reinforcing metropolitan fragmentation and thus the competitive context in which cities operate. If intercity competition compels cities to pursue developmental policies, and if developmental policies stimulate intercity competition, then there is a cyclical process at work in which the pursuit of developmental policies propels the pursuit of still more developmental policies. Water and sewerage systems serve to reinforce the later construction of shopping malls, industrial parks, and sports stadiums. I will extend this argument in the Conclusion to suggest that, paradoxically, the pursuit of developmental policies serves to reinforce municipal borders while at the same time blurring the distinction between cities and suburbs.

On the one hand, proponents of metropolitan fragmentation argue that greater intercity competition compels local governments to better match the services they provide to the needs of their residents and to supply those services more efficiently.[7] On the other hand, a number of authors have argued that metropolitan fragmentation leads to a socioeconomic "sorting" in which some cities, often outlying suburban municipalities, become middle- and upper-class enclaves, while other cities, often the older ones that form the central core of a metropolitan region, become repositories of the lower class.[8] Both sides of this debate treat metropolitan fragmentation as either an independent or an exogenous variable: regional inequality of local government resources (or greater efficiency through competition) is caused by metropolitan fragmentation; or metropolitan fragmentation provides the framework by which local government resources can be unequally distributed (or more efficiently provided). In contrast, the argument that I make in this book treats metropolitan fragmentation as an intermediary process in which urban services are not merely conceived of as things that might be provided efficiently or inefficiently in an equitable or inequitable manner, but are also viewed as evolutionary processes that transform the context in which they were formulated. Central city infrastructural development that ostensibly benefited all city residents may have also inadvertently facilitated a socioeconomic sorting through metropolitan fragmentation that created greater inequality in local service delivery within metropolitan regions. Thus the connection between infrastructural development and suburban autonomy suggests possible constraints under which contemporary urban policy operates.

Other authors have been more attentive to the motives for, and causes of, suburban autonomy, which has been explained with reference to such things as residential demand for racial, ethnic, and socioeconomic homogeneity; realtors and land developers who sought to capitalize on residential demand; or entrepreneurial town officials and business leaders.[9] While these explanations are no doubt valid, they are narrowly conceived, because they all hold that the motives for suburban autonomy arise from individuals or other actors who are at most only tangentially related to the central city. By contrast, I discuss suburban autonomy in this book as a product of city government policy and thus as an inherent part of urbanization, at least within a specific legal and political context. Whatever the motives for suburban autonomy, they were most often expressed through suburban infrastructural development, which was itself a product of central city infrastructural development.

For instance, nativism may have motivated the suburbanite "Yankee middle class" to prefer municipal autonomy in order to remain free of the city's "Celtic machines."[10] But suburbanites also wanted adequate water and sewerage. If the suburban officials were able to provide public works while maintaining municipal autonomy, they were often able to do so only because technological advances, based on the experience from public works in cities, had made infrastructure systems affordable for smaller communities. Thus the ability to express nativist sentiments through a municipal border depended on city government policy. Where suburban communities were not able to provide themselves with adequate infrastructure, residents' desire for municipal services could lead them to eschew concerns about ethnicity and approve annexation to the city, as happened when Bergen City residents approved the annexation of their community to Jersey City, a topic discussed at greater length in Chapter 4. In other instances, infrastructural development might maintain suburban autonomy even where there were no class and ethnic differences between the municipalities to be annexed, as was the case with the failed Greater Orange movement, discussed in Chapter 5.

Infrastructural development also serves to qualify the link that historians have traditionally made between transportation and metropolitan growth. Speaking of the turn-of-the-century transformation of the "walking city" into one "segregated by class and economic function and encompassing an area triple the territory," Kenneth Jackson claims that "the electric streetcar was the key to the shift." Likewise, Sam Warner claims that "the building of the metropolis can be analyzed in terms of the street railway alone."[11] In fact, my argument suggests that transportation served a much different role in "building the metropolis" than did other forms of infrastructure. A sewerage system that serves all of the neighborhoods of a city or all of the municipalities within a metropolitan region will bring those communities closer together, at least in the sense that those communities will have to make decisions jointly on the public good that they share. But each of the neighborhoods in a city, or each of the municipalities within a metropolitan region, may be served by separate sewerage systems that effectively keep those areas separate from one another, both physically and socially. Disregarding questions of economies of scale, it makes no difference whether an area is served by one or several sewerage systems in terms of the good provided, sewage disposal. By contrast, the good provided by a transportation system, moving people and goods from one place to another, depends directly on how far that transportation system extends. Thus sewerage can separate communities as much as it can bring them together; transportation, practically by definition, always serves to connect communities in new ways.

Suburban residents in the New York metropolitan region who were opposed to annexation typically argued that they would gain nothing from being absorbed into the neighboring central city, because their community already had adequate water, sewerage, and street pavement. Those in favor of annexation usually touted more adequate and less expensive public works as the main benefit of being part of a larger city. Hardly ever did transportation come up in suburban annexation debates, in large part because rail systems served both cities and suburbs without threatening suburban autonomy. Rail companies hardly cared if they served a metropolitan community fragmented into numerous separate municipalities as long as they reached the most customers. In Brooklyn and Vailsburg (a suburb annexed to Newark), transportation did figure into annexation debates, and I discuss why these are special cases in the relevant chapters. But in general, although there is also little doubt that transportation systems contributed to urban growth in a variety of ways, there is also little evidence that they had much impact on suburban autonomy and metropolitan fragmentation.

The connection that I make between infrastructural development and suburban autonomy also reverses the traditional understanding of the relationship between city politics and "the larger socioeconomic and political context."[12] As Peterson and others have argued, social and economic processes over which cities have no control largely determine the character of urban politics. Moreover, cities have no legal authority beyond what they are granted by their state government. As we will see throughout the case studies of the New York metropolitan region, actions taken at the state level had a significant impact on city politics.[13] Thus it is no doubt true that we can explain city politics in large part through processes beyond the city limits, but by arguing that a developmental policy within the central city played a significant role in shaping the city's geographic limits, I am suggesting that there is a recursive path between city politics and at least part of the larger context—the metropolitan region—in which city politics takes place. I am thus proposing a new way in which we can link the study of politics within cities to the study of those external factors that affect city politics.

The Urban Origins of Suburban Autonomy offers four case studies of expansionist efforts by three central cities in the New York metropolitan region, each of which met with varying levels of suburban acceptance, resistance, or rejection. (See Figures 1–3.) If infrastructural development is one of the defining elements of urbanism, then it is appropriate to examine public works in the New York metropolitan region, which has long defined what it means to be urban in the United States. The New York metropolitan region is also a useful subject for analysis because it had multiple central cities that were recognized as such even in the nineteenth century. Given that cities operate within the confines of state policy, it is also advantageous that the three central cities examined here are spread across two states. Thus central city infrastructural development can be compared across different contexts, yet within the same metropolitan region, which also means that possible variations in such things as geography, climate, and date of European occupation will not affect the comparisons.

Figure 1. Newark, Jersey City, and New York City in 1865, with surrounding suburbs

The definition of central city depends on context. Brooklyn was much larger than Jersey City, but because of its location in New York State, next to Manhattan, it was also a suburb of New York City. Jersey City may have been in large part a residential suburb of New York City as well, but it was the largest and most industrialized city in Hudson County, and Newark was likewise the largest and most industrialized city in Essex County. Specific behaviors also marked central cities. Newark, Jersey City, and New York

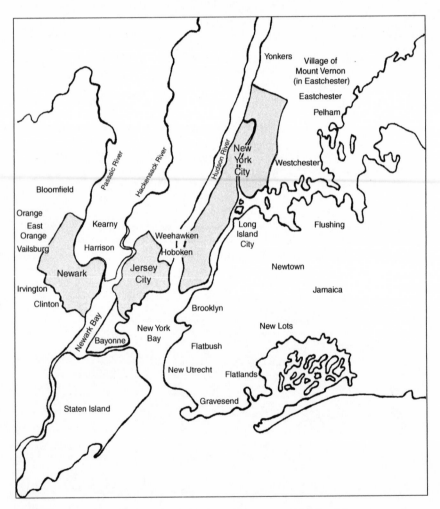

Figure 2. Newark, Jersey City, and New York City in 1875, with surrounding suburbs

City all acted more like central cities than surrounding municipalities, principally, for my purposes, because these were the three cities that were most interested in annexing outlying territory. Finally, my definition of Newark, Jersey City, and New York City as central cities follows contemporary descriptions of these cities in the nineteenth and early twentieth centuries.

Prior to the case studies, Chapter 1 provides a more comprehensive and detailed version of the argument made in this Introduction. It uses "rational

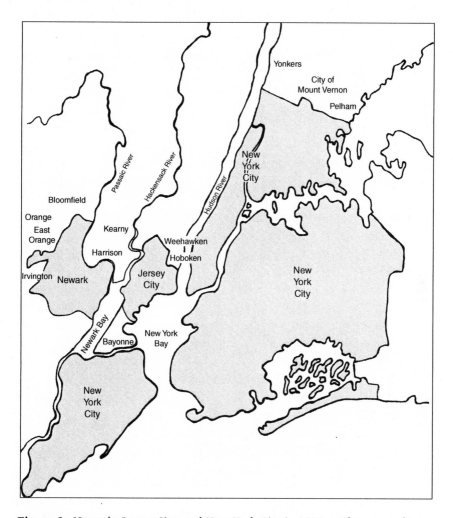

Figure 3. Newark, Jersey City, and New York City in 1905, with surrounding suburbs

choice" or "public choice" notions of public goods and collective action to establish a theoretical link between central city infrastructural development and metropolitan fragmentation and presents examples of infrastructural development from other metropolitan regions with which the case studies from New York and New Jersey can be compared.

Chapters 2, 3, 4, and 5 each provide a separate case study. Chapter 2 covers infrastructural development in New York City up through the Tweed Ring, the reform movement that followed, and the various attempts to expand the city into lower Westchester County that ultimately resulted in the annexation of Morrisania, West Farms, and Kingsbridge. Yonkers is compared with the annexed townships as a community that thwarted annexation and remained independent. Chapter 3 continues with New York City, this time examining the 1894 referendum on Greater New York, with a specific focus on Mount Vernon, Flushing, Long Island City, and Brooklyn.

The analysis moves across the Hudson River in Chapter 4 to Hudson County, New Jersey, where in 1869 residents in eleven municipalities voted on whether their communities should be annexed to Jersey City. The chapter focuses specifically on Hudson and Bergen Cities, where a majority of residents voted in favor of annexation; Hoboken and Bayonne, where residents voted by majorities against annexation; and Greenville, where residents initially voted against joining Jersey City, but then reversed themselves and approved annexation in 1872. Chapter 5 moves over to Essex County to discuss infrastructural development in Newark, leading up to the largely unsuccessful Greater Newark movement in the first decade of the twentieth century. I argue that the proponents of Greater Newark failed to achieve their expansionist goals in large part because Newark officials and businesses targeted for annexation communities that were already developed and thus had the least interest in consolidating with the central city.

The Conclusion expands the argument presented in Chapter 1 to propose that public choice arguments regarding the benefits of metropolitan fragmentation can be extended and qualified by the case studies to suggest that growing suburban autonomy as a result of central city infrastructural development can be understood as an evolutionary explanation of urban government and politics. Unlike public choice arguments that argue for the benefits of metropolitan fragmentation, an evolutionary explanation only suggests the reasons for change, although it certainly also can be used to inform contemporary urban policy.

CHAPTER 1

Private Benefits, Public Goods

Waterworks, sewerage, street lighting, and street paving have often been defined as an inherent responsibility of government in an urban milieu—a "public good." Infrastructure systems are costly, so often only a government can afford to build them. Because infrastructure systems have high economies of scale, they tend to be "natural monopolies," a fact that has also served as a rationale for government ownership or regulation. Finally, many of the benefits that infrastructure systems provide (sanitation, public health, public safety) are nondivisible and nonexcludable. Thus in many instances, private actors have no incentive to provide infrastructure systems, and if they are to be provided at all, they must be supplied by a government that can force people to pay for them through taxation.[1]

Like all public goods, the provision of infrastructure systems faces a possible collective action dilemma, since each individual actor has an incentive to shirk the responsibility for providing them or for pressuring the government to provide them. As Mancur Olson has famously explained, collective action dilemmas can often be overcome if "selective incentives"—private, noncollective benefits—are provided to the individuals who would supply the public good.[2] In this chapter I sketch out a general model of how various actors realized private benefits that provided the motivation for them to supply the public goods of waterworks, sewers, streets, and streetlights.

It is also my purpose in this chapter to explain how central city infrastructural development had systematic and unintended consequences that facilitated suburban autonomy, or metropolitan fragmentation. The notion that collective action is motivated by selective incentives provides a theoretical link between central city infrastructural development and metropolitan fragmentation. Metropolitan fragmentation can be described as a collective action dilemma: municipalities, separately pursuing their own individual

11

benefits, do not act collectively to realize larger, metropolitan public goods.[3] As cities overcame the problem of collective action in building infrastructure systems, they created a new collective action dilemma in the larger metropolitan region.

Public and Private Interests in Infrastructural Development

When benefits are more private than public (that is, more divisible and excludable), interested actors are more likely to take proactive steps to provide themselves with the good in question. When a good is more public than private, actors receive greater benefit if they themselves do not provide the good. Yet if all actors wait for someone else to provide a public good, it will obviously never be supplied, and a collective action dilemma results. The type of prospective benefits expected from a good determines the actions of interested parties and thus the type of good actually provided.

A case in point is gas street lighting. From the very beginning in the early nineteenth century, most American cities relied on private companies to supply gas for street lighting. Private companies were motivated to provide gasworks and distributing systems because they expected to profit from the sale of gas to private customers. But companies' distribution networks relied crucially on the city's previous work of opening and grading the streets. The private provision of gas thus depended on the larger public good supplied by the city's street system. For the right of gas companies to use the streets to lay out their distribution networks, cities compelled the companies to also provide gas for streetlights. Thus provision of the public good of street lighting depended on the individual benefits that companies expected from selling gas as a private good.[4]

While the profit-making motives of gas companies could be harnessed to supply the public good of street lighting, the same was not true of water companies. At least in the nineteenth and early twentieth centuries, where private companies rather than the city government supplied water, those companies provided water of lesser quality to fewer people and for fewer city services, such as street cleaning and fire fighting, in order to lower costs and thus increase their profits. As city populations increased, and as water became more essential for fulfilling such public functions as sanitation and street cleaning, most major cities either built public waterworks or purchased waterworks from the private companies that had previously served the city. By 1860 three-quarters of the sixteen largest American cities had municipally owned water supply systems.[5]

Public ownership did not eliminate the profit motive in water systems. Many municipalities, including Philadelphia, Milwaukee, and Jersey City, sold their water as a private good to neighboring municipalities.[6] Moreover, some cities had public waterworks, but bought their water from private companies. For example, many suburban municipalities around Newark bought their water from the East Jersey Water Company, a subject that will be discussed at greater length in Chapter 5. Many American cities have also essentially sold street pavement on a piecemeal basis. From approximately the late eighteenth to the late nineteenth century, streets were paved when property owners representing some majority (usually two-thirds) of the property abutting a street petitioned the city council. The property owners specified the type of pavement, and the city had the streets paved, collected a special assessment from the property owners, and took responsibility for maintenance. The result, as one might expect, was that streets were more often paved in wealthier neighborhoods than in poorer ones. In some cities, such as Newark, sewers were also provided through special assessments on the basis of resident petitions.[7]

Piecemeal infrastructural development may have made sense from the standpoint of short-run financial concerns and indeed was often the only economically feasible option, but from the standpoint of long-run concerns for efficiency, economy, and public health, cities fared better with a more comprehensive, general plan for infrastructural development. Piecemeal street paving motivated residents to choose gravel pavement, which was cheaper to install than asphalt or block pavement, but was more expensive to maintain and thus cost city governments more in the long run than if they had centralized operations and used low-maintenance pavement on all city streets. Similarly, comprehensive, citywide infrastructural development lowered per-unit costs because it took greater advantage of economies of scale.[8]

If comprehensive, centrally planned infrastructural development approximated a public good more closely than piecemeal construction, there were still plenty of individualized, private benefits to be had on the supply side of public works in the form of jobs, contracts, and bribes involved in building and maintenance. If the goods produced by a government service cannot be consumed privately, compensation for providing them (that is, money) might be. Political scientist Matthew Crenson has argued that city government is distinctive for this very reason. Having evolved from centralized, top-down "machines," city bureaucracies are distinguished by the relative "purity" (that is, nonexcludability and nondivisibility) of the public goods they supply, such as public order, safety, and cleanliness in the forms of police patrols, sanitation, and public schooling. This purity is maintained because city services are provided to a disorganized public at large rather than to any particular clientele group. Consumers of city services are therefore unlikely to shape government-supplied goods and services to their more private, individualized needs, as happened in many areas of national government policy.[9]

The relatively pure public goods provided by city governments offer little in the way of private benefits to the individuals who consume them, and thus, as Olson has argued more generally, these individuals have little motivation to organize into interest groups to shape them.[10] The police officers, sanitation workers, and teachers who supply these goods, however, receive private benefits in the form of paychecks and have been notably successful at organizing through unions to shape the contracts from which they all collectively benefit. As Crenson comments, "Like a production line being run in reverse, urban governments often seem to produce public services and facilities primarily for the sake of consuming the raw materials needed to manufacture them."[11]

Of course, a union-negotiated contract can only be produced within the context of a bureaucratic agency where employees receive fixed annual salaries. It is, in other words, a collective good "nested" within the institutional structure of city government.[12] Before this system, municipal service providers such as police officers and street cleaners worked essentially as private contractors to the city, which paid them on a piecemeal basis for work performed. Piecemeal service provision by contract prevented organization among workers because they were in constant competition with one another to catch criminals or clean streets. Instead, workers would organize vertically along the production line. Police officers, for instance, would make deals with thieves where the thief would, with immunity, turn over the stolen property to the officer for a cut of the reward money.[13] Although one of the touted benefits of the private contracting system is that the competition between contractors produces higher-quality services delivered more efficiently than city employees organized into unions and protected by civil service laws, a powerful criticism of this form of privatization is that it motivates graft and corruption as contractors attempt to organize by other means.[14]

As the construction of urban infrastructure systems was mostly by contract, we would expect this policy area to be characterized by such vertical organization along the production line, and there is indeed some evidence to show that this was the case. Unlike the previous example in police work, private contractors in the field of infrastructural development organized upward, with city council members, departmental personnel, or others who awarded city contracts and jobs. New York City's Tweed Ring is famous for letting contractors overcharge the city in exchange for a cut of the profits. This process was later continued within the constraints of the law under Tammany boss Charles Murphy. "Tammany men became open or secret partners in contracting firms, using the pressure of political power to have large contracts awarded to their concerns. It was not necessary for these leaders to know anything of contracting . . . their one aim was to get the contracts; the actual skilled work could be done by hired professional men."[15] In Cincinnati, utility companies regularly employed politicians who could award them franchises with the city. In *The Shame of the Cities,* Lincoln Steffens reported that "boodlers" in the municipal governments of both Philadelphia and St. Louis intended to sell out their respective waterworks "to a private concern" at a vastly discounted price in exchange for a healthy kickback. By colluding with the providers of public goods formally external to the government process, city officials might capture some of the private benefits of supplying public goods.[16]

The Beneficiaries

In short, in discussing the benefits of public works, it is important to distinguish between those benefits on the demand side (public health, order, safety, sanitation, economic development) and those on the supply side (wages, contracts, kickbacks). Supply- and demand-side benefits together determine the beneficiaries of infrastructural development. How these beneficiaries act, or fail to act, in relation to one another determines the politics of infrastructural development.

If actors are more likely to provide a public good when they receive private benefits, we would expect to see a more active politics on the supply side of infrastructural development, generated by the private benefits of wages, contracts, and kickbacks. The more diffuse public benefits provided on the demand side would be less likely to create political action. Political scientist Paul Peterson has suggested another reason why infrastructural development would be unlikely to generate much in the way of demand-side politics. Infrastructural development is a classic developmental policy because waterworks, sewerage, streetlights, and street pavement make cities economically viable and competitive. According to Peterson, developmental policies benefit all city residents and are therefore largely apolitical, "developed in a consensual fashion," and carried out by "respected community leaders" with the tacit consent of the general public.[17]

To a great extent, Peterson's argument about the politics of developmental policies is confirmed by the history of infrastructural development in the United States. By the late nineteenth century there was certainly wide agreement that cities' viability and sustainability depended on adequate water, sewerage, street pavement, and street lighting. Especially before germ theory had weakened the claims of moral environmentalists, better city sanitation through greater quantities of water, better sewers, and paved streets were seen as important elements in the establishment of social order. Yet there was at least some resistance to public works on the demand side. As historian Christine Rosen notes, "Once basic public services were established, people tended to make do with what they had, no matter how unsafe, inadequate, or inconvenient it was."[18] Other historians have found residential resistance to large-scale waterworks out of a sense of attachment and pride in neighborhood pumps, and resistance to new street pavements that would increase vehicular traffic, since that limited alternate uses for streets, such as play areas for children.[19]

Residents also often had legitimate concerns about major new public works projects that might incur ruinous municipal debts.[20] Indeed, as will be illustrated in the chapters that follow, public officials' interest in building infrastructure systems for the selective benefits they would receive (for example, kickbacks from contractors or insider information that would help them make profitable real estate transactions), rather than for the public good provided, could serve as prima facie evidence of fiscal recklessness that would result in high debt and onerous tax hikes. Peterson's "respected community leaders" were often in short supply, and city residents perceived that their officials were operating as self-interested actors. It is one of the ironies of infrastructural development that the same private benefits that generated the motivations for public officials to provide public works also created resistance among residents and businesses on the demand side.

Among actors on the supply side of infrastructural development, engineers may have had the least reason to resort to graft. Rather than guaranteeing their role in public works by providing private benefits to public officials, engineers established themselves as neutral experts, without whom infrastructural development could often do more harm than good. Expertise also served as a source of power within city government. In numerous cities during the late nineteenth century, most notably in New England and in larger cities throughout the country, municipal engineers served continuously through different administrations of different parties, retained because of their expertise and knowledge of that city's infrastructure. City engineers were independent enough that they could serve as consultants to other cities without threatening their position at home.[21]

Possibly professionalism did not so much absolve engineers and other experts from the politics of infrastructural development as it placed them in separate but overlapping political realms. For instance, the efforts of physicians to gain a voice in Cincinnati government, specifically concerning the city's water supply, were thwarted by a coalition of business organizations and the local engineers' club. This suggests that engineers used business connections to maintain their professional turf. In speaking of the advent of uniform asphalt street paving at the turn of the century, historian Clay McShane comments that "the arguments made by engineers for smooth pavements to serve public health needs seem to be largely political propaganda," disguising a somewhat blind and irrational belief in technological advancement, an obsession they apparently shared with most city planners. Finally, in an area of emerging and unproven technologies, there was plenty of room for debate that could move quickly into personal sniping where competing experts attempted to discredit one another's claims by questioning their professional ethics, as engineers questioned George Waring's promotional efforts on behalf of the separated sewerage system, to which he held the patent.[22]

On the demand side, infrastructure systems created a variety of public benefits and thus a variety of beneficiaries. Residents experienced the benefits of infrastructural development primarily as part of the "use value" of property—it provided them with quality water supplied through an indoor faucet, indoor water closets that drained properly, and better heating and lighting through gas and, later, electricity. By contrast, real estate brokers and developers experienced the benefits of infrastructural development as an "exchange value" because it enhanced the sale price of property at the expense of taxpayers.[23] Fire insurance companies had a vested interest in upgrading of cities' water supply systems.[24] Business in general, organized into chambers of commerce, for instance, supported infrastructural development as an economic development policy that made the city more attractive to labor and capital.

Different demand-side interests had varying levels of ability to organize collectively in order to secure the benefits of infrastructural development. When residents were aware and accepting of the benefits infrastructural development offered, they faced daunting challenges to articulating their demand. As previously noted, demand for government services had traditionally been fragmented geographically into streets and neighborhoods, as well as wards, a product of the method by which political machines maintained control. Thus in the case of Baltimore, ward-based parochialism was strong enough that "the city first envisioned a set of eight sewerage systems rather than a single comprehensive system." When neighborhoods did organize for the sake of infrastructural development or the improvement of other city services, they often operated counterproductively by competing with one another for city services.[25] The collective action dilemmas that impeded the articulation of demand for comprehensive infrastructural development could thus be embedded within the institutional structure of a city's political system.

In contrast, insurance companies, real estate developers, and other business interests had more resources and more cohesive organizational structures through which they could articulate their demands for infrastructural development more effectively than individual residents. Fire insurance companies organized at both local and national levels in the form of boards of fire underwriters "to pressure municipalities into upgrading their fire-fighting forces, increasing their water supplies, adopting building codes that prohibited flammable construction, and enacting ordinances outlawing fire hazards." Likewise, "Powerful corporations and business district property owners enjoyed privileged positions . . . that generally gave them an advantage in demanding that improvements be made."[26]

Interested parties also attempted to alter the institutional structure of city government itself to make it more likely to undertake citywide infrastructural development projects. For instance, the ward-based system of service delivery in Baltimore resulted in a plan for eight separate sewerage systems, as previously mentioned, but the charter reform of 1898, which empowered the mayor relative to the city council and reorganized the administration of municipal services along functional lines, facilitated the development of a single, comprehensive system, a bond issue for which was approved by referendum in 1905. The centralization of power under the auspices of the 1898 charter was reinforced by the creation of a special Burnt District Commission appointed by the mayor and authorized to redevelop Baltimore's downtown after the city's devastating 1904 fire. The city council's power over the commission was limited to approving its redevelopment plans without amendment. By thus centralizing power, the Burnt District Commission was able to implement most of the planned improvements to the burned-out area, including the widening of streets, the redevelopment of the harbor, and the laying of drains in preparation for the previously mentioned new sewerage system.[27]

Urban Infrastructure Games

Figure 4 is a general outline of the flow of private benefits that created the public good of infrastructural development. The radial distance of the different interests from the center of the figure is a rough indication of the relative strength of their relationships to city government. For instance, the relatively great overlap of personnel in the active membership of political parties and in city government is represented by their placement in adjacent concentric rings, while the lesser extent of overlap in personnel between the city government and the general residential population is shown by their positions in rings more distant from one another. Figure 4 also indicates that

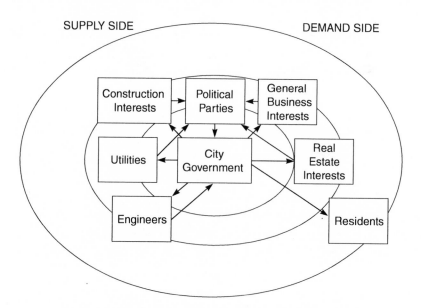

Figure 4. The flow of private benefits from public works

most of the graft by which private firms secured city government contracts was probably mediated through political party organizations.[28]

Each box in Figure 4 represents a cluster of interests who shared some common characteristics and motivations, but who also actively competed with one another for the private benefits that flowed from infrastructural development. For instance, within the "city government" box, the executive and the legislature might be involved in a power struggle with each other, while simultaneously the legislature might be attempting to thwart the efforts of a semi-independent commission to usurp discretionary power over a given infrastructure project. The executive, the legislature, and the commission might each be involved in different disputes with different resident groups or in different contract negotiations with construction companies or materials suppliers, any of which might shape the actions of the legislature, the executive, and the commission in relation to one another.

Political scientist and game theorist George Tsebelis has generalized the network of different actors who compete in different yet interlocking institutional contexts exemplified in Figure 4 as "games in multiple arenas." Tsebelis conceives of different "games" as situations where individual actors make choices between different actions that have prescribed "payoffs" (expressed as numbers on an ordinal scale in more rigorous analysis). The dilemma each actor faces is that the payoff from any given action he or she takes is affected by the actions other actors take. The classic story in such situations is the "Prisoner's Dilemma," which has been recounted in enough places that a detailed description here is unnecessary. It suffices to say that when two actors each have a choice between two actions (for example, to confess or not to confess to a crime), and when each actor's action determines not only the payoff he or she receives but also the payoff that the other actor receives, the two actors each face four possible payoffs (that is, the payoff if [1] one confesses and the other does not and [2] vice versa, and if both either [3] confess or [4] do not confess). The outcome will depend on the relative payoffs for each possible action an actor can make, given what that actor believes the other actor will do. With games in multiple arenas, each actor is involved in several games at once, the payoffs of which are interdependent.[29]

At least as I use the concept here, the prisoner's dilemma and other such "games" are simply more specific applications of the general problem posed by public goods: the private interests of individuals often preclude the benefits that could be realized through cooperative behavior. The advantage of thinking about public goods in terms of games is that this approach simplifies a complex process by reducing an institutional context to a combination of payoffs and defining actors in terms of those payoffs. The relative values of the different payoffs then determine the extent to which individual self-interested actors will be able to realize a public good.

To return to the situation represented in Figure 4, imagine that a city councilman at the turn of the twentieth century faced the choice of voting for or against a certain infrastructure project. The councilman was involved in a legislative game with other council members in which his vote determined to some extent whether or not the project would be undertaken. The payoffs to the councilman in this game were determined in part by how much he perceived the infrastructure project would contribute to his chances for reelection. If he believed that the residents of his ward were more concerned about the increased taxes they would pay because of the project than the benefits that they might receive, he might have voted against it. Yet by voting for the project, he might also have been doing one or more of his fellow councilmen a favor, for which he would expect a future payback. Thus in his voting for or against the proposed project, the councilman was playing a legislative game, the payoffs of which were determined by the electoral game he was also playing with each of the voters in his ward, where his vote would determine the payoffs they perceived in voting for or against him in the next election.

We can complicate the situation of the councilman in two important ways. First, the councilman was of course aware that voters had only imperfect information about his actions on the city council, and thus his reelection did not depend directly on how he voted. Second, voters' imperfect information opened up the possibility that the councilman could benefit personally from infrastructural development. By voting for a large-scale infrastructure project, for instance, the councilman might have gotten to choose some of the contractors for the project. In their gratitude for being chosen, the contractors might have contributed to the councilman's next reelection campaign, perhaps using funds that they received from their contract. The contractor might also have been willing to hire laborers from the councilman's district, thereby increasing the councilman's chances of reelection. It is even conceivable that the councilman could have dispensed with an intermediate party and simply have awarded a contract to himself.

The more ways in which a councilman might have expected to benefit personally from infrastructural development, the higher his payoff in voting for a given infrastructure project, thus making infrastructural development in the city a more likely outcome. However, the extent to which a councilman could personally benefit from infrastructural development was inversely proportional to the level of voter information about the councilman's actions. If voters were aware that their elected representative on the city council was benefiting personally from his relationship with contractors, they might have suspected that the councilman was not working on the voters' behalf.

The example of a highly publicized infrastructural development campaign in the District of Columbia in the 1870s suggests that the greater the extent to which government officials were benefiting personally from infrastructural development, and thus the greater the extent of infrastructural development, the more information voters would have about government actions. Residents in the District became active participants in the infrastructural development process, not only because of the high property assessments that resulted but also because homeowners had to pay for property renovations in order to adjust to changes in street grades. Thus affected by infrastructural development, residents were receptive to allegations that Alexander Shepard, the president of the board of public works and previously a city councilman, who was himself a contractor with ties to the city's street-paving industry, had let favored contractors overcharge the city. Several notable mistakes—a sewer main that ran uphill in places and wooden street pavements that began to rot within two years—only reinforced the image of incompetence and corruption. Although Shepard was not then an elected official, the revelations that resulted from the infrastructure projects he authorized and oversaw led Congress to disband the board of public works, thus putting Shepard out of a job.[30]

In order to avoid accusations of incompetence and corruption, government officials turned over much of the responsibility for infrastructural development to city engineers. Protected by their expertise, city engineers, as previously mentioned, were insulated from city politics and could use infrastructural development to establish national reputations and build consulting practices. Indeed, in the case of Washington, D.C., after firing Shepard, Congress hired the "acclaimed sanitary engineer Rudolph Hering" to fix the city's sewers.[31] Historians have argued that the construction of comprehensive sewerage and water supply systems elevated the importance of engineers in city government who dealt with the city as an organic, unified whole and thus provided the initial physical and intellectual basis for later progressive reforms such as comprehensive city planning, citywide elections, administrative centralization, "scientific management," and civil service reform.[32] However, these later reforms were in large part designed to undermine the power of traditional politicians; the game between reformers and politicians involved each party either winning or losing. Engineers and politicians, on the other hand, benefited in a reciprocal fashion from infrastructural development. Without politicians, engineers did not have the political and financial means to build infrastructure systems upon which they could base their careers. Without engineers, politicians lacked the cover of legitimacy they needed to build infrastructure systems that they could use to reward themselves, their friends, and their allies. Engineers and politicians thus played a cooperative game (what Tsebelis calls an "assurance" game) in which they advanced their respective careers and provided a public good in the process.[33]

If city officials got too greedy and extracted too much graft in the process of infrastructural development, the city might risk financial disaster, residents would suffer higher taxes, and the officials might lose their jobs or even end up in jail. Moreover, shoddy planning and construction could create public works that did more harm than good. But if city officials kept graft to a reasonable minimum, and if infrastructure systems worked as they were supposed to, the city would experience an increase in industrial and residential capacity that would expand its export potential, attract more labor and capital, create more jobs, increase property values, and improve the quality of life. In the latter case, infrastructural development was a classic developmental policy. In line with Peterson's argument, as long as infrastructural development served a developmental function, public works probably proceeded with little residential input. Yet with less residential input, public officials could extract more private benefits in the form of graft.

City officials may have benefited so much from public works that they looked for new ways to justify infrastructural development, even after all the streets were paved and all the water and sewer pipes were laid. In order to create new demands for infrastructural development, over which they would have control, city officials could attempt to annex outlying areas that had not yet been built up. Previous authors have often pointed out that suburban residents were motivated to approve the annexation of their communities to neighboring cities in order to gain access to urban services. As Kenneth Jackson notes in *Crabgrass Frontier,* "In the absence of decent sewerage, water, and educational systems, land speculators looked to annexation as a sort of guarantee to potential buyers that the suburb would eventually possess the comforts of the city." Sam Bass Warner states that the residents of Roxbury and West Roxbury approved the annexation of their communities to Boston in 1868 and 1873, respectively, because they wanted to gain access to services provided by the central city. Ann Durkin Keating relates of the suburbs surrounding Chicago that "residents found annexation . . . particularly appealing during the mid-1880s because the city had been rapidly extending its infrastructure."[34]

What has not yet been adequately explained is why cities were interested in annexing largely undeveloped land for which they would have to supply services. In the absence of a good rationale, historians have relied on a nebulous "booster spirit" or an "urban imperialism." On a more practical level, it has also been suggested that city officials and residents thought that municipal service delivery might achieve economies of scale in larger cities.[35] Yet the case studies in this book indicate that the search for more efficient service delivery is at best only a partial explanation of why city officials and residents suggested and approved annexations. Moreover, it was clearly obvious to many city residents and officials that their taxes might increase as a result of the supply of services to newly annexed territories.

If infrastructural development is understood as a process motivated by private benefits, a new explanation for annexation suggests itself. In order to maintain infrastructural development from which they personally benefited, city officials (along with engineers and contractors) needed new land to develop. The interests of the city overall, whether explained as boosterism, imperialism, or economies of scale, were only of secondary importance. "The city" made no decisions. Individuals made decisions, and individuals sought individual benefits.

Suburban residents were interested in annexation because they wanted new and better services. The lower the cost of these services, the greater the benefit to suburban residents. For city officials, the possibility of benefiting personally from public works increased along with the cost of public works, since that left more money to skim off the top. In another irony of infrastructural development, the motives that inspired both suburbanites and city officials to desire annexation also brought them into conflict over public works. Thus suburbanites faced a dilemma—in some cases, a Faustian bargain. Annexation was one of the easiest ways to gain access to new services that could increase property values and improve the quality of life, yet these benefits might be compromised by graft and corruption that came along with big-city government.

Infrastructural Development and Suburban Autonomy

Suburban communities might also remain independent municipalities and build their own infrastructure systems. Thus while Roxbury and West Roxbury had been annexed to Boston in part so that the city would extend its infrastructure to their residents, other suburban communities that had built or purchased their own infrastructure systems, such as Somerville and Cambridge, remained independent. Indeed, independent infrastructural development was sometimes a conscious strategy for maintaining suburban autonomy. In California during the first two decades of the twentieth century, political leaders in East Bay municipalities feared that if they were supplied water from the Hetch Hetchy aqueduct, they would risk a loss of independence and future consolidation with San Francisco; fears of consolidation provided at least part of the motivation for undertaking a separate aqueduct project.[36]

East Bay residents only had to look to Los Angeles to see that the geographic expansion of a central city was enabled by its water supply. In what has been described as the most important decision "ever made by the City of Los Angeles," voters approved $25 million worth of bonds in 1905 for the purposes of building the Los Angeles Aqueduct, which would supply the city with water from the Owens River. Upon completion of the Los Angeles Aqueduct in 1913, the city found itself with a surplus of water. The city council decided that outlying communities could be supplied with water from the Los Angeles Aqueduct, but only if they were annexed to the city. Shortly thereafter, residents in the San Fernando Valley and Palms voted in favor of annexation, and thus Los Angeles more than doubled in size. Until 1927 "Annexation campaigns were waged in every surrounding community . . . In long-established communities, both sides fought as though their future survival were at stake." The annexation movement came to a halt before the city of Los Angeles became coterminous with the county due to the construction of the Colorado River Aqueduct, which began supplying water to the residents of southern California in 1941. Operated by an independent, multistate governing body, the Colorado River Aqueduct could supply water to the communities around Los Angeles without the threat of their being annexed to the central city.[37]

A relationship between infrastructural development and suburban autonomy is also evident in the southeastern United States, for example, in the case of two neighboring suburbs of Birmingham, Alabama, Fairfield and

Ensley. A number of Birmingham suburbs were annexed to the city in 1910. Suburban residents around Birmingham supported annexation because, in the words of historian Carl Harris, "improved city services would make the higher city taxes worthwhile and would perhaps enhance the value of their property." Ensley was one of the communities annexed, while Fairfield remained just beyond the city's expanded borders. Both communities were company towns, Ensley for the Tennessee Coal, Iron, and Railroad Company (TCI) and Fairfield for a subsidiary of U.S. Steel. Both companies evidently did not want their property to fall within the limits of Birmingham and thus be subject to the higher city taxes. In the case of Ensley, TCI had enough political clout to make sure that its property remained outside the city limits, while the residential portion of the town was annexed to Birmingham. Unlike Ensley, in Fairfield, as one contemporary described, "all the fundamental utilities—streets, sidewalks, water, sewers, gas, electricity, etc.—were installed." Houses in Fairfield came "all equipped with bath, hot and cold water, electric light, and modern sanitary conveniences."[38] By establishing Fairfield as a community capable of providing the essential services its residents needed, business interests reduced the incentive for residents to demand annexation to the central city and thereby protected themselves from the city tax.

The relationship between infrastructural development and municipal autonomy is not simple or direct. Infrastructure systems were constructed and maintained through a variety of institutional arrangements. Anticipating what would become a major trend in infrastructural development by the mid-twentieth century, the water supply and sewerage systems that served the Boston area were placed under the control of independent metropolitan districts in the 1880s and 1890s, which allowed them to be extended to new areas without endangering home rule. A suburb might also have a central city extend its infrastructure into its jurisdiction for a fee, while remaining politically independent, or be supplied with water from a private company. According to census data, by 1915, of the 204 cities in the United States with populations of more than 30,000, 26 percent were served primarily by private water systems, 30 percent were served by municipally owned systems that served only city residents, and 44 percent were served by municipally owned systems that served residents both inside and outside the city limits. No cities besides those in the Boston area were served by a metropolitan district by this time.[39] While these statistics tell us very little definitively, they do suggest that there was no single arrangement that characterized the relationship between cities and suburbs in terms of infrastructural development. The arrangements by which water was supplied in a metropolitan region were no doubt varied and complex, and any explanation can therefore only capture a part of reality.

Technology and Autonomy

By the late nineteenth century, advancing infrastructure technology was making it progressively easier for suburban communities to remain independent. Previous authors have attributed the ability of suburbs to maintain their autonomy from central cities to permissive state incorporation laws, a growing affluence among suburban residents, which meant that they could afford their own municipal services, or the power of local business interests to shape municipal boundaries to their economic benefit, as was suggested in the cases of Ensley and Fairfield.[40]

What has largely been ignored in discussions of suburban autonomy is that not only increasing wealth but also the decreasing cost of infrastructural development provided by technological advances made the independent provision of municipal services possible for progressively smaller communities. For instance, the journal *Paving and Municipal Engineering* (which later became *Municipal Engineering*) reported in 1890 that the popularity of George Waring's separated sewerage system was "in a measure due to its comparative cheapness, which is a distinctive merit, because it enables places to have the benefits of sewerage which would otherwise not have them." In the same year, the journal also reported that "there was a time when water-works plants were thought of as being desirable only for cities and towns of large growth, but now in every progressive community of any considerable number of people, water-works are being brought into use as a convenience, if not a necessity . . . the reduction in the cost of plants, and the great improvement in the systems over all other kinds of water supply will make the business more general in the future." Likewise, the introduction of cheaper forms of asphalt and concrete, such as Portland cement, and more efficient lighting systems, such as the Welsbach incandescent gas light, reduced the costs of street paving and street lighting and gave smaller municipalities the opportunity to install infrastructure systems that were not only within the constraints of their budgets, but also had been technically refined and thus provided better services than the older systems in cities.[41]

In an analysis of why smaller and smaller towns in New England began to invest in water supply systems in the 1870s, economist Letty Anderson rejected the hypothesis that "a possible decline over time in the per capita cost of investment" led to the diffusion of waterworks into smaller communities. Anderson found that the per capita costs of water supply systems actually increased more than threefold from 1860 to 1897. Acknowledging changes in waterworks technology, Anderson was careful to note that her "figures may reflect only a change in the *type* of investment a town was likely to make . . . since characteristics of waterworks constructed after 1880 may not have been the same as those constructed earlier."[42] Increases in the per capita costs of water supply systems by no means preclude the possibility that the prices for water supply systems themselves were decreasing, as the previous passages from *Paving and Municipal Engineering* suggest. Decreasing prices would have brought waterworks within the budget constraints of smaller and smaller communities, even though these smaller communities were still paying higher prices per capita than larger communities.

According to Anderson, one factor that likely did have an impact on investment in waterworks was "the probability of a given town's receiving relevant technical information." Both the technological advancement of infrastructure and the diffusion of that technology were made possible by the emergence of a national and international engineering profession.[43] Professional journals and societies provided a medium through which individual experiences of infrastructural development could be accumulated, generalized into a unified body of knowledge, and codified into a professional language.[44] Prominent "cosmopolitan" engineers such as George Waring, Rudolph Hering, and Ellis Chesborough disseminated their knowledge and techniques personally through extensive consulting work, advancing their profession as a whole while enhancing their own personal status as professionals. The emergence of national trade associations related to municipal infrastructure in the 1870s, starting with the American Gas Light Association but spreading quickly to "waterworks, street railways, and electrical systems," also served to "speed up the diffusion of the latest advances in the industry to the hinterland."[45]

Many engineers who became prominent in the field of municipal infrastructure had built their reputations upon innovative work they had done in larger cities. For instance, Chesborough was perhaps best known for his work in Chicago, where "he built a two-mile tunnel under Lake Michigan to supply fresh water, dredged the river to provide adequate drainage, and used the fill to raise the streets," and Waring's reputation and consulting practice were both greatly enhanced by the separated sewerage system that he first installed in Memphis. Regarding the diffusion of infrastructure technology, historian Harold Platt notes that "most innovations in the gas business originated in cities with the biggest mass markets."[46] Since cities were the places where infrastructure systems were first needed, and city governments were among the few institutions with the resources and authority necessary to at least initiate the construction of such systems, the urban origins of infrastructural development should come as no great surprise.

The progression of infrastructural development into suburban communities was both a local and national process. Cosmopolitan engineers such as Waring became consultants to communities across the entire country, not to mention the rest of the world. Likewise, by the 1870s at least some forms of urban infrastructure were being sold as "complete systems" across the country by "national manufacturing companies."[47] In contrast to these nationalizing processes, however, infrastructural development was often dependent on the unique circumstances of a given area, such as the availability of water or of high-grade coal for gas lighting. There were many less prominent engineers who consulted on a regional or metropolitan level, were knowledgeable about the unique problems involved with infrastructural development in their areas, had ties to local construction and real estate industries, and also charged less than a Waring or a Hering. As Anderson notes, "Most engineers confined their consulting activity to one region, but not to the larger towns."[48] If suburban communities that were installing infrastructure systems consulted with international engineering talent and purchased the components for their infrastructure systems from national companies, the location of the suburban community did not matter for the development of its infrastructure. To the extent that suburban communities depended on the availability of local engineering talent, contractors, and materials suppliers, infrastructural development was a location-bound process.

While engineers played an important role in facilitating suburban autonomy, I have also argued that engineers were crucial to the success of central city infrastructure development, and successful central city infrastructural development created the motivations within the central city to annex suburban communities. It was only through annexation that city officials could benefit from suburban infrastructural development. By contrast, engineers working as consultants could benefit from infrastructural development regardless of whether it was in the city or in independent suburban municipalities. Thus as technological advances facilitated independent suburban infrastructural development, the previously mentioned compact between politicians and engineers over infrastructural development probably began to fray. Possibly it was at this point that engineering could serve as the basis for political reform.

There is good reason to think that suburbanites, if they had the choice, would opt to have the engineers but not the city officials. They would, in other words, choose independent infrastructural development rather than annexation. Civil engineers were markedly successful at fusing their personal ambitions with the public duties of their profession. As historian Raymond Merritt has written, "Civil engineers, . . . entrusted with million-dollar investments and held accountable for the health and safety of thousands of citizens, were chiefly responsible for establishing the profession's spirit of *noblesse oblige*."[49] By contrast, if city officials were perceived to be working for their own personal benefit, they were also considered, practically by definition, corrupt. Only a few years after the last of the great municipal annexations, Lincoln Steffens noted that "the corruption that shocks us in public affairs we practice ourselves in our private concerns."[50] If both city officials and engineers engaged in suburban infrastructural development out of self-interest, only the self-interest of engineers was socially acceptable. Suburban residents might welcome engineers into their communities to build public works for a fee, but not city officials, whose fee was corruption and graft.

Like engineers, contractors from the city probably facilitated suburban infrastructural development. Suburbs needed contractors who could build public works, and if a central city had engaged in infrastructural development to a relatively great extent, this conceivably would have stimulated more people to get into the infrastructure contracting business. If more contractors competed against one another for jobs, their services would ostensibly have been bid down in price, thus lowering the cost of infrastructural development for the city, as well as neighboring suburbs. But contractors were also political actors who won contracts through their connections and were often implicated in municipal corruption scandals, and they did not enjoy the same reputations for professionalism as did engineers. Thus suburban communities may have been reluctant to rely on the city's market of contractors if they were seen as tainted by big-city corruption. Moreover, there is some evidence that suburban officials were partial to local contractors rather than those from the neighboring city.[51] Thus more competitive markets for contractors generated by central city infrastructural development may have lowered costs for suburban communities and thus stimulated suburban public works, but probably to less of an extent than did a readily available pool of engineers.

Several other possible factors served to mitigate the relationship between infrastructural development and suburbanites' decisions over annexation. The quality of services provided by a suburban versus a central city government might vary, as would the costs, depending, for instance, on the available watersheds from which water could be drawn or the ability of suburban officials to negotiate contracts with gas or water companies. A central city might be able to supply better-quality services at a lower price, and thus annexation might be preferable, but the corrupt practices that could accompany infrastructural development under the auspices of the city government could also lead to excessive taxes for shoddy public works. Suburban officials, however, were often just as likely to use public works as vehicles for graft, although the smaller size of their communities may have made graft less feasible.

These mitigating factors do not appear to have eliminated a nationwide relationship between central city infrastructural development and outlying suburban population growth. Regression analysis using census data on cities with populations of more than 30,000 in the early twentieth century shows that cities that had invested more in infrastructural development by 1907 experienced greater population growth immediately outside their borders during the 1930s and 1940s.[52] This suggests that greater levels of infrastructural development within cities stimulated greater infrastructural development in the suburbs and thus provided suburbs with a greater capacity for population growth, which became especially evident later in the twentieth century.

Regression analysis of census data can demonstrate a relationship between central city infrastructural development and suburban population growth, but it cannot explain why that relationship exists. Thus the case studies in this book are efforts at understanding specifically how the politics of public works mediated the relationships between cities and suburbs. In order to clarify the evidence provided by the case studies, Figure 5 provides a diagrammatic outline of the general argument made in this chapter. Figure 5 indicates that the availability of engineering expertise, construction experience, and the development of infrastructure technology are all depicted as causes of both decreasing costs and increasing availability of suburban infrastructural development. As noted previously, a greater supply of engineers, contractors, and more technologically advanced infrastructure systems may not have lowered per capita costs for suburban infrastructural development; instead, they may have brought the overall cost of infrastructure systems within the budget constraints of smaller communities. Increasingly affordable infrastructure sys-

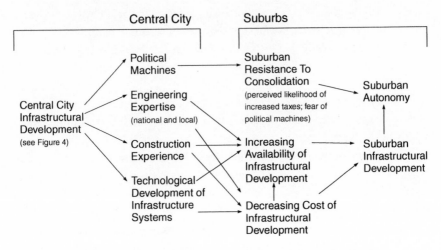

Figure 5. Relationship between central city public works and suburban autonomy

tems may have made a greater range of public services available for independent suburbs, which may have actually raised suburbanites' taxes.

The case studies are accompanied by similar outlines that show what parts of the general argument they provide evidence for. The simple diagrammatic outline cannot capture the full complexity of the varied relationships between infrastructural development and municipal autonomy that will be discussed in each of the case studies. Nevertheless, the diagram does provide a focal point through which the evidence provided in the case studies can be unified and applied to the general argument.

Infrastructural Development, Suburban Autonomy, and the Public Good

To the extent that infrastructural development made suburban autonomy possible, it also contributed to metropolitan fragmentation—the proliferation of independent municipalities within a metropolitan region. Charles Tiebout has argued famously that metropolitan fragmentation provides one solution to the public goods dilemma presented at the beginning of this chapter. Noting that prior discussions of public goods assumed that they were provided by a single, central government, Tiebout speculated that if public goods could be provided in a decentralized fashion, by "city managers" in different "communities," this would approximate the functioning of a private market. More specifically, individual "consumer-voters" move to those communities where public goods expenditures best match their preferences. Assuming, among other things, that there are no costs involved in moving between cities, that all consumer-voters are "living on dividend income" so that they are not constrained by employment, and that they have "full knowledge" of the public goods supplied in all communities, "the consumer-voter moves to that community whose local government best satisfies his set of preferences. The greater the number of communities and the greater his variance among them, the closer the consumer will come to fully realizing his preference position." Because the only thing in Tiebout's model that would determine the choice among communities would be the public goods provided, by moving to a given community, the consumer-voter has signaled his or her true preference for the supply of the public good, which can then be provided accordingly and efficiently.[53]

Because the central city was a single municipality, and because the government of that municipality was in most instances the only organization with sufficient power within the city to enable the construction of large infrastructure systems, different interested parties had to cooperate with one another if they wanted to receive the benefits, both public and private, of infrastructural development. With the fragmentation of the metropolitan community into separate municipalities, interested parties no longer had to cooperate in infrastructural development, because infrastructural development had been privatized by metropolitan fragmentation. Residents, for instance, no longer had to rely on the city council to provide infrastructure systems. If the city did not provide infrastructure systems that met the preferences of a resident, the resident could simply move to that neighboring municipality where the level of infrastructural development best matched the resident's preferences.

On the supply side, metropolitan fragmentation provided more customers for the services offered by engineers, contractors, and materials suppliers and made them all less dependent on the city government for their livelihoods. Similarly, metropolitan fragmentation meant that municipalities were less dependent on the services of contractors, suppliers, and engineers within the city. Municipalities could now purchase the services needed to supply infrastructure from engineers, contractors, and materials suppliers in neighboring municipalities or from the neighboring municipalities themselves.[54]

From an economic standpoint, the impact of metropolitan fragmentation on infrastructural development depends crucially on the extent to which

Tiebout's assumptions hold true. If there were perfect mobility and economic equality among all parties involved, metropolitan fragmentation would lead to an optimal outcome for infrastructural development. Residents could register their desires for infrastructural development more accurately by moving to the community that offered what they desired. Municipalities could supply infrastructural development more efficiently because metropolitan fragmentation would increase competition among contractors, suppliers, and engineers. In addition, breaking up the market for contractors among different municipalities would decrease the likelihood of collusion between contractors and government officials. Competition between municipalities would increase the penalties for side payments such as kickbacks from padded contracts because these would increase the costs of infrastructural development, thereby making a given municipality less attractive to residents. Furthermore, contractors would not be compelled to offer bribes and other side payments to government officials, since there would now be other buyers for their services.

To the extent that Tiebout's assumptions do not hold true, the impact of metropolitan fragmentation on infrastructural development becomes less beneficial. For instance, to the extent that mobility is restricted within a metropolitan region, residents will not be able to register their true demands for infrastructure by moving to the appropriate community. Municipalities will not have access to a range of contractors, and contractors will be confined to seeking jobs within their own municipalities. Restricted mobility within a fragmented metropolitan region could conceivably exacerbate political corruption within infrastructural development by creating separate fiefdoms ruled by small groups of elites with coteries of favored contractors, ultimately raising the overall price of infrastructural development.

Moreover, if we assume that resources are distributed unequally within the population, metropolitan fragmentation could be seen to underwrite the spatial segregation of different socioeconomic groups. Some municipalities within the metropolitan region will become centers of concentrated poverty that are unable to adequately supply themselves with infrastructure. Other municipalities within the metropolitan region will become havens for affluent residents with the resources to create communities at the cutting edge of infrastructure technology. Thus without the assumption of equal resources, infrastructural development within a fragmented metropolitan region might not reflect residential preferences so much as the unequal distribution of residential wealth. To the extent that infrastructural devel-

opment underwrites metropolitan fragmentation, it compounds and reinforces social and economic inequalities with municipal borders. Metropolitan
fragmentation could thus be seen as simply moving the collective action
dilemma of infrastructural development from the level of the municipality to
the level of the metropolitan region as a whole.

From a political standpoint, the implications of metropolitan fragmentation also depend crucially on the initial assumptions. To the extent that municipal boundaries reflect social and economic inequalities, they are political
divisions that reflect the battle for resources within the metropolitan region.
If central city infrastructural development was in large part a game of who
got the private benefits from a public good, the metropolitan fragmentation
that resulted from central city infrastructural development simply carried
this game into a new arena. On the other hand, to the extent that metropolitan fragmentation reflects not social and economic inequality but different preferences for styles of life and bundles of public goods, it serves to
replace a public process with a private one. Residents, contractors, and
other interested parties no longer come together with various agendas in
order to create a public good, but instead have the freedom to choose public
goods in a private market.

The implications of the privatization of infrastructural development
through metropolitan fragmentation depend on the assumptions that we
make about the political processes that metropolitan fragmentation replaces.
On the one hand, the fact that different interests within a city had to come
together to fight over the benefits of a public good may have been beneficial.
In the struggle over infrastructural development, different interests within
the city engaged in a collective dialogue about the basic necessities of urban
life and created a more expansive understanding of the public good in the
process. On the other hand, the battle for the private benefits of infrastructural development may simply have devolved into a situation where some
parties were winners and other were losers, with no greater collective outcome. In the former case, metropolitan fragmentation diminished some of
the benefits of public interaction over an important topic. In the latter case,
metropolitan fragmentation provided a resolution to an insoluble conflict.

CHAPTER 2

Independent Yonkers, Expansionist New York

In the summer of 1665, one year after he had seized New Amsterdam from the Dutch, Colonel Richard Nicolls declared "that the Inhabitants of New Yorke, New Harlem, with all other His Majesty's Subjects, Inhabitants upon this Island, . . . are, and shall bee for ever, accounted, Nominated and Established, as one Body Politique & Corporate, under the Government of a Mayor, Aldermen and Sheriffe."[1] Thus the island of Manhattan became the exclusive domain of a single city and remained so for the next 209 years, after which New York City's jurisdiction began to expand. While New York's present-day boundaries are the product of the famous 1898 consolidation, the city first expanded its jurisdiction beyond Manhattan Island in 1874 by annexing three towns in Westchester County—Kingsbridge, Morrisania, and West Farms—that would form a part of what later became the Bronx. A fourth town, Yonkers, was also considered for annexation, but instead incorporated as a city in 1872 and remained independent of its expanding neighbor to the south.

New York City's boundaries are a product of both expansion and delimitation, which were intimately related to infrastructural development. The various pressures wrought by population growth on Manhattan throughout the early nineteenth century compelled the municipal government to authorize an increasingly elaborate infrastructure of streets, sewers, and water and gas lines. Population growth in the communities surrounding New York created demands for infrastructure similar to those that had developed earlier on Manhattan. Suburban residents increasingly desired that their communities be annexed to the central city so that the city's infrastructure systems, primarily water and sewerage, would be extended into their streets.

Outlying communities, however, might resist annexation to New York by building their own infrastructure systems and remain independent municipalities. Thus the residents and local government of Yonkers opposed annexation and supported their incorporation as an independent city because their community had already invested in infrastructural development to a degree sufficient to supply essential services. Incorporation as a city facilitated further infrastructural development, which reinforced Yonkers's autonomy and independence and thus limited the geographic expansion of New York. In contrast, Kingsbridge, Morrisania, and West Farms were relatively undeveloped at the time that New York City considered geographic expansion. Annexation for these towns represented a more viable option by which they could be supplied with infrastructure and other services.

The case of Yonkers indicates that infrastructural development in New York not only served to provide an incentive to suburbanites for annexation, but also spurred suburban infrastructural development and thus suburban autonomy. New York City's increasing claims over the water supply of Westchester County generated part of the incentive for the city of Yonkers to build a waterworks, which in turn helped Yonkers remain independent of New York. There is evidence as well to suggest that Yonkers's residents were wary of annexation because of the political corruption that characterized street improvements in New York, especially during the reign of the Tweed Ring. Thus central city infrastructural development could actually delimit the boundaries of the central city by creating a suburban backlash against expansion. This is significant because it suggests that pro-growth, "developmental" policies also served, inadvertently, to set the limits to city growth.

The delimitation of the central city through infrastructural development was a variable process that took shape in different ways, given the specific context. The expansion of New York City into lower Westchester County and the reaction that this created in Yonkers is one such context. The story begins with the physical development of New York as the city grew northward and eventually met up with lower Westchester County.

The Physical Development of a Central City

Infrastructural development in New York City dates back to the seventeenth century. The first street was paved in 1658, sewers were installed as early as 1676, and "most of the city's major thoroughfares were covered with cobblestones" by 1707.[2] Even before the American Revolution, the municipality had begun construction of what was then the most ambitious public water supply system in the colonies, consisting of a steam-engine pump that would fill a reservoir in the northern part of the city, from which water would flow through bored wooden logs laid under "every Street and Lane" of New York. The water project was abandoned during the British occupation of the city.[3] After the Revolution, several major projects served to define infrastructural development: the 1811 street grid plan, the Croton Aqueduct, Central Park, and the adoption of a comprehensive sewerage plan after the Civil War. Finally, the increase in infrastructural development during the reign of the Tweed Ring immediately preceded, and thus set the stage for, the annexation of lower Westchester County. Collectively, these public works projects gave New York City a distinct physical form; each also served as an important juncture in the definition of municipal responsibilities and the public good.

The 1811 Manhattan street plan laid the groundwork for the comprehensive development of other infrastructure systems. Rapid population growth in the city after 1790, combined with yellow fever epidemics in 1803 and 1805, convinced local officials that the city, in its inexorable northward growth, should develop along streets wide enough to permit the healthy circulation of air and with a predictability that would encourage investment. Without the authority itself to impose new streets that would infringe on the rights of property holders, the common council petitioned the New York legislature in 1807 to prepare a street plan for Manhattan that would be legally binding upon the city. The legislature responded by appointing three commissioners who, in 1811, presented their plan for Manhattan Island: a street grid extending up to 155th Street, broken only by one 240-acre park and four smaller squares. Accepted by the common council without debate, the 1811 grid became the official plan along which the city developed.[4]

Historians have argued that the success of New York's street grid lay in its promotion of "republican as well as realtor values."[5] As the head surveyor of the plan, John Randel Jr., noted, the grid provided for "safety from conflagration, beautiful uniformity, and convenience" and "must have greatly enhanced the value of real estate on New York Island." The grid plan was thus a classic developmental policy, one that is beneficial to almost all city residents because it improves the "economic position of a community in its competition with others." Indeed, Erastus Benedict, in his *New York and the City Travel* (1851), argued that rapid development of the streets along the grid plan would stem the tide of out-migration from the city, which had contributed to the growth of neighboring Brooklyn.[6]

Foreseeing a time when New York City would be supplied with water from an external source by aqueduct, the commissioners designated an open space in the street grid that was to be reserved for a reservoir.[7] The common council had in fact proposed to build an aqueduct that would supply the city with water from the Bronx River in Westchester County and had sent a bill to the legislature in 1799 requesting authorization to raise money for the project. The proposed Bronx River aqueduct system would have been the most ambitious waterworks in the United States and the first public water supply system in a major American city. In Albany, however, state senator Aaron Burr redrafted the common council bill to provide for the creation of a private corporation, the Manhattan Company, whose ostensible mission was to supply the city with water, and included a clause giving the company the right to use its "surplus capital" in any way it saw fit. Under the direction of Burr, the bill passed successfully through the legislature and thus created the most expansive charter for a bank that had ever been enacted in New York State up to that time, and one that would provide for a Republican competitor to the other banks in the city, all of which were controlled by Federalists.[8]

Historians have debated the motivations and interests that surrounded the creation of the Manhattan Company.[9] There is little doubt, however, that the company never satisfied the requirement in its charter to "furnish and continue a supply of pure and wholesome water" to all residents willing to pay for the service. Most of the $2 million in capital that the company was authorized to raise was diverted away from building a waterworks to more profitable banking operations. Instead of turning to a source outside the city for water, such as the Bronx River, the company purchased the well that had originally been intended for the prerevolutionary waterworks, which had been designed for a population of approximately 22,000. By 1800, however, New York City's population had exploded to 60,489. The Manhattan Company had originally proposed to build a reservoir with a capacity of 1 million gallons that would deliver water to city residents through iron pipes. The reservoir the company actually built could hold 132,600 gallons and delivered water through bored wooden logs. By 1808, when the city's population was probably close to 80,000, the Manhattan Company had 2,316 customers, who complained frequently about the service provided and the quality of the water.[10]

To say that Aaron Burr and the Manhattan Company deprived New York City of an adequate water supply is probably an unwarranted imposition of contemporary assumptions about city services on a time when people had a different understanding of municipal responsibilities. The fact that the Bronx River aqueduct was first proposed as a municipal project suggests that there was at least an emerging understanding that an adequate urban water supply was a public responsibility. Yet of all American cities at the turn of the nineteenth century, only Philadelphia had a public water supply. The first few decades of the nineteenth century saw only the dawning of the "municipal revolution," when city governments began to take on new responsibilities for the public good.[11] Indeed, as early as 1804, De Witt Clinton, who was then both mayor of New York and director of the Manhattan Company, expressed interest in selling the waterworks to the city, but enough common council members were concerned about the profitability of water to vote down the proposal in 1808. In 1824 the common council voted down a new plan for a Bronx River aqueduct system, once again on account of its cost.[12]

A comparison of water and gas service in New York City suggests how some services came to be understood as municipal responsibilities, and how that understanding affected their future development. At its earliest stages, the municipal government attempted to provide both water and gas. The municipal government tried to establish public water service in both 1774 and 1799, and the common council experimented with a "crude gas works" in 1816 that lit up "several street lamps and store windows on Broadway," after which it decided that public gas service was infeasible. In 1823 the common council granted an exclusive franchise to the New York Gas Light Company to supply gas south of Grand Street for thirty years. In exchange for the right to sell gas to residents, the company was required to provide gas for street lighting.[13] Thus in the early part of the nineteenth century, gas and water service were both provided by private companies who held exclusive franchises and were required by the municipal government to provide at least some minimal public service.

From the 1830s to the 1850s both gas and water service changed fundamentally, though in different ways. During the 1830s the responsibility for supplying water to the residents of New York was transferred from private to public hands. In 1834 the legislature, acting on a proposal made by the New York City Common Council, authorized a state-appointed water commission to develop and propose a new water supply system for the city. In 1835 the water commissioners proposed to build an aqueduct that would supply water to the city from the Croton River in Westchester County. The proposal was approved by the common council and received majority approval in a referendum; by 1837 the commissioners were advertising bids for construction, and by 1842 the residents of New York City were being supplied water from the new, public system. Like the 1774 plan and the 1799 Bronx aqueduct plan, the Croton Aqueduct system was unprecedented in the United States for its size and capacity. Despite previous concerns over the cost of supplying water, the Croton system was built at tremendous expense—first estimated at about $5 million, the final cost came to a bit more than $10 million.[14] New York was also one of the first American cities to establish water as a public service; most other large municipalities built or acquired public waterworks a generation later.[15]

If New York City was precocious in the establishment of a public waterworks, the same cannot be said of gas. As was the case with waterworks, though on a much smaller scale, the trend during the mid-nineteenth century was for cities to establish municipal gasworks. The first city to establish a public gasworks was Philadelphia, in 1841. After Philadelphia, twelve other municipalities also established public gasworks throughout the nineteenth century.[16] In New York City, the Gas Consumer Association proposed a municipal gasworks in 1851, which apparently aroused little public enthusiasm.[17] Yet the city did seek to improve gas service through competition. In 1855 the common council granted a franchise to the Metropolitan Gas Light Company that allowed it to sell gas throughout Manhattan Island and thus compete with the other three companies operating in the city, all of which were constrained by mutually exclusive territories: the New York Gas Light Company, operating south of Grand Street; the Manhattan Gas Light Company, granted a franchise in 1833 to supply gas between Grand and 79th Streets; and the Harlem Gas Light Company, granted a franchise in 1855 to operate north of 79th Street, among "the far-flung villages of Harlem, Yorkville, Manhattanville, Carmansville and Bloomingdale."[18]

The attempt to induce competition is perplexing, since the gas industry had long been identified as naturally monopolistic. The common council indicated as much in 1830 when it turned down a request by the Manhattan Gas Light Company for a franchise that included the right to supply gas in the territory of the New York Gas Light Company. In denying the proposed franchise, the Law Committee of the council relied on the experience of London, where "serious evils grew out of the operations of different Gas Companies in the same district, the breaking up of the pavement for two sets of mains [in] the place of one[,] the confusion and disorder produced by pipes crossing and intersecting each other, the disputes and delay in identifying . . . leakages, altogether became so great an inconvenience that it proved absolutely necessary to separate and confine the different companies to different districts."[19]

The findings from London were confirmed when the Manhattan and the Metropolitan Gas Light Companies, after a prolonged legal battle, split the Manhattan Gas Light Company's territory, giving the Metropolitan all the gas business between 34th and 79th Streets. After the Civil War, technological developments, such as the naphtha process and water gas, prompted new companies to enter the New York market. The industry became more monopolistic, however, when all of the gas companies serving New York City merged in 1884, forming the Consolidated Gas Company as part of a peace treaty designed to end the price wars between them.[20]

The monopolistic nature of the industry suggested to some that gas should be provided as a municipal service. Indeed, water was a monopolistic industry much like gas and had been made a public service in most large American cities. Yet something distinguished gas service from water service—in New York and most other cities—that provided for a common understanding that the former was a commercial industry and the latter a public responsibility.

One thing that evidently distinguished water from gas and defined water as a public service was that water was perceived as a solution to the periodic disease epidemics that swept the city, notably yellow fever and cholera. The 1799 and 1824 Bronx River aqueduct plans were both inspired by yellow fever epidemics, in 1798 and 1822, respectively. The official generally given credit for the Croton Aqueduct plan, Myndert Van Schaick, was both a member of the common council and treasurer of the board of health during the cholera epidemic of 1832. The cholera epidemic convinced Van Schaick that "New York must at once, if possible, be supplied with good and wholesome water."[21] By contrast, there is little evidence to suggest that gas street lighting was ever conceived of as a solution to any crisis. Street lighting may have been important for providing public safety, and there was certainly a crisis in public safety during the riotous 1830s and 1840s, but the main solution to that problem was the establishment of a municipal police force in 1845. In fact, "brightly lighted streets" could be morally ambiguous, since they might facilitate nefarious nighttime activities.[22] Thus a comparison of gas and water indicates that recurrent crises of public health eventually served to redefine water service as a municipal responsibility. A private water company did not have the incentive to use water for public health purposes, since that required supplying water to poor neighborhoods, where there was the greatest risk of disease, yet the least ability to afford water.[23]

At the same time that the Croton Aqueduct provided the general public good of public health—and thus promoted "republican values" in the same way as the street grid—it also provided individualistic, private benefits to a diverse and broad array of groups. Bakers, sugar refiners, taverns, hotels, brewers, distilleries, tanners, dyers, soap and candle makers, and especially fire insurance companies each had a special interest in being provided with water of a quality and in a quantity sufficient for drinking, fire protection, manufacturing, and other purposes—even gas companies needed an ample water supply in order to condense gas. The water commission had a special interest in the uses of Croton water for fire protection, it seems, since three of the commissioners were either executives or large shareholders of fire insurance companies, as were many members of the common council.[24]

The benefits of the Croton Aqueduct were not limited to the water it provided. There were also plenty of benefits to be had in building the aqueduct, in the form of kickbacks and political alliances made possible through the jobs and contracts that had to be awarded in the process of construction. In New York, by the 1850s, the term "laying pipe" referred specifically to the patronage and corruption that had become associated with construction of the aqueduct.[25] Here was a distinction that developed between water and gas as a result of water having become a public service. Since provision of gas was controlled by private companies, the profits that were to be made from supplying gas came from fees paid by customers. Residents in New York also had to pay for Croton water, but no one profited directly from these revenues, since they went to pay off construction bonds or else went back to a general fund. If a public official were to profit from Croton water, he would do so indirectly, through kickbacks and political alliances gained in exchange for jobs and contracts. Thus the politics of the Croton Aqueduct centered on having control over construction. The authorizing legislation had given the state-appointed water commission control over construction of the aqueduct, the reservoirs, and at least part of the distributing system. While the water commissioners appointed by a majority Democratic legislature in the 1830s agreed that their authority ended at 42nd Street, new commissioners appointed by "anti-Jacksonians" in 1840 claimed control over construction further south on the grounds that the city had performed its part of the construction inadequately.[26]

The incentive structure for officials interested in profiting from a public waterworks would have significant implications for suburban residents. For the directors and shareholders of gas companies, more customers meant more revenues and thus more profits. Gas companies therefore gladly extended their services into the suburbs in order to capture new customers and increase their profits. By contrast, public officials responsible for New York's water supply only had an incentive to expand the customer base of the waterworks if this involved new construction or new opportunities for employment, over which the officials maintained control. Public officials had little incentive to provide suburban residents with Croton water, even if those residents were willing to pay a premium for the service, since the profits did not go back to the officials. Public officials could only profit by supplying Croton water to the suburbs if they had control over construction of the infrastructure necessary to deliver that water, and control was best maintained by annexing the suburb to the city.

In 1849, as part of a new city charter, the waterworks were placed under the authority of a newly created Croton Aqueduct Board whose members were appointed by the mayor, upon the approval of the common council, for five-year terms. The first president of the Croton Aqueduct Board, Nicholas Dean, was an early advocate for a large, centrally located park, which he believed should be created as an embellishment to a new, proposed reservoir, to be located immediately north of the old reservoir on Seventy-ninth Street. There is thus an intimate connection between the development of the city's waterworks and the origins of Central Park. Central Park was also an important improvement to the 1811 street plan. While the street plan envisioned a grid that continued up through the center of the island, the actual land there was rocky and of irregular topography, rendering grading expensive. Since it was unfit for development, the land was comparatively inexpensive, and as a park, it would serve as a catalyst for northward development on either side of the island, thus fulfilling the street grid's initial promise of promoting realtor values. As one historian has put it, Central Park would "induce the construction of infrastructural networks on all sides until the sewers, streets, grades, gas and water mains of northern Manhattan connected with existing grids downtown."[27]

Central Park was not only intimately related to the waterworks and the street grid; it was also a public good in the same fashion as the other two public works projects. Both the street grid and the waterworks were considered important assets in the struggle for public health. Similarly, a large city park was in part justified by the health benefits that it would bring to residents by serving as the "lungs of the city." Both the street grid and the waterworks were developmental policies that improved the economic position of New York in its competition with neighboring cities; park advocates argued similarly that a large park, along the lines of those in London and Paris, would stem the tide of out-migration from the city into Brooklyn and New Jersey. The park plan that ultimately succeeded in winning legislative and public approval did so because it had developed a broad and diverse array of supporters, as had the Croton Aqueduct. An initial plan that would have provided for a smaller park located on the eastern side of the island was defeated by West Side residents and downtown interests, who would have experienced little benefit from the eastern park. Working-class interests were initially opposed to a large park that would mostly benefit wealthy elites and speculators who owned northern property. However, as the economy worsened during the 1850s, workingmen began to see the large park project "as a source of jobs during a recession."[28]

In 1853 the legislature authorized the use of eminent domain to create Central Park on the 778 acres between Fifth and Eighth Avenues and 58th and 106th Streets. In 1855, in response to concerns over the public purse during a recession, the common council voted to cut down the size of the park by twelve blocks in length and 800 feet in width. In what is often cited as his "one creditable act," the infamous and newly elected Democratic mayor, Fernando Wood, vetoed the council provision and thus "saved" the park. Wood did not necessarily act purely out of regard for the public good, however, since he did own a good deal of property on the West Side that stood to appreciate from a larger park. Moreover, a larger park provided more jobs and contracts, which initially fell under the control of Mayor Wood and Street Commissioner Joseph Taylor.[29]

As was true of the Croton Aqueduct, the politics that surrounded the construction of Central Park centered primarily around patronage. In 1857 the Republican-controlled legislature passed a new charter for the city that took away most of the mayor's patronage resources by placing responsibility for the city's port, construction of the new city hall, and construction of Central Park into the hands of state-appointed, nonelective commissions and by transferring responsibility for street improvements to the Croton Aqueduct Board.[30] The city still maintained responsibility for issuing construction bonds, however, which gave Wood the opportunity to retaliate against the creation of the Central Park Commission by refusing to raise money for park construction. The commission retaliated in turn by issuing IOUs to its laborers, "payable whenever the Common Council should vote the appropriations,"[31] which undermined Wood's efforts to promote Central Park as a jobs program. Wood thus capitulated to the commission and approved a $250,000 appropriation by the common council for park construction, which kept more than 1,000 men employed after the panic of 1857.[32]

The 1857 charter did not take away all of the patronage resources of the mayor. The *New York Times* noted in 1860 that the city's street department had "annual disbursements exceeding three millions of dollars" and employed "thousands of laborers," and the "peculiar nature of its work" made it the "largest field for peculative jobbery" in the city.[33] Yet during the 1860s much of the physical development of the city proceeded through agencies that were at least semi-independent of the mayor and the common council. For instance, under the direction of Andrew Haswell Green—an early and stalwart reformer whose impact on the physical development of New York has often been compared to that of Robert Moses—the Central Park Commission became a planning agency for upper Manhattan and lower Westchester County. In 1859 the legislature, overriding the veto of Mayor Daniel Tiemann, authorized the commission to extend Central Park up to 110th Street and to take responsibility for the widening, grading, and development of Seventh Avenue north of the park to the Harlem River. After the Civil War, between 1865 and 1867, the legislature granted the commission control over the planning and construction of the entire West Side north of 59th Street, St. Nicholas Avenue north of 110th Street, and all of upper Manhattan north of 155th Street, where the 1811 street plan had left off.[34]

In 1868 Green wrote a report to the Central Park Commission in which he recommended the consolidation of Manhattan and lower Westchester County under one municipal government as the best means to develop "the water supply, the sewerage, the navigation of the interjacent waters, the means of crossing these waters, and the land ways that should be laid on each side so as to furnish the best facilities for both."[35] While the legislature did not at that time take Green's advice concerning consolidation, it did grant the Central Park Commission "the exclusive power to survey, map, and lay out the street pattern of lower Westchester, improve the Spuyten Duyvil Creek and the Harlem River for navigation, and prepare plans for the construction of bridges over the waterways."[36] Thus the origins of the 1874 annexation can be found in the Central Park Commission and the role it played as a planning agency.

Besides the Central Park Commission, the Croton Aqueduct Department (governed by the Croton Aqueduct Board) also gained additional control over the physical development of the city, both in the 1857 charter, as previously mentioned, and in 1865, when the legislature authorized the department to design and construct a comprehensive sewerage plan for all of Manhattan. The mayor had at least some formal authority over the Croton Aqueduct Board, since he appointed its members to five-year terms, but it seems likely that mayoral control was minimized by the fact that the engineers who worked under the board actually had much of the control over the aqueduct and other public works. For instance, Alfred Craven, appointed chief engineer of the Croton Aqueduct Department at its inception in 1849, became the "chief lobbyist" for the department, "waging an unrelenting campaign for its autonomy." Using the claim of expertise, Craven was able to withstand an attempt by Mayor Wood (voted out in 1857, but reelected in 1859) to remove him from office in 1860. Craven was also able to maintain the department's control over the city's sewers, despite Andrew Green's attempt to lobby the legislature to give the Central Park Commission control over sewerage.[37]

Control over the Croton Aqueduct, the sewers, Central Park, and most other public works returned to the mayor and the common council under a new "home rule" charter that was passed by the legislature in 1870. Central Park fell under the purview of the new Department of Public Parks, while water, sewers, and streets were placed within the new Department of Public Works. The first commissioner of the Department of Public Works was William Tweed, who also happened to be the state senator generally credited with passage of the 1870 city charter.[38]

William Tweed is of course remembered less for the home rule charter than he is for being the supposed center of the "Tweed Ring," which began its rapid descent in 1871 after an exposé in the *New York Times* provided evidence of financial improprieties on the part of Tweed, Mayor A. Oakey Hall, City Chamberlain Peter Sweeny, and Comptroller Richard Connolly. In response, the city's economic elites formed a reform group, the Committee of Seventy, which succeeded in getting an injunction that prevented the city from raising or spending money. The anti-Tweed and anti-Tammany campaign led to the general electoral defeat of Tammany Hall in the city and state in 1871. Tweed was reelected as a state senator, but resigned as public works commissioner. He and his associates faced various civil and criminal charges relating to the $6 million out of which the city had been defrauded. Tweed was brought to trial twice in 1873, was sentenced to twelve years in prison, was then released on an appeal in 1875, but was immediately rearrested on civil charges and sent back to prison, held on $3 million bail. After escaping for a year, Tweed was sent back to prison, where he finally died in 1878. Mayor Hall survived unscathed through four trials and remained in the city, working as a "newspaperman and attorney." Connolly and Sweeny both fled the country.[39]

Before he left, Connolly turned on his associates and in 1871, on the recommendation of the Committee of Seventy, appointed Andrew Green acting comptroller, who remained in that position through 1876. As comptroller, Green spearheaded a severe fiscal retrenchment campaign, so that the city—despite a treasury depleted from five years of graft, combined with the effects of the financial panic of 1873 and the ensuing depression—could restore its credit, meet bond payments, and pay its employees. Ironically, fiscal retrenchment did not make for popularity at the polls, and the reform mayor elected after the fall of the Tweed Ring, Andrew Havemeyer, lost the mayoral election of 1874 to William Wickham, a candidate backed by Tammany Hall, which had been centralized and revitalized under the leadership of John Kelly.[40] Thus Green stayed on as comptroller—a position from which he was able to facilitate his previous plan of consolidating New York City with lower Westchester County—at the same time that Tammany Hall returned to power in the city.

The charges against the Tweed Ring centered on the physical development of New York: the city was vastly overcharged for its public works because contractors padded their bills and kicked back some of the profits to the ring. Historians have explained these padded contracts in different ways,[41] but there is little dispute that they coincided with a marked increase in infrastructural development. An average of 55,000 linear feet of sewer pipe had been laid annually in the city from 1850 to 1865, but the average during the first four years of the Tweed Ring, from 1866 to 1869, was 68,000 linear feet.[42] As Figure 6 shows, the length of sewers for which the city contracted increased sharply from 1867 to 1870. In 1869 state senator Tweed was able to get a provision passed in the legislature that allowed the city to pay for street improvements from general revenues rather than through special assessments levied on the owners of adjacent properties, thereby facilitating development by spreading its cost over the entire city population.[43]

While infrastructural development under the Tweed Ring may have served as a vehicle for graft, it also empowered a corps of city engineers who were allowed "considerable discretion to direct policy" and who continued their work after the ring was gone—an example of the symbiotic relationship between politicians and engineers discussed in the previous chapter.[44] The available data on infrastructural development certainly indicate that city engineers were busy after the fall of the Tweed Ring. Figure 7 shows, for instance, that while there was a sharp drop in the square yards

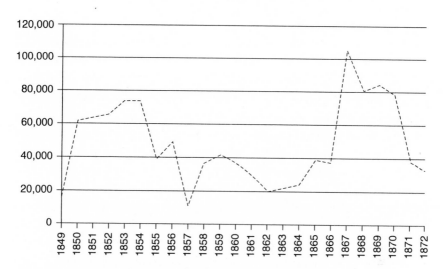

Figure 6. Linear feet of sewers contracted for New York City, 1849–72. *Data source:* New York City Department of Public Works, *Third Annual Report for the Year Ending April 10, 1873* (New York: Martin B. Brown, 1873), p. 270.

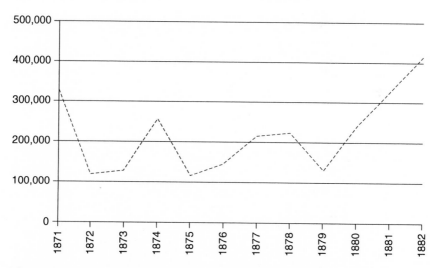

Figure 7. Square yards of pavement laid annually in New York City, 1871–82. *Data sources:* New York City Department of Public Works, *Quarterly Report,* December 31, 1880, p. 17; New York City Department of Public Works, *Quarterly Report,* December 31, 1882, p. 18.

of new pavement laid after 1871, the amount laid remained relatively level through the 1870s and then increased in the 1880s, suggesting that the Department of Public Works was able to resume infrastructural development at "Tweed" levels after the depression of the 1870s. Even more suggestive is Figure 8, which shows that the length of water pipe laid annually increased under the Tweed Ring, then dropped sharply in 1873, but still remained at a level higher than that of the pre-Tweed years. Figure 9 shows that a higher level of water pipe continued to be laid during the rest of the nineteenth century. In contrast to street pavement and water pipe, however, Figure 6 shows that while there was a marked increase in the length of sewer pipe contracted for during the Tweed Ring, the level dropped back to pre-Tweed levels after 1871, where, as Figure 9 indicates, it stayed through 1896.

By the 1870s an odd combination of reformers and machine politicians, exemplified in the persons of Green and Tweed, respectively, had facilitated the northward development of New York to the point that the city was beginning to cross the barrier of the Harlem River and extend into the lower townships of Westchester County. These townships had also grown rapidly in population, and their residents faced a choice in how to meet their growing public needs. Either they could accept the offer of annexation by New York City, in

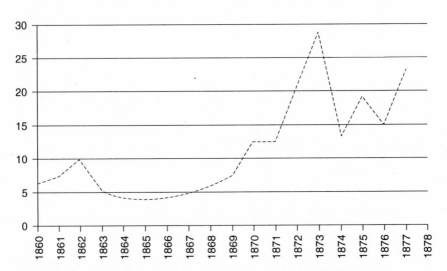

Figure 8. Miles of water pipe laid annually in New York City, 1860–78. *Data source:* New York City Department of Public Works, *Quarterly Report,* June 30, 1879, p. 56.

which case the city's infrastructure systems would be extended into their streets, or they could attempt to finance and build their own independent infrastructure systems. Annexation might make suburban communities the underserved and overtaxed tools of a vilified political machine. Yet by 1874 very few people could have missed the fact that infrastructural development proceeded rapidly under the rule of Tammany Hall, but slowly under a reform regime. In order to better understand how suburban residents made the choices that they did, we now turn to an examination of the first suburbs annexed to New York City.

The City of Yonkers and the Annexation of Lower Westchester County to New York City

Throughout the metropolitan region that was developing around Manhattan Island in the nineteenth century, a typical response to urbanization was a division of existing political jurisdictions into smaller units. In lower Westchester County, the western half of the town of Westchester split off in 1846 to form the town of West Farms, and in 1855 the southwestern portion of West

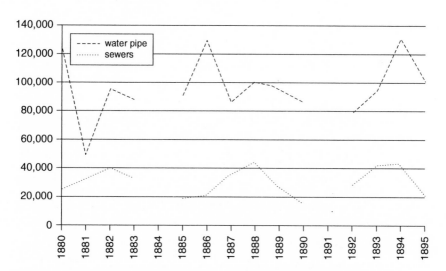

Figure 9. Feet of sewers and water pipe laid annually in New York City, 1880–95. *Data sources:* New York City Department of Public Works, *Quarterly Reports,* March 31, 1880–December 31, 1895, and *Annual Report,* 1896.

Farms that lay across the Harlem River from Manhattan split off to form the town of Morrisania (see Figure 1 in the Introduction). Various spots of concentrated settlement within these towns incorporated as villages, such as Riverdale and Spuyten Duyvil, in order to gain greater control over the opening, grading, and paving of streets and over other public works. The concentrated area of settlement located along the Hudson River and midway between the northern and southern ends of the town of Yonkers, north of West Farms, incorporated as the village of Yonkers in 1855 and would serve as the nucleus for the city of Yonkers.[45]

Real estate promotion and the introduction of rail service that connected to New York City tripled the population of lower Westchester County during the 1850s. Of the twenty-four towns that comprised the county in 1858, Yonkers, West Farms, and Morrisania ranked first, fifth, and sixth, respectively, in terms of the value of assessed property. The population of the town of Yonkers alone increased from 4,160 in 1850 to 18,318 in 1870. In response to increasing urbanization after the Civil War, the northern portion of the town of Yonkers, led by the village of Yonkers, incorporated as a city in 1872, and the southern portion of the town became the town of Kingsbridge. In 1874 Kingsbridge, Morrisania, and West Farms were annexed to New York City.[46]

Several factors came together to make the area that would become the city of Yonkers the largest settlement in lower Westchester County. Blessed with "an excellent supply of water power," the area became a locus for industry by the early nineteenth century, attracting some sawmills, gristmills, and blacksmiths. This industry in turn made the area a "stopping-off point" for stagecoaches traveling between New York City and Albany and then, in 1849, the first stop on the Hudson River Railroad. A wealthy newcomer to the city, Robert Getty, built a large hotel near the railroad depot and became one of the most prominent boosters for the creation of a village of Yonkers. Getty envisioned incorporation as a village as a first step toward the area becoming the "Queen City of the Hudson," second only to New York. When the city of Yonkers was created in 1872, Getty was serving as village president. With the introduction of rail service, the village of Yonkers became increasingly a center for industry, especially for the manufacture of elevators, carpets, hats, and, as a result of the Civil War, firearms.[47]

Yonkers was the largest and wealthiest of the villages in lower Westchester County, but it was similar to neighboring villages in its role as a suburb of New York. As early as 1857, the New York correspondent of the *Missouri Republican* described life in Yonkers as follows:

Breakfast at half past seven, A.M., New York morning papers and cigar till 8, steamboat at 8, a sail down to the city at one hour's length, past a panorama of exceeding beauty. A disgorging of passengers at the foot of Warren street . . . A vigorous battle with the dust, dirt, noise, bulls, bears, mock auctions, Peter Funks, and Jeremy Diddlers, of the city, till 5 P.M. Steamboat up to Yonkers, supper at 6, then talking, laughing, sailing, rowing, fiddling, flirting, dancing, etc., etc., till midnight, or as much later as may seem proper. Then a sweet, sound, country sleep, without mosquitos to molest or make afraid.[48]

Twelve years later a local Yonkers newspaper also described the growing village as a suburb "spread over a tract about two miles long, by a mile wide, nearly every street and avenue being thickly studded with residences, mostly of people doing business in New York."[49] Morrisania has been described similarly as "an affordable opportunity for New Yorkers to escape their congested city."[50]

Historians and others have often assumed that the annexation of industrial suburbs to the central city was practically inevitable. Historian Edward Spann, for instance, claims that Morrisania's "railroad spur, lumber yard, crowded housing, and spindly trees omen[ed] its eventual absorption into Greater New York at the end of the century."[51] Yet the case of Yonkers indicates that an industrial suburb might also remain independent. Furthermore, the fact that two industrial suburbs developed such different relationships with New York City suggests that we cannot explain annexation or resistance to annexation in Westchester County in the 1870s simply in terms of class differences between the city and its suburbs.[52]

The idea of incorporating as a city first emerged as a partisan issue in the village and town of Yonkers. In 1870 the Democratic town paper, the *Yonkers Gazette*, endorsed a proposed city charter introduced into the legislature by local Democratic senator William Cauldwell. The proposed city would include all the land in the town of Yonkers. A mayor and common council, consisting of ten aldermen and five county supervisors, would govern the city and appoint two fire wardens and constables for each of five wards. While admitting that the charter was "capable of some judicious amendments," the *Gazette* argued that a city government could provide, among other things, "A uniform system of streets, avenues and sewers, a new code of civil and criminal ordinances, new wharfage privileges and power over the speed of trains passing through."[53] In contrast, Yonkers's Republican newspaper, the *Statesman*, came out against the charter, arguing that it was designed to increase Democratic representation on the county board of supervisors and to bring advantage to some town Democrats with large real estate holdings, and that it would increase taxes for unnecessary services and create a corrupt government bloated with patronage positions, thus hampering the progress of the town. After Republicans won control of the town government in the elections of March 1870, the *Gazette* lamented that "there is no use of pressing the matter at present."[54]

At least as it was reported in the local press, this first debate over the creation of a city of Yonkers centered on local political issues. There was, however, an external factor looming on the horizon—New York City—that would turn the incorporation debate on its head. At the end of 1870, the *New York Times* reported that

> in the green pastures of Westchester County, the "Ring" sees fresh mines of future wealth . . . Once let those pastures be "annexed" and become a part of this City, and there will be such an upturning of Westchester soil as the plodding farmers of that region never dreamt of . . . : magnificent streets will traverse their waste places, laid out at right angles, nicely graded, and paved with "Nicholson," "Russ," "Belgian," or "Fiske concrete," as one or another of those pavements shall furnish the most profitable "job."[55]

Here was the incentive system for public infrastructural development at work: if politicians from New York could not sell the city's infrastructure to the suburbs, they could at least profit indirectly by annexing the suburbs and gaining control over the jobs and contracts that would come with the extension of the city's streets, sewers, and water lines. Indeed, the *Times* reported that "certain influential political leaders" from New York City and Westchester County were planning to present a bill to the legislature early in 1871 that would authorize New York to annex Westchester, Eastchester, New Rochelle, Pelham, Morrisania, West Farms, and Yonkers—the "seven most populous and wealthy towns in Westchester."[56]

The *Yonkers Gazette* resumed its case for incorporation, this time as a method to defend the town's independence from New York City. The Democratic newspaper argued that annexation would raise taxes and lead to greater corruption.[57] Yonkers's Republican paper was no longer opposed to a city charter when it was presented as an antiannexation measure. In January 1871 the *Statesman* declared, "We do not wish to be annexed to New York," but argued that a proposed city charter must be subject to public approval.[58]

Simultaneously, and in contrast to the growing incorporation movement in Yonkers, an annexation movement was developing in the towns to the south, immediately north of New York City. Early in January 1871 there were signs of resistance to annexation in the towns of Morrisania, West Farms, and Westchester. A group identified in the *Gazette* only as "influential property owners" proposed that the three towns be incorporated as a single, independent city. The *New York Daily Times* reported as well that "Morrisania, West Farms, and Westchester have protested in emphatic terms against the scheme for annexing them." By the end of January, however, there was movement in favor of annexation. Citizens' committees in the towns of Morrisania and West Farms sent a joint committee to Albany to lobby in favor of passing the annexation bill and offer some amendments. On January 28, 1871, the *Gazette* wrote simply that "Morrisania craves annexation."[59]

The annexation bill presented to the legislature in 1871 was voted down in the Senate Committee on Cities in early February, but it had clearly served to beat the bushes and flush out those towns that were interested in annexation. Thus the following year a new bill was presented to the legislature, proposing only that West Farms, Morrisania, and Yonkers be annexed to New York. The *Gazette* urged once again that "what we want, and must have, to save us from being 'gobbled' by New York city, is a city charter."[60]

A special committee of the Yonkers village government had been formed in December 1871 to "prepare such amendments to the charter as they might deem necessary." At the end of February 1872, while the new annexation bill was pending in the legislature, the special committee reported that "they had prepared a charter for a city government for the town of Yonkers . . . with a recommendation that it be printed." Since most of the resistance to the 1870 city charter had been concentrated in the southern portion of the town, the new charter proposed the creation of a city that included only the northern half of the town of Yonkers. As a result, the *Statesman* commented that the new charter was "a great improvement over the charter presented two years ago, and will meet with very general endorsement." Sent to Albany soon thereafter, the charter worked its way through the legislature in the following four months, passed, and was signed by Governor John Hoffman in early June. The village board of trustees held its final meeting later in the month, and the common council assumed its position as the governing body of the city of Yonkers.[61]

Almost immediately after Yonkers became a city, residents in what had been the southern portion of the town lobbied successfully at the first session of the county board of supervisors in 1873 to have their area reincorporated as the town of Kingsbridge. A prominent landowner and member of a citizen's committee in the new town, H. F. Spaulding, expressed his relief and gratitude at a public meeting: "The board of supervisors had made them the free and independent township of Kingsbridge. Thank God for that. We are no longer bound to the nest of office-seekers in the city of Yonkers, no longer held in their aspiration for water-works, docks, etc., for which they would spread their butter over the whole township, if they had been able to annex us."[62]

Immediately after thanking God that the residents of Kingsbridge were free from Yonkers, Spaulding recommended that the new town join with Morrisania and West Farms in their "efforts . . . to get annexed to New York City." By May this annexation bill had passed the legislature, by September the governor had signed it, and in November the residents of the three towns voted in favor of annexation, as expected. On January 1, 1874, they became part of the city of New York.[63]

Spaulding's comments indicate that residents in Kingsbridge faced the choice of joining either Yonkers or New York and chose to join New York. The residents of Morrisania and West Farms desired annexation in large part because they then expected to have access to New York City's water supply.[64] Yet in Kingsbridge—if Spaulding spoke for the sentiments of the community, as he clearly intended—residents rejected the Yonkers city charter specifically because it meant that they would be supplied water from Yonkers. For Kingsbridge residents, then, the choice to join New York City was not a decision to be supplied with water, but a decision on how to be supplied with water, or, more broadly, a decision as to whether they wanted their community to develop physically as Yonkers or as New York. Thus for Yonkers, the physical development of the city served to alienate a portion of the community who drew themselves outside the city boundaries; infrastructural development thus served to limit the expansion of Yonkers as it contributed to the growth of New York.

Possibly the residents of Kingsbridge chose to separate from Yonkers and join New York because they could then take advantage of economies of scale that went along with public services in a large city. For instance, at a town meeting in 1871 convened to discuss the first proposed city charter for Yonkers, one resident argued that "the taxes of small cities . . . were very much larger in proportion, than those of large ones." Another resident, James Sanders, suggested that city taxes were not just a question of economies of scale, but also of political corruption, and Yonkers had as corrupt a "ring" as did New York. Sanders claimed that it was the Yonkers ring that was using the threat of annexation to attempt to push incorporation. It does not appear that Sanders's claims about the Yonkers ring—made in early 1871, at the height of the Tweed Ring—were taken very seriously. Sanders was rebuked for being "grievously troubled because he was neither in the New York ring or the Yonkers ring . . . his (Mr. S's) sole anxiety was to form a ring for himself."[65]

By 1873 the Tweed Ring was gone, and any "ring" that may have existed in Yonkers would have looked relatively worse by the time Kingsbridge, Morrisania, and West Farms voted to consolidate with New York. Indeed, the *New York Times* noted in January 1873 that "the proposition to annex Westchester County to this City, it appears, has lately been viewed with increasing favor by the residents of West Farms and Morrisania. As New-York has been rescued from the grip of Tweed and his gang, it is now thought that annexation would be calculated to greatly benefit the towns named."[66] Suburbanites probably used the presence or absence of a "ring" as a heuristic device for understanding the otherwise confusing array of costs and benefits that came with annexation. In order to evaluate the economic impact of joining New York, residents would have had to compare the benefits of projected increases in property value that would arise from additional services with the costs of special assessments for street improvements, increases in property tax rates, or higher taxes resulting from higher property assessments. Yonkers apparently had a higher property tax rate than New York, yet the benefits of a low property tax could be eliminated by higher assessments. David Hammack, who has provided perhaps the most careful political analysis of the creation of Greater New York in 1898, contends that "the enormous number of microeconomic calculations needed to assign precise values to consolidation's economic impact would make a very doubtful contribution to knowledge." The same can be said of the 1874 annexation of lower Westchester County. In both cases, newspaper accounts certainly suggest that rather than making microeconomic calculations, residents relied on the presence or absence of "rings" and "bosses" to estimate whether they would be taxed in fair proportion to the services they expected to receive.[67]

Suburban reactions to political corruption can thus be used to explain a good deal about municipal boundaries in Westchester County. Residents in Yonkers, fearful of political corruption in New York, incorporated as an independent city. After the fall of the Tweed Ring and the establishment of a reform regime, New York City seemed a better option than Yonkers to the residents of Kingsbridge. Still, political corruption cannot explain everything; by the time Yonkers residents voted in favor of incorporation, members of the Tweed Ring were being tried in the courts, Green was comptroller, and Tammany had suffered significant electoral defeats. In short, if New York City looked to be a better option than Yonkers to the residents of Kingsbridge in 1873, there is also good reason to believe that annexation to New York would have looked like a good option to the residents of Yonkers in 1872, especially since the original justification for a city charter in Yonkers was that it would protect the city from corruption. The local press had certainly made it apparent to the residents of Yonkers that annexation to New York City was an available option for their community. There may have been a "ring" in Yonkers whose power was threatened by the prospect of annexation, and that had enough clout to get a city charter passed through the legislature, even against residents' wishes. Indeed, there is no clear evidence that there was ever a referendum on the Yonkers city charter. The fact that both the Republican and Democratic press came out in favor of the city charter suggests, however, that the measure had popular support and was not the product of a political cabal.

In order to better understand why the residents of lower Westchester County opted to become part of New York City, but the residents of Yonkers opted to create an independent city for themselves, we need to look not only at rings and bosses, but at reformers as well, namely, Andrew Green. It was in response to Green's 1868 plan to consolidate New York City and lower Westchester County that the legislature granted the Central Park Commission authority over the planning and opening of a street system for Manhattan north of 155th Street and adjoining territory in Westchester County. Even before 1868 town officials in Morrisania had developed a street plan that continued the numbered streets of Manhattan's grid from approximately 125th to 170th Streets.[68] In both cases, it is likely that the physical unification of New York and Westchester County made the political unification of these areas more likely. The *New York Times* noted in 1869 that the unified street plan provided for the "practical, if not political, annexation" of lower Westchester County to New York City.[69]

The collective development of street, water, and sewerage systems was a "path-dependent" process: high fixed costs meant that an initial investment in a capital plant would determine the shape of future investments.[70] Significant investments had been made in the village of Yonkers, even before the Civil War, that in large part determined its destiny as an independent city. Indeed, when it was created in 1855, the village of Yonkers became a "road district" separate from the highway commission of the town of Yonkers.[71] By the late 1850s sewers had been laid in many of the principal streets, and the board of trustees was agitating for greater control from the town commissioners over the opening and improving of streets in the village. By mid-1857 the village had passed an ordinance regulating the width of sidewalks and gutters relative to streets so as to create a more uniform village street system. By at least one account, Yonkers was, by the early 1870s, "one of the best governed, best graded, best lighted villages in the country."[72]

The fact that Yonkers was larger and wealthier than Morrisania and West Farms meant that it could better afford to engage in infrastructural development. As mentioned previously, however, wealth alone cannot explain why an outlying area of a central city would resist annexation to the central city. Wealth did not, in other words, create a spurious association between infrastructural development and resistance to annexation. The city of Brooklyn had a substantial industrial tax base and ranked as one of the largest cities in the United States in the 1890s, yet voted in 1894 to consolidate with New York City, albeit by a very slim majority. More telling for the discussion here is the fact that Long Island City, which was an industrial city very close to Yonkers in size, voted overwhelmingly in favor of consolidating with New York City in 1894. One thing that distinguished these two cities from Yonkers was the fact that in both Long Island City and Brooklyn, for very different reasons that will be discussed in Chapter 3, residents received inadequate urban services because local officials had been unable to provide the necessary infrastructure.

Infrastructural development was not only a matter of wealth, but also of available resources. For instance, concerns about available water resources compelled Yonkers to build an independent water system, and here again Andrew Haswell Green played a role. The question of providing an adequate water supply to Yonkers preceded the issue of annexation. Widespread support for a waterworks began to build after a fire during the summer of 1869 burned down an entire block of the village. That September Yonkers residents voted overwhelmingly in favor of granting the board of trustees "authority to provide water" for the "purposes of fire." An engineer was hired to prepare a report on how Yonkers could best be supplied with water "for household or fire purposes, or both," and in December the board of trustees appointed a special committee to draft a bill that relied on the engineer's suggestions. Instead of granting the village the authority to raise money for building a water supply system, however, the legislature only passed a bill allowing for a special election to determine whether or not residents would agree to give the board of trustees the authority to issue $225,000 in bonds for that purpose. The election, held on January 9, 1872, decided by a margin of twenty-five votes (258 to 233) against authorizing bonded indebtedness for the purposes of supplying the village with water. Both the *Statesman* and the *Gazette* editorialized that the vote did not reflect the true wishes of the majority of village residents.[73]

As a city, Yonkers had more authority to raise money and more discretion over what it could use that money for. By 1873 the common council had prepared a bill authorizing the city of Yonkers to raise a maximum of $250,000 for the purpose of constructing a water supply system and to appoint five members to a semi-independent commission that would determine the proper source for the city's water and the method for distributing it. The bill passed the legislature early in 1873, and the common council had appointed the five commissioners by mid-March.[74]

Most of the important city officials in Yonkers were members of the local business elite, who probably stood to benefit personally from a public waterworks that would serve not only residential but also industrial and commercial purposes. The fact that these officials were serving under a city charter that had apparently never been approved in a referendum and the fact that the city charter allowed them to engage in the financing and construction of a waterworks that had previously been rejected in a local referendum suggest that the creation of the city of Yonkers may have been in large part an end run around local opposition to infrastructural development.[75] Yet there is good reason to believe that residents in Yonkers also had an interest in a water supply system. It would not only help to prevent a repeat of the 1869 fire but would also significantly reduce the cost of fire insurance. In 1872 the Nationwide Board of Fire Underwriters included in its rate sheet lower insurance rates for communities that had water supply systems. Furthermore, the "water question" in Yonkers was resolved simultaneously with the last widespread outbreak of cholera in the United States. The 1869 fire may not have provided enough impetus among residents to approve a waterworks bond issue because the last serious cholera epidemic had occurred three years previously, in 1866. The growing threat of cholera in 1873 may have increased demand for a water supply in Yonkers.[76]

In any case, a significant threat to Yonkers's ability to develop an adequate water supply system was that New York City might usurp the best sources of water in Westchester County for itself. In 1872 members of the Yonkers Common Council had met with an official from the Croton Aqueduct

Department to look into the possibility that Yonkers could receive water from the Croton Aqueduct. They were informed that not only did the Croton Aqueduct Department have no water to offer them, but Yonkers "had better seize on the Nepperhan while [it] had the chance, for [Comptroller] Andy [Green] had an eye on it." The officials from Yonkers were informed that were Yonkers to be annexed to New York City, it would be supplied with water from whatever new source the city ultimately decided to use.[77]

As previously discussed, Green had seen the consolidation of New York City and lower Westchester County, including Yonkers, under a single municipal government as the best means by which a water supply system could be developed for the entire area. It thus seems likely that Green was pursuing the water resources of Westchester County with the hope that this would force Yonkers to consolidate with New York City. Indeed, it was in large part the need for a greater supply of water that ultimately forced Brooklyn to consolidate with New York City thirty years later.[78]

Consolidation with New York was not to be Yonkers's fate, however. In May 1873 the *Statesman* reported that in order to supply water to the area of Westchester County that was soon to be annexed, New York City was considering using the Bronx and Saw Mill Rivers. The threat that New York City would "deprive Yonkers of its natural source of supply" compelled the *Statesman* to urge the water commissioners to action: "Nearly two months ago Commissioners were appointed but they move slow; and we feel justified in saying that they are not meeting the public expectation. They will incur a grave responsibility if, by their inaction, they permit our natural supply to slip away from us."[79] By August the water commissioners had decided on the Sprain Brook for the water supply; by the end of the month they had contracted for the necessary pipes, stopcocks, hydrants, and labor; and in September work had commenced.[80]

Yonkers's water commissioners were moved to action at least in part by the fear that New York City would take over the best sources for water in Westchester County. Their haste provides an example of how infrastructural development could work to reinforce the boundaries between cities. As has already been argued, infrastructural development in the form of streets and sewers appears to have played a significant role in Yonkers's decision to incorporate as an independent city rather than be annexed to New York. Furthermore, by incorporating as a city, Yonkers was better able to proceed with infrastructural development in the form of a waterworks, thus differentiating itself further from New York City. To the extent that Yonkers had been moved to action, in turn, by New York's plans to extend its water supply system to additional sources in Westchester County, infrastructural development in New York facilitated infrastructural development in Yonkers that further differentiated these two cities from each other.

New York City as a Resource for Infrastructural Development in Yonkers

Infrastructural development in New York City not only provoked infrastructural development in Yonkers (at least in the case of waterworks) but also appears to have served as a resource upon which the smaller city could draw. For instance, infrastructural development in New York City provided a model from which Yonkers could learn. When the *Statesman* made a plea in December 1869 that sewerage in Yonkers "should be planned as a whole, with its main stem and collateral branches," it used as a warning against piecemeal sewer construction the example of New York, where, "without sufficient foresight, or provision for the future needs of the population . . . large sewers emptied into small ones!" Earlier in 1869 John Oliver, a member of the board of trustees, argued that based on the experience of the Brooklyn Water Works, brick sewers were significantly less expensive than tile sewers, and based on the experience of both "the Croton and Brooklyn Water Boards," vitrified Scotch pipe was the "most suitable" type of pipe for proposed sewers that were to be installed in two of Yonkers's main avenues. On the subject of streets, when the village board of trustees was at one point discussing alternative pavements in 1869, one member "suggested taking experience by neighboring cities, who are using broken trap rock to great advantage."[81]

Yonkers could of course rely on more than the experience of New York City in developing its physical infrastructure. Indeed, in determining what sort of water distribution system should be used for Yonkers, members of the board of trustees visited the waterworks of four cities in New York State (Syracuse, Buffalo, Dunkirk, and Lockport), three cities in Michigan (Detroit, Jackson, and Kalamazoo), two cities in Illinois (Peoria and Chicago), and one city in Ohio (Columbus). In addition, the waterworks of numerous other cities were discussed, as were different pumping systems, used both in Europe and the United States.[82]

The materials for infrastructural development also came to Yonkers from relatively long distances. All the contractors who submitted bids for supplying pipe, hydrants, and stopcocks for the waterworks were located on the east coast, the farthest away being B. S. Nichols and Company of Burlington, Vermont, which did not submit the lowest bid. The company that supplied the pump for the waterworks, the Holly Manufacturing Company, was from Lockport, New York, and had sold similar pumping systems to more than thirty small to midsize cities by the early 1870s, including ones in states as far away as Michigan, Iowa, Georgia, Kentucky, Ohio, Indiana, and Illinois.[83]

The experts employed in the development of the water supply system were drawn from a smaller radius. The first engineer to report on supplying Yonkers with water was the village engineer, M. K. Couzens (one of four engineers in Yonkers in 1887 listed in the earliest available business directory for Westchester County), and the second engineer to make recommendations on a water supply system, William H. Grant, was from New York City. J. S. Newberry, who was hired "to make an examination of the geological structure of the Nepperhan valley," was the geologist in chief of the state of Ohio and a professor at Columbia University's School of Mines.[84] The contractors who did the bulk of the grading and opening of streets, laying of sewers, and other physical development projects—J. and G. Stewart, James Horner, and George Frazier were some of the most frequent bidders—appear to have been primarily from the city and village of Yonkers. The Yonkers business directory, however, lists only six "contractors and builders" in Yonkers in 1887. If it is assumed that there were fewer contractors in the city in the 1870s, Yonkers may very well have required the assistance of outside contractors for larger public works projects.[85]

Conclusion

The argument presented in this chapter is that the expansion of New York City's physical infrastructure systems laid the groundwork for annexation in Morrisania, West Farms, and Kingsbridge but provoked Yonkers to differentiate itself physically and legally from the larger city. The difference between Yonkers and its neighboring towns was that Yonkers had already established itself as an independent urban community, in large part through its program of public works, by the time New York City was considering annexation.

The evidence suggests that the presence of a local business elite that controlled the village and later the city government appears to have been the main force behind both Yonkers's physical development and its independence from New York City. Infrastructural development and independence worked in tandem. Control of the local government, which would be lost through annexation, facilitated economic development, including public works, and those public works projects reinforced Yonkers's independence from New York City.

Except for the very narrow defeat of the first proposed waterworks bond issue, there is little evidence to suggest that in pursuing infrastructural development or Yonkers's municipal autonomy, the local business elite were operating contrary to the general wishes of the residents. In fact, if the local newspapers, both Republican and Democratic, are any indication, the policies of infrastructural development and municipal autonomy proceeded for the most part with the consent of village residents.

Yonkers appears to have used New York City as an example of infrastructural development, although it also relied on examples from other cities near and far. It employed labor and supplies from sources closer to home, yet the town did not rely disproportionately on New York City. Yonkers may have drawn on New York City's pool of civil engineering talent, as would have been expected. As the home of the American Society of Civil Engineers and Columbia's School of Mines, New York was a national center of civil engineering talent.[86] New York City served as a resource for infrastructural development in Yonkers, although New York City was only one of many municipalities from which Yonkers drew experience, materials, and expertise.

In short, the case of Yonkers provides evidence for the argument that infrastructural development facilitated municipal autonomy. Moreover, it appears that infrastructural development in New York City served as encouragement and provided some of the means for infrastructural development in Yonkers, though in some unexpected ways. Yonkers's experience, of course, is to some extent unique and provides only a partial picture of the general relationship between infrastructural development and municipal autonomy. By examining other municipalities in the following chapter, namely, those considered for consolidation into a "Greater New York" in the 1890s, I begin to present a more complete test of my argument.

CHAPTER 3

Greater New York and
Later Annexation Schemes

In 1894 residents of the cities, villages, and towns surrounding New York City voted on whether they would like to be included in a "Greater New York" that would encompass all the land in lower Westchester County up to the cities of Yonkers and Mount Vernon and the town of Pelham and all the land on western Long Island up to the towns of Hempstead, North Hempstead, and Oyster Bay in Queens (later Nassau) County. Despite some pockets of resistance, Greater New York came into existence in 1898. Unsuccessful attempts were later made to annex some of the bordering cities and towns to the newly expanded city.

Reactions to the Greater New York plan in municipalities surrounding New York City add several new insights into the relationship between infrastructural development, annexation, and municipal autonomy. First, infrastructural development was a central theme that ran through most of the other issues raised in regard to consolidation with New York City, including tax rates, property assessments, municipal debt, corruption, and the loss of a sense of place identity. Second, infrastructural development was not only intimately related to tax rates, property assessments, and debt levels but, as we began to see in Chapter 2, was also the most important policy area for graft in New York City, as well as in outlying communities. Relative levels of perceived corruption in New York City and surrounding municipalities played an important role in the debates on consolidation. Third, not only did New York City have less to offer a community that had already supplied itself with essential urban services, but in developing its own infrastructure systems, that community defined itself as a place with a distinct sense of identity—in most cases a distinctly suburban identity—that engendered an opposition to consolidation. Finally, infrastructural development in municipalities surrounding New York City was made possible, in large part, because New York and other cities throughout the country provided markets large enough to sustain available supplies of expertise, materials, and possibly even labor that outlying communities could use.

As infrastructural development in New York City facilitated infrastructural development in outlying municipalities, the benefits of being annexed to New York decreased, and thus suburban opposition to the consolidation plan increased. Yet the legislature simply ignored local opposition to consolidation when it authorized Greater New York in 1896. The fact that the legislature could act unilaterally to nullify any relationship between infrastructural development and suburban autonomy seriously qualifies the argument made in Chapter 1. However, the creation of Greater New York was a special case of consolidation because it had statewide significance. Later annexation schemes around New York City, discussed toward the end of this chapter, were of only local import, and the state took a less proactive role. These later annexation schemes indicate that in normal cases of consolidation, infrastructural development was an important factor in maintaining municipal independence.

The 1894 Referendum on a Greater New York

The Tweed Ring, the panic of 1873, and the economic depression that followed all made it difficult to raise money through municipal bonds and thus discouraged public capital investment in New York City during the 1870s and early 1880s. As a result, geographic expansion did not receive serious attention in New York City for more than a decade after the 1874 annexation of West Farms, Morrisania, and Kingsbridge. Moreover, the area that had been annexed in 1874 was not developed as rapidly as had been hoped. Ironically, Yonkers first began to supply Kingsbridge and West Farms with water, starting in 1882.[1]

By the mid-1880s New York City had once again begun to extend its reach into outlying areas. In 1885 construction started on the New Croton Aqueduct, described as "the greatest engineering achievement of its kind." The New Croton Aqueduct served not only to supply New York City with more water, starting in the early 1890s, but also as an important point in the development and diffusion of water infrastructure technology. Engineers throughout the country who were working on smaller water systems flocked to the new aqueduct.[2] The geographic expansion of New York City was revived as an issue by the New York State Chamber of Commerce in conjunction with Mayor Abram S. Hewitt's dramatic announcement in 1888 of a new public works initiative that included an array of improvements to the city's port and transportation facilities.[3]

With the call for consolidation, Andrew Haswell Green came forward in 1889 to reclaim his role as the chief proponent for a Greater New York. Largely due to Green's efforts, the New York legislature created the Consolidation Inquiry Commission in 1890. Five of the six commissioners appointed by Governor David B. Hill were handpicked by Green. The commission proposed that Greater New York include the town of Westchester and portions of the towns of Eastchester and Pelham in Westchester County; the towns of Flushing, Jamaica, Jamaica Bay, and Newtown, part of the town of Hempstead, and Long Island City in Queens County; the towns of Flatbush, Flatlands, Gravesend, New Utrecht, and Jamaica Bay and the city of Brooklyn in Kings County; and the towns of Castleton, Middletown, Northfield, Southfield, and Westfield on Staten Island (See Figure 2 in the Introduction).[4]

In order to build support for its plan, the commission scheduled a referendum on consolidation as part of the general elections in 1894. The referendum asked residents in all the areas proposed for inclusion in Greater New York to simply cast a vote "For Consolidation" or "Against Consolidation," without reference to any details, such as the form that the new municipal government would take. The ambiguity of the initial question makes the meaning of the referendum itself ambiguous. Moreover, the referendum was not binding. Areas that voted for consolidation did not guarantee themselves admission to the larger city, nor did areas that voted against consolidation thus guarantee their continued independence. Because it was ambiguous and nonbinding, the meaning of the referendum vote is questionable, although it does provide at least a rough measure of the extent to which the communities in the region supported their inclusion in a Greater New York.[5]

Overall, the referendum showed a majority of approximately 55 percent in favor of consolidation, although the vote varied significantly between different areas. Staten Island showed the greatest support, with 79 percent of the vote in favor of consolidation. In Queens County 62 percent of the total vote was in favor of consolidation, although the town of Flushing voted by 55 percent against the measure. In New York City the vote was 58 percent in favor of consolidation. In Kings County consolidation won with only a 277-vote lead, or less than 1 percent of the total vote, with most of the opposition coming from the city of Brooklyn. In Westchester County the town of Westchester registered a majority of one vote against consolidation, while the towns of Pelham and Eastchester voted in favor of consolidation by 62 and 59 percent, respectively.[6]

The Referendum in Westchester County

It is not clear why the vote on consolidation differed so markedly between the town of Westchester and the towns of Eastchester and Pelham, although one factor may have been that the entire town of Westchester was proposed for inclusion in Greater New York, while only parts of Eastchester and Pelham were to be annexed. In fact, only the relatively undeveloped southern end of Pelham, which became Pelham Bay Park, was included in the proposed consolidation. In Eastchester the area proposed for consolidation had recently been estranged from the rest of the town by the incorporation of the village of Mount Vernon as a city in 1892. In becoming a city, Mount Vernon separated itself from Eastchester and split the town into noncontiguous upper and lower portions. Residents in the lower portion of the town of Eastchester voted in favor of consolidation in 1894.

Although Mount Vernon was not originally included in the plan for Greater New York, residents in Mount Vernon who favored annexation were able to get the consolidation question on the ballot in their city.[7] Mount Vernon is thus unique because it did not have the referendum imposed on it by the state, as was the case in all of the other outlying municipalities. The presence of residents with strong-enough feelings in favor of consolidation who had the power to get the referendum on the ballot, suggests that the issue of consolidation with New York was an especially salient one in Mount Vernon. Thus Mount Vernon serves as an important case for examining the issues that residents considered when they voted for or against Greater New York.

Mount Vernon residents had been agitating for their annexation to New York City as early as 1892, for a host of common reasons: "a sufficient supply of pure, wholesome water at cheaper rates, better fire protection, lower insurance rates, a better sewage [sic] system, a larger police department, lower fares, and far less taxes."[8] As in the case of Yonkers, the question of Mount Vernon's annexation to New York City was contemporaneous with a proposal to incorporate the village as an independent city. If Yonkers serves as any example, incorporation as a city or annexation to New York were likely posed as the two alternatives by which Mount Vernon, whose population had increased from 4,586 to 10,830 between 1880 and 1890, could confront the issues that arose from rapid urbanization. As in Yonkers, the residents of Mount Vernon confirmed their desire for municipal independence by voting in favor of incorporation in 1892 by a majority of 78 percent (1,485 to 428) and against consolidation in 1894 by 56 percent (2,017 to 1,602).[9]

We may be able to explain, at least in part, the fact that the lower portion of the town of Eastchester voted in favor of annexation while the city of Mount Vernon voted against the measure by reference to an 1893 map that shows the majority of the streets in the most densely settled area of Mount Vernon supplied with water, gas, and sewer lines that end abruptly at the southern city limits. The most densely settled area of lower Eastchester was known as South Mount Vernon, and while its street grid was largely contiguous to that of the city of Mount Vernon, it had no sewerage, water, or gas service.[10] If residents in Mount Vernon had agitated for annexation in order to receive a better water supply and sewerage system, it would seem likely that the demand for annexation to New York City would be greater in an area such as South Mount Vernon that had no water supply or sewerage system at all. The possibility of being included within New York City's proposed public works program would thus have benefited lower Eastchester more than Mount Vernon and may have tipped the scales in favor of consolidation in that area.

Water was first supplied to Mount Vernon by the Mount Vernon Water Supply Company, formed in 1882. One of the initial supporters of the company, Joseph S. Wood, a prominent attorney with large property holdings in the village, was also a leader of the annexation movement in 1892. Unable to attract enough customers to pay off the $5,000 debt that it had incurred in building its waterworks, the Mount Vernon Water Supply Company was bought out in 1886 by investors from New York City, Boston, and Philadelphia who organized as the New York and Mount Vernon Water Company and received a "20 year exclusive franchise" to supply the village with water. The new company impounded approximately three square miles of the drainage area of Hutchinson River, which it judged adequate to supply 35,000 people with water. In 1892 the New York and Mount Vernon Water Company consolidated with a water company that served New York City's 24th Ward, or Kingsbridge Heights. The newly consolidated company became the New York City Suburban Water Company.[11]

The water from the Hutchinson River "had a horrible look and a worse taste" and was judged by the health officer of the town of Eastchester to be polluted by animal and human wastes, among other things. Nevertheless, the pressures of urbanization forced the residents of the growing village to abandon their local wells and subscribe to the water company's service. Possibly even more disturbing than the quality of the Hutchinson River water was its growing scarcity as numerous water companies and municipalities competed for the water resources of Westchester County. Mount Vernon's water supply was seriously threatened when the New Rochelle Water Company purchased water rights to the Hutchinson above the intake of the New York City Suburban Water Company, with the result that the company was sent scrambling to find other sources for water, including the polluted Bronx River and the artesian well of the old Mount Vernon Water Supply Company.[12]

It was thus in the context of a possibly catastrophic water shortage that residents in Mount Vernon began to agitate for annexation to New York City. It is notable, however, that by utilizing other sources, the New York City Suburban Water Company prevented a water crisis and was in fact taking proactive steps to improve the water supplied and ensure an adequate water supply for the future, including the purchase of new water sources such as Tom Paine Creek and the installation of innovative new filter beds, at a cost of $200,000, that received national attention.[13] The renowned filter beds may also have served as part of a larger booster movement to promote the city as a healthy place of residence. To the extent that the residents of Mount Vernon were making a choice against annexation when they voted for incorporation as an independent city in 1892, it seems likely that that choice was in large part based on their belief that their city could provide itself with an adequate supply of water without the help of New York City, and that belief was at least in part inspired by the progressive steps taken by their water company. Moreover, many of the other issues that Mount Vernon residents considered when they voted to incorporate as an independent city in 1892, such as fire protection and insurance rates, were intimately connected to the issue of water supply.

Sewerage was another important issue for the city, and here Mount Vernon was also relatively advanced, having installed sewers under the village streets in 1886–87. While the sewerage system was reported to have "apparent defects," the city's first full-term mayor, Edward Brush, could claim in his inaugural address of June 1892 that "we were all glad when the sewerage system was inaugurated, and many of the citizens doubtless feel that the system has been completed." The village had also been actively improving its streets, many of which were paved with macadam by the time

Mount Vernon became a city. Street improvements were no doubt facilitated by the fact that affected property owners were only charged special assessments for one-third of the cost of street paving, a policy that had stimulated street paving in New York City twenty years earlier.[14]

If Mount Vernon, like Yonkers, had reached a point of physical maturity that provided residents with a supply of local services and a distinct sense of place identity sufficient to make them vote for incorporation in 1892, it was not necessarily clear that this would be sufficient to make them vote against consolidation with New York City in November 1894. Substantial problems had arisen since 1892 that consolidation might solve. For instance, many residents believed that both the gas and water companies charged exorbitant fees for services; one annexationist claimed that "it was cheaper to sprinkle our lawns with whiskey than with water." Problems with the city's sewers were also escalating. In the same month as the consolidation referendum, a county grand jury began investigating claims that Mount Vernon's sewage discharge into local waterways was damaging the health of people who lived downstream from the city. According to Joseph Wood, only by becoming residents of Greater New York could Mount Vernonites confront the water and sewerage issues "without running ourselves into bankruptcy." Wood's contention that the water supply problem would bankrupt the city was reinforced when, approximately one month before the referendum, the New York City Suburban Water Company declared itself financially insolvent and was put into receivership.[15]

We may be able to explain at least part of the majority vote against consolidation in Mount Vernon by suggesting why the arguments in favor of annexation made by Wood and others may not have convinced voters. First, it was Wood's contention that in order to solve the city's pollution problem, the city of Mount Vernon was going to have to build a new "system of outlet sewers." Wood was a prominent and active member of the Mount Vernon community and was no doubt well aware of the problems his city faced, but it is not clear that the average resident would have considered the construction of new outlet sewers an imperative. Most of the individuals harmed by the city's sewage discharge lived outside the city. Furthermore, the grand jury investigation began (and was reported in at least one local paper, the *Mount Vernon Daily Argus*) only after the consolidation referendum. Finally, complaints regarding Mount Vernon's sewage had been made practically since the introduction of the sewerage system, and the city had been successfully avoiding the issue since that time.[16]

In regard to water, the ostensible assumption behind Wood's claim that providing an adequate water supply would bankrupt the city was that it was the city that would build and operate the waterworks.[17] If the *Daily Argus* is any indication of public opinion in the city, however, it does not appear that many residents shared this assumption. In its frequent criticisms of the high fees charged and the poor service provided by both the water and gas companies, the *Daily Argus* never mentioned municipal ownership of these utilities, but instead demanded more vigilance from the municipal government to make the utilities operate in the public interest. This is in fact the strategy the city followed. For instance, the city of Mount Vernon had "several times" through writs of mandamus compelled the water company to lay new mains. In October 1894, at the behest of the common council, the city's corporation counsel had taken legal action "to protect citizens against the excessive charges of the Water Company." It was, according to the *Daily Argus*, in response to these legal proceedings, and not because of financial difficulties, that the company was put into receivership: "to retain the benefits of the contract and to lay down its burdens; to collect dues, but to discharge none."[18]

Pursuing legal action against utility companies may have been one of the few economically feasible options for improving municipal services during the 1890s, but it could also serve to validate municipal independence. If (contrary to Wood's argument) the public provision of water proved unnecessary, then the city had no need to consolidate with New York and in fact could negotiate with private suppliers better as an independent municipality. As the *Daily Argus* commented, "If the city authorities shall succeed in bringing these corporations to a lively sense that a monopoly has obligations to perform which can be enforced, as well as money to take in, we shall do pretty well under our local government, yet awhile."[19] Moreover, many Mount Vernon residents probably made the connection between the slow provision of services to the areas annexed to New York City in 1874 and the likelihood that they would be supplied with services from New York during a similar economic downturn.[20] As one prominent Mount Vernon antiannexationist, Judge Isaac N. Mills, noted, "The New York water supply with the present demands upon it and with the prospective demands upon it from territory, imperatively needing water, will not be diverted in any part to Mount Vernon."[21]

As a community gained in population and became increasingly urban, water was needed for more public purposes, and thus the establishment of a municipal waterworks became more imperative.[22] In the case of New York

City, urbanization certainly seems to have required the public provision of water, and as we will see in Chapter 5, the same can be said for Newark. In the case of Mount Vernon, however, the reliance on a private water company appears to have been not only a result of that city's smaller size, but also of the fact that it was a different type of community than New York City—namely, a suburb. As Mayor Brush said of Mount Vernon in his 1892 inaugural address,

> This city is purely a place of residence, a home. The hum and noise, the smoke and steam, with the hurry and bustle of traffic, which show the immense importance of a commercial city, is all absent here. The quiet of the villa, the park, the pleasant lawn, the modest, substantial and beautiful home characterize Mount Vernon. A large majority of our citizens go into the great metropolis daily, and there amid the din and strife, fight the battle of life, leaving their peaceful homes meantime in our care.[23]

In a "city of homes" that might remain relatively small and low density, a municipal waterworks was not an inevitable necessity. Indeed, by the 1890s, while two-thirds of American municipalities with populations of more than 50,000 had public waterworks, municipalities with less than 50,000 people were roughly equally split between public and private water systems, and "in towns of from 20,000 down private works have the strongest footing."[24] Thus the preference for private water in Mount Vernon was distinctly suburban in nature. Infrastructural development and a suburban identity worked in tandem to differentiate Mount Vernon from New York City, increasing residents' resistance to annexation.[25]

What may also have compelled many Mount Vernon residents to vote against consolidation was the fact that by the 1890s Tammany Hall was once again in power in New York City. Many residents may have seen little difference in being provided water by a private company that charged exorbitant fees or by a municipal government that levied exorbitant taxes in order to finance a reviled political machine; they would at least have more control over a local company. Moreover, at the time of the consolidation referendum, corruption and vice in New York City were receiving an unusually high level of attention through the Lexow committee (named after committee chair and state senator Clarence Lexow), authorized by the legislature and funded by the chamber of commerce to investigate municipal corruption. A week before the consolidation referendum, the *Brooklyn Daily Eagle* noted that "it is extremely unfortunate for the advocates of consolidation that their efforts . . . happen to coincide with the shocking revelations being made from day to day before the Lexow Committee." These revelations did help elect a reform candidate, William L. Strong, as mayor of New York in 1894.[26] Since the consolidation referendum was scheduled as part of the general election, however, the residents of Mount Vernon would not have known that New York City had elected a reform administration until after they had voted on consolidation. In any case, Tammany Hall had become a much larger and more effective political machine under the direction of John Kelly and Richard Croker, and in comparison, any reform administration looked that much more fleeting.

The Referendum in Queens County

The fear that consolidation would mean control by Tammany politicians was prevalent in Queens County. In 1892 "prominent Flushing men" told the *Flushing Journal* that the primary reason for their disapproval of the Greater New York scheme "was their fear of Tammany."[27] The majority vote against consolidation by the residents of Flushing in the 1894 referendum supported the *Flushing Journal*'s findings.

Residents in the other towns of Queens County also voiced opposition to consolidation because it would likely expand the control of Tammany over their communities, but it is notable that only in Flushing did a majority vote against consolidation in the 1894 referendum. Something obviously distinguished Flushing from the other towns in Queens County that made it vote against consolidation. As in Yonkers and Mount Vernon, at least one thing that distinguished the town of Flushing was the fact that with the possible exception of Long Island City, it was more advanced than the other towns in terms of infrastructural development.

Flushing's well-developed infrastructure compared with that of other towns in Queens County was evident as early as 1873. An advertisement for the Flushing and North Side Railroad highlights the development of infrastructure only for the two largest villages in the town of Flushing. Of the village of Flushing, which then had a population of approximately 8,000, the advertisement notes that "gas was introduced a number of years ago and water is about being [*sic*] introduced." In College Point, which had a population of approximately 4,000, "The streets are well regulated, curbed and guttered, sewers and gas pipes are laid throughout the village, and a special act has been obtained from the Legislature for introducing water."

For five other villages along the railroad's route, no mention is made of local infrastructure.[28]

Flushing's waterworks were operational by 1874, and the local water sources that it used were expanded as the village grew. By the 1890s the village had a sewerage system. The Flushing Gas Light Company supplied gas for streetlights, starting in 1860. Mostly through the organizing efforts of the Flushing Village Association, an influential civic group, the village trustees issued bonds for street improvements, and by 1897, "with few exceptions, all of the streets were macadamized and in perfect order." Like Mount Vernon, street paving in Flushing was in large part centrally financed, thus avoiding piecemeal development that might have impeded infrastructural development.[29]

In short, there is at least circumstantial evidence to suggest that like Mount Vernon and Yonkers, Flushing's rejection of consolidation with New York City in the 1894 referendum was connected to infrastructural development in that town. The fact that the residents of the villages of Flushing and College Point were already supplied with independent water, sewerage, and street lighting systems should have lowered the perceived benefits of consolidation that might otherwise have provided a countervailing force against fears concerning Tammany Hall. Moreover, like Mount Vernon, Flushing was notably suburban and thus distinct from New York. As one resident described Flushing in the 1890s, "Those institutions have been fostered that would render the village attractive to persons seeking homes: manufacture has not been encouraged."[30]

Unlike suburban communities such as Flushing, Long Island City's name suggests that its founders envisioned it as a rival to New York, but the name was probably the only thing that suggested urban greatness along the western edge of Queens County.[31] As one author noted in 1882, "Long Island City . . . comprises the localities known as Astoria, Hunter's Point, Ravenswood, Dutch Kills, Blissville and Middletown. The more populous of these places are still geographically distinct, the spaces intervening between them not having been built up as yet, and the new city name is by many ignored in consequence."[32] If Long Island City did not inspire much shared sense of identity among its residents, it did serve to unite them on their desire to be a part of Greater New York. In 1894 the residents of Long Island City voted overwhelmingly in favor of consolidation, by 82 percent—3,529 to 792.[33]

Long Island City was incorporated in 1870 and consolidated the separate communities of eastern Queens County under one municipal government, thus separating them from the town of Newtown. The area that would become the commercial center of Long Island City, Hunter's Point, existed as undeveloped, low-lying meadowlands until 1852, when the area was graded, leveled, and staked out into streets—an effort by owner Eliphalet Nott to sell his land off in lots. By 1860 enough streets had been opened to form fourteen city blocks, and by 1865 the population had reached approximately 1,500. Population growth and lot sales at Hunter's Point were facilitated by the introduction of rail service to Flushing and ferry service to Manhattan, starting in 1854. The unique combination of rail and ferry service with massive population growth on previously undeveloped land furthered the commercial and industrial development of Hunter's Point, thus distinguishing it from the older communities in Queens County that resisted the encroachment of industrialization.[34]

Rapid population growth also highlighted the need for infrastructural development and local government. As one resident of Hunter's Point noted in 1869, "there is one fact patent to all and that is there is a daily increasing demand for some kind of local government, some way in which we may have our principle [sic] streets curbed and guttered, repaired and kept in passable order and sewered and such other projects as are needed inaugurated and successfully carried out." The "citizens of Hunter's Point and vicinity" first endeavored to have the legislature incorporate their area as a village. The "owners of all the large manufacturing establishments" were initially opposed, since the measure was likely to raise their taxes, but residents overall voted in favor of incorporation (299 to 150) in a local referendum. Possibly on account of the manufacturers' resistance, the village charter was defeated in the legislature in the spring of 1869. Yet defeat only escalated the battle for incorporation. In the summer of 1870 proponents of incorporation sought to have Hunter's Point annexed to the village of Astoria, and by winter the plan had grown to a city charter, encompassing "so much of the Town of Newtown as lies between the East River and Bowery Bay Road." That spring Governor John Hoffman held hearings on the Long Island City charter after the measure had already been approved unanimously in both houses of the legislature. Opponents of the charter, reportedly all large property holders who were concerned about city taxes, testified that the charter had been "prepared in secret and . . . smuggled through the Legislature," while proponents countered that it had been "submitted to and approved by the residents of each of the proposed wards." Governor Hoffman took the proponents' side and signed the bill, thus creating Long Island City on May 4, 1870.[35]

The city the governor created was hardly impressive. The common council was restricted to raising and spending $25,000 annually. The limit was raised to $75,000 in 1871, but this was still insufficient for a city that needed street pavements, street lamps, street signs, sewers, and water-works. Instead, residents could petition the legislature to create "special commissions" that had the authority to issue bonds for specific local projects, thus keeping public works decentralized. The commissions served as convenient vehicles for graft for local politicians and contractors. For instance, a First Ward Improvement Commission was created to finance street improvements in Hunter's Point. Grading the streets of Hunter's Point, including raising one of the main thoroughfares, Jackson Avenue, five feet, required approximately one million cubic yards of fill dirt and involved heavy expenses for property owners who had to raise their buildings to the new grade. One local businessman, James Thomson, was informed by his lawyer, Henry Debevoise (who also happened to be mayor of Long Island City from 1875 to 1883), that the city was going to need large amounts of fill dirt for Jackson Avenue. Thomson thus bought local farmlands for $100,000, and the city bought dirt from Thomson's land for ten cents a cubic yard. By 1880 Thomson had made back his initial investment. In the process of removing fill dirt, the city had also brought the land to grade, thus increasing its value significantly, at no cost to Thomson.[36]

The relationship between Thomson and Mayor Debevoise surfaced again in relation to the city's water supply. In 1870 the residents of Long Island City depended on street hand pumps that produced water of varying quality, "depending on their location and nearness to salt water and industrial pollution." Under a revised city charter in 1871, the legislature authorized the establishment of a water board for Long Island City, with the authority to build and manage a waterworks, financed with a maximum $300,000 bond issue. The water board easily fell within the control of the mayor, as he served on the board along with two commissioners he appointed, as well as a city judge and the city's commissioner of public works. Thus when Debevoise became mayor, the water board opted not to make use of forty acres of water-rich land donated to the city, but purchased various properties within the city limits from Thomson for a total of $90,000. Thomson later bought back some of his land at a reduced price, from which he proceeded to sell more fill dirt to the city. Questionable sums were also paid for surveying, equipment, and a useless reservoir, with the result that another bond issue of $50,000 was required to install a pumping station and seven miles of water main.[37]

One contemporary noted of the water supplied by the Long Island City waterworks that it "proved to be the best and coldest water introduced by main into any of the cities in the United States. It is now admitted by all that the system has proved a marvelous success." Even this sympathetic author had to admit, however, that "the water board of Long Island City, having but limited means, could not enter upon a plan of waterworks sufficiently extensive to meet the future wants of a large and populous city." That flagrant corruption, not "limited means," resulted in an insufficient water supply is suggested by a comparison with the Yonkers waterworks, which were built at the same time and used the same system (a Holly pump) for a city of comparable size, yet required only a $250,000 bond issue to build a water supply system that could meet the water supply needs of Yonkers's entire population, and indeed of people living outside the city as well. In contrast, the Long Island City waterworks were built on a $350,000 bond issue (the actual debt incurred ultimately was $362,000) and did not extend throughout the entire city but were supplemented by private waterworks, such as those built by the Steinways in the mid-1870s. Not only did the Long Island City waterworks saddle the city with an exorbitant amount of debt, but the inadequacy of the system also increased the risk of fires, thus raising insurance rates.[38]

Mayor Debevoise was removed from office in 1883 when the state supreme court found him guilty of electoral fraud in the 1880 election. Debevoise's challenger from that election, reform candidate and "prosperous hardware dealer" George Petry, assumed the mayoralty, which he won again in 1884. Petry brought at least some efficiency and competence to Long Island City government, but he lost the mayoral election in 1886 to Patrick Jerome Gleason, an alderman, regular Democrat, and classically corrupt political boss who became the defining figure of politics and infrastructural development in Long Island City. Gleason served as mayor from 1887 to 1892 and again from 1895 until the city was absorbed into Greater New York. During the first part of his mayoralty, Gleason refused to abdicate his position as an alderman and also appointed himself the presiding officer of the boards of education, police, and water, among other offices.[39]

Under Gleason the water board went from running surpluses to deficits within five years. None of the annual reports required by law were ever published. Expenditures went unexplained, and wells dug to an insufficient depth polluted the city's water supply "with surface water drawn from the quagmire at Bowery Bay." While the "Gleason Water Board" poisoned the public water supply, Gleason himself profited through his interests in local water and electric companies. Gleason's Woodside Water Company was incorporated in 1890 and received an $80,000 contract to supplement the inadequate supply of the city's waterworks. The commissioner of public works was later charged with having disconnected some of the city's pumping stations in order to create more business for Gleason's company. In 1893 the *Long Island City Weekly Star* reported that Gleason's electric company, the Gleason Electric Illuminating Company, had illegally tapped one of the city's water mains and had been using from 8,000 to 10,000 gallons of water a day, free of charge. Another electric company in which Gleason had an interest, the Long Island City Illuminating Company, was awarded a five-year street lighting contract in 1891 "without bidding in an open violation of the Charter; passed 5–1 by Gleason's men."[40]

Long Island City's population had increased from 17,129 in 1880 to 35,629 in 1892, yet the municipal government appears to have been incapable of meeting the increasing needs of the population through infrastructural development. Indeed, in the case of the Gleason water board, infrastructural development frequently did more harm than good. The shoddy and insufficient infrastructure systems of Long Island City were not cheap either, but had made a substantial contribution to an enormous municipal debt—$1.2 million as early as 1876, compared with $10 million for the "whole state of New York"—and a comparably high tax rate. In 1891 the *Long Island City Weekly Star* asked, "Have we not reached the limit of burden bearing? . . . [W]ould it not be advisable to proclaim: not another dollar's addition to the public debt, for any purpose whatsoever, no matter how plausible the argument or seemingly urgent the purpose[?]" A reform administration was elected in 1892, but the Democratic machine remained sufficiently entrenched to get Gleason reelected in 1895.[41] In short, there is little evidence that Long Island City had met residents' needs sufficiently throughout its twenty-seven-year history as an independent municipality. It seems entirely likely that this fact was registered in the overwhelming support that consolidation received in 1894.

The Referendum in Kings County

Long Island City was very close in population size to Yonkers (30,506 to 32,033 in 1890, respectively), and thus the idea that such a city might be annexed to New York was not unprecedented. That a city of Brooklyn's size might be annexed to a still larger city was, however, unprecedented in the history of the United States. First "recognized by the state Legislature" as a town in 1788, then incorporated as a village in 1816 and again as a city in 1834, Brooklyn had a population of 96,838 in 1850, making it the seventh-largest city in the nation. In 1855, after Brooklyn had annexed the city of Williamsburgh and the town of Bushwick, it became the third-largest city in the country, with a population of approximately 200,000. By 1890 Brooklyn's population exceeded 800,000—more than twenty times the size of Long Island City at the time of the referendum vote in 1894.[42]

Brooklyn and Kings County stand in interesting contrast to Long Island City and Queens County because the pattern of the vote in the 1894 referendum in these two cities and counties was the reverse image of one another. In contrast to Queens, where the urbanized sections of the county closest to Manhattan voted by vast majorities in favor of Greater New York, the ten wards farthest away from New York in Brooklyn provided the bulk of support for consolidation. Of the twenty-one wards in Brooklyn closest to Manhattan, only four gave a majority vote in favor of consolidation. Indeed, the only reason that the overall vote in Brooklyn came out in favor of consolidation (and only then by the slimmest of majorities) was that three outlying towns that had been annexed to the city earlier in 1894—Flatbush, Gravesend, and New Utrecht—provided large pro-consolidation majorities. As one Brooklyn resident noted after the referendum, "New Utrecht and Flatbush, which have only just come into the city [,] cast so large a vote for consolidation that they swamped the old city majority against it."[43]

One possible explanation for Brooklynites' opposition to consolidation was that despite its estimable size, Brooklyn was, like Flushing and Mount Vernon, a suburb of New York City. Like Mount Vernon, Brooklyn was known as a "city of homes," where a sizable proportion of the population left each morning for work in Manhattan.[44] For at least some Brooklynites, the suburban nature of their city appears to have generated a distinctly different sense of place identity than that of New Yorkers. Brooklyn historian Harold Syrett has explained, for instance, that nineteenth-century Brooklynites were inclined to believe that "the life of the average New Yorker was essentially immoral," while New Yorkers held that "Brooklyn was merely an ambitious, but none the less ludicrous, country cousin."[45] As the anti-consolidationist *Brooklyn Daily Eagle* put the case for Brooklyn, "Here the rich and the poor meet together and the Lord is the maker of them all. New York is the city of palaces and of unimproved tenements. There the rich and the poor keep separate, growling at one another, and the devil is to pay . . . in New York the condition of earnest and happy living is dependent upon the exploitation of Brooklyn qualities."[46]

Unlike Flushing and Mount Vernon, however, Brooklyn's suburban identity undermined its justifiable claim to being a major American city and created what Syrett has called a "feeling of insecurity" in relation to New York City.[47] In his monumental work on Brooklyn completed just after the Civil War, Henry Stiles explained that

> although Brooklyn had, at a single bound, jumped from the seventh to the third position among the cities of the American Union, it could by no means claim the same relative position in point of wealth, business or commercial importance; being outranked, in these respects, by several cities of less population. Nor had it risen to its eminence by virtue of its inherent vigor and enterprise. Candor certainly compels the acknowledgment that it was chiefly attributable to the overflowing prosperity and greatness of its giant neighbor, New York.[48]

Thus Brooklynites were caught between lauding the suburban virtues of their city and boosting Brooklyn as a booming metropolis—and in both instances seeking to differentiate themselves from New York. One booster publication in 1890 sought to dispel the common notion that Brooklyn was merely a suburb by noting that "she ranks as the fourth largest city of the country in manufacturing and commerce." The president of the League of Loyal Citizens of Brooklyn, William C. Redfield, stated emphatically in 1894 that "the manufactories of Brooklyn are not largely run by New York capital. Brooklyn has achieved within ten years very largely her own independence. Our business interests are in no sense dependent upon New York."[49]

Part of Brooklyn's claim to being distinct and independent from New York relied on the city's ability to build comprehensive infrastructure systems, in which city officials took obvious pride. Street improvements started as early as the 1820s, and by 1840 there were some thirty-five miles of paved streets supplied with oil lamps. In 1848 gas service was introduced into the city and construction on the Gowanus Canal began, which would drain off 1,700 acres of land, thus greatly facilitating housing construction in the southern part of the city. In 1855 the mayor of the enlarged city, George Hall, boasted in his inaugural address that Brooklyn had 3,766 streetlights ("of which 2,609 are gas lamps"), five miles of sewers, "157 public cisterns and 547 wells and pumps." In 1855 alone, fourteen miles of new streets were opened, nine miles of streets were "graded and paved; 426 new gas lamps and posts set," and sixteen public cisterns were constructed.[50]

The wells and cisterns constructed in the 1850s were outmoded shortly by a new water supply system that commenced operation in November 1858. In regard to Brooklyn's new waterworks, the *New York Herald* declared that "the citizens of our city, who are so justly proud of their Croton Department, will be astonished to hear that Brooklyn will, ere long, have not merely a far larger supply, but will be enabled to furnish the lower part of New York with much advantage over its present supply, both as regards effective head and annual cost."[51] Not only was Brooklyn's water system more advanced than New York's, but in conjunction with the waterworks, the legislature also authorized Brooklyn's water commissioners to plan and build a sewerage system for the city. As a result, the city was divided into four drainage districts, and the miles of sewer pipe laid in the city increased from 5 in 1857 to 149 in 1870.[52]

Plans to build a comprehensive water supply system for Brooklyn had been proposed since the 1830s. The first formal action was taken in 1847, when Major David B. Douglass prepared a report for the common council that recommended that the city draw its water from "monster wells" that were to be dug "somewhere near the south-east base of the Flatbush hills" on Long Island. After a devastating fire in the city in 1849, the legislature authorized Douglass's system, at an estimated cost of $830,000, but construction never began. A new plan, developed by William J. McAlpine with the assistance of John B. Jervis, was presented to the common council at the end of 1851. McAlpine recommended that water be pumped from streams in southern Long Island to a reservoir on Prospect Hill, "thence to be distributed through the city." A referendum in July 1853 rejected the new plan for a water supply, the cost of which had been estimated at $4 million. The common council, apparently undeterred, submitted a new plan (the principal difference being a change in location of the distributing reservoir) for a referendum in 1854, which was also rejected.[53]

Faced with voter resistance, Brooklyn officials ultimately secured a water supply by collaborating with private interests through a succession of water companies. In 1852 the Williamsburgh Water Company was incorporated for the purpose of constructing a waterworks, "costing not over $500,000, for the supply of Williamsburgh alone." In an action similar to what McAlpine had proposed, the company purchased several streams on the south side of Long Island. In 1853 the Williamsburgh Water Company was "absorbed and succeeded" by the newly created Long Island Water Company, which, with a capital stock of $3 million, was authorized by the legislature to supply both Brooklyn and Williamsburgh with water. The Long Island Water Company became the Nassau Water Company in 1855, and the new corporate charter authorized the city of Brooklyn to purchase $1.3 million worth of the new water company's stock, which it did in 1856. In February 1857, by another act of the legislature, "the contracts, property and rights, of the Nassau Water Company" were transferred to the city of Brooklyn, and the seven directors of the company were named to a new board of water commissioners that was authorized to construct a city waterworks.[54]

The planning and construction of Brooklyn's water and sewerage system was clearly aided by the knowledge and experience gained from building the Croton waterworks. The author of the first official plan to supply Brooklyn with water, Major Douglass, was "the distinguished engineer of the Croton Works of New York." John Jervis, who assisted William McAlpine with the second plan for a Brooklyn water supply, had also been an engineer for the Croton system. The president of the Long Island Water Company was "Nicholas Dean, Esq., for many years connected with the Croton department in New York." Engineers from both the Croton Aqueduct Department and the Jersey City Water Works lent their assistance in determining the appropriate materials and equipment to use for Brooklyn's sewerage system.[55] Thus to the extent that Yonkers officials relied on the advice and example of Brooklyn in the physical development of their city, as discussed in Chapter 2, they may actually have been indirectly following the example of New York City, indicating a pattern of infrastructure technology transfer from larger to progressively smaller cities in the metropolitan region.

Despite the city's impressive growth, even sympathetic authors were compelled to note by 1870 that "Brooklyn has not been made beautiful without heavy expense to her citizens," reflected in high taxes and a large municipal debt. Because infrastructural development had a greater impact on the value of land used for industrial purposes, public works in a city such as New York could be financed in large part through increased revenues from higher land valuations. In a "city of homes" such as Brooklyn, the cost of infrastructural development was met more by higher residential property taxes than by higher valuations on industrial property. Thus in the same year as the referendum on Greater New York, local state senator William H. Reynolds could call Brooklyn "the highest taxed city in the Union." Moreover, the city was rapidly approaching its debt limit.[56]

The problem of high debt and taxes was a central issue in the consolidation referendum in Brooklyn. Advocates for Greater New York argued that consolidation would equalize taxes between New York and Brooklyn and lower Brooklyn's tax rate in the process. However, as it stood in 1894, the Greater New York bill had no provisions for equal taxation, Senator Reynolds's amendment for this purpose having been defeated in the legislature. Anticonsolidationists could thus argue that Brooklynites' taxes would not be lowered as a result of consolidation. Indeed, because it had the largest population, the old New York City would still maintain majority control over Greater New York and would have little interest in equalizing tax rates for the benefit of Brooklynites.[57]

Brooklyn's weak tax base exacerbated the problems of an inefficient administrative structure that practically invited corruption. Like New York City, Brooklyn was regularly Democratic, and as a result, the regularly Republican legislature sought to usurp local patronage resources. Control over such essential services as police and public works was given over to state-appointed commissions, while Brooklyn's city officials were left with little real power. As in Long Island City, local infrastructure projects in Brooklyn were carried out by special commissions that were created by petition of interested parties and passed by rote in the legislature. The Brooklyn city government, however, had the responsibility of collecting assessments and paying back the bonds issued by the special commissions. With responsibility for local infrastructural development thus fragmented, the election of a reform mayor in 1868 who campaigned on a platform of fiscal retrenchment (Martin Kalbfleisch, for whom "good government was tantamount to cheap government") made little difference. Brooklyn's mayor could not control the expenditures of commissions created by the legislature.[58]

Although the legislature did begin to return some control over public works to city officials in the late 1860s, infrastructural development in Brooklyn remained in large part a vehicle for Republican patronage and "one of the most corrupt branches of the local government." The system was reformed under the 1882 city charter, which provided for city department heads appointed by the mayor, over whom the common council had no confirmation authority. Administrative centralization coincided with the reform administration of Seth Low, who served as mayor from 1882 to 1885. Low's administration did little to lighten Brooklynites' tax burden, however. The new mayor pursued municipal efficiency along with a new program of public works that actually increased tax rates.[59]

If Low could increase taxes to pay for infrastructural development in the 1880s, by the 1890s the debt and tax rates were high enough to impede needed public works. As Senator Reynolds claimed, it was especially Brooklyn's debt that, "from the standpoint of needed improvements, is a serious obstacle." The debt blocked new street pavements and schools and improvements to the city's fire department and water supply and closed off the possibility of constructing bridges over the East River to Manhattan. If consolidation could equalize taxes and debt, it would facilitate infrastructural development by loosening Brooklyn's financial constraints. As one Brooklyn annexationist noted in regard to the outlying wards of the city, "With New York and Brooklyn consolidated, we can better afford to grade, pave and build up these farm lands. Brooklyn alone could not afford the cost. New York City, if wise, would decline, but the chances are that they will be very willing." It was one of the planks of the Brooklyn Consolidation League that as part of Greater New York, Brooklyn would attain "a comprehensive system of public improvements, such as *bridges, tunnels, waterworks, parks, roadways and means of rapid transit.*"[60]

As the Brooklyn Consolidation League indicated, transportation was at least one of the rationales given for consolidation. Municipalities in Kings and Queens Counties were unique in this regard because their economic and commercial development depended on an increasing volume of traffic coming to and from New York City, which required bridges across the East River. In most situations transportation was not an issue in annexation because rail companies served both cities and suburbs. Yet rail companies did not have the capital to build bridges that could cross the East River, so transportation required government investment, which was facilitated if it was undertaken by a single city.

More important than bridges to the consolidation debate in Brooklyn were other forms of infrastructure. In their recent and monumental history of New York City, Edwin Burrows and Mike Wallace note of Brooklyn in the 1890s that "the transport dilemma . . . was as nothing compared to the water crisis."[61] Wards most in need of public works cast some of the largest majorities in favor of Greater New York. For instance, of all the wards in Brooklyn lying along the East River, the 17th, which included most of Greenpoint, had both the highest vote for consolidation and the most residential areas without adjoining water and sewer lines. In the eastern section of the city, the 26th Ward (New Lots) had no sewers and the second-highest vote for consolidation in the entire city. Moreover, while most of the 26th

Ward was served by water, it was not the city's system, but that of the Long Island Water Supply Company, which charged exorbitant fees for apparently poor service.[62]

Areas that had no sewer or water lines were not the only ones that had reason to be concerned about the infrastructure of Brooklyn. As towns and villages farther out on Long Island made increasing use of the water sources that Brooklyn also used, water shortages became a concern for the entire city. In May 1894 the *Brooklyn Daily Eagle* listed twelve fires between December 1889 and May 1894, the damage from which could have been reduced with adequate water pressure and supply.[63] The threat of a water shortage was apparent during the notably dry summer prior to the consolidation referendum. Because the Brooklyn water system relied on small ponds and streams, it was relatively sensitive to dry periods. In addition, water consumption in the city had increased from the previous summer by approximately 7 million gallons per day. By the end of June the *Eagle* was reporting on numerous complaints about the "dusty conditions" in Prospect Park and rumors that "the water supply in the park has given out." There were also reports that the increase in water consumption had forced the Department of City Works to use water of poor quality "from ponds or streams about Jamaica and Hempstead."[64]

In order to address the city's water problem, City Works Commissioner White presented a plan to the board of aldermen for a $2.5 million extension of the waterworks that would tap into water resources farther east on Long Island (mostly from driven wells) and increase the available water supply by an estimated 25 million gallons per day. In order to address the longer-term water needs of the city, White also requested $10,000 to investigate possible water sources for the future, including "the Ramapo region, Lake George, and . . . the Connecticut watershed." Several Republican aldermen were reluctant to make an appropriation for White's plan and blocked its consideration in the final regular session of the board before their summer recess.[65]

According to the opposing aldermen, the problem with White's plan to extend the waterworks was that the money requested might be used to support the "ring" of "old engineers and contractors." The *Eagle*, reproaching the aldermen for their intransigence, noted of this "ring" that "nobody can find out what or whom they are talking about." Yet infrastructural development in Brooklyn had been characterized by graft in the recent past. In 1887 the city's political boss, Hugh McLaughlin, picked Alfred Chapin to run for mayor as a compromise candidate between independent and regular Democrats. As mayor, Chapin initiated a new round of public capital investment; during three years more than $6 million were spent for "schools, parks, public buildings, pavements and sewers." Chapin's public works program addressed a dire need in Brooklyn and most probably contributed to his reelection in 1889, but Chapin also used his public works program in large part to reward party loyalists, especially in the area of street improvements. Contractors friendly to the Democratic machine repaved Brooklyn's streets with used Belgian block that had been pulled out of the streets of downtown Manhattan. The work was often evidently shoddy and incomplete.[66] Thus public works in Brooklyn created opportunities for graft that justified the reluctance of the Republican aldermen to expand the city's water supply.

Chapin was not nominated for a third term as mayor because of revelations that he had been secretly negotiating to buy the Long Island Water Supply Company (the previously mentioned water company of the 26th Ward) on behalf of the city at a price significantly above the company's estimated value. McLaughlin had Chapin nominated for a seat in the U.S. House of Representatives, and the incumbent congressman, David Boody, was run as mayor in 1891. Elected by a large majority, Mayor Boody reappointed all of the city commissioners who had been in office under Chapin. Graft and malfeasance flourished under the Boody administration, increasing the city's debt to unprecedented levels and providing the opportunity for a Republican reform candidate, Charles A. Schieren, to win the mayoralty in 1893.[67]

The election of Schieren may very well have had an impact on the consolidation referendum, since perceived levels of corruption were no doubt used by Brooklynites to judge the expected benefits or losses to come from consolidation. The *Eagle* contended, for instance, that "if tied to New York, Brooklyn would be a Tammany suburb, to be kicked, looted, and bossed as such." With Schieren, Brooklyn had a reform administration that, one letter to the editor of the *Eagle* claimed, was "more vigorous" than the reform administration of Seth Low and would last for "six, and may reach ten" years.[68]

In regard to Brooklyn's water supply problem, Mayor Schieren called a special session of the board of aldermen on July 23, 1894 to vote on a $750,000 appropriation for White's extension plan, which passed unanimously. Yet Brooklyn's consolidationists still used the issue of water to argue in favor of Greater New York. Commissioner White himself had argued that Brooklyn would soon have to look beyond Long Island for its water needs, at which point the consolidation of the cities would be a great advantage. Edward C. Graves, a Brooklyn attorney and possibly the most outspoken proponent of Greater New York, argued that building a new aqueduct from Lake George or Ramapo would cost less for both Brooklyn and New York if they were consolidated into a single city. Even the *Eagle* recognized that in regard to water, "the needs of the two cities are the same and they must be met in the same way." However, the *Eagle* also contended that Brooklyn could "co-operate with New York on a common system of water supply, whether politically then in union with that city or not."[69]

As an independent city, of course, Brooklyn did not have the financial means to "co-operate" with New York City in building a new aqueduct. The question was in fact moot, since by 1894 New York City had just completed the New Croton Aqueduct, thirty-one miles long and capable of supplying an additional 300 million gallons of water per day. With its new aqueduct, New York City had enough water for "New York and Brooklyn and one million people more." Reflecting the disparate financial conditions of the two cities, the New Croton Aqueduct was estimated to cost more than $14 million, while Brooklyn's council members deliberated spending $750,000 on their waterworks. One Brooklyn resident made the astute observation that his city could be "likened very much to a merchant who has a large store with an insufficient capital to run his business . . . to avoid bankruptcy the merchant wisely takes in a rich partner."[70]

Like Long Island City, infrastructural development in Brooklyn had been characterized by inefficiency and political corruption and had brought the city to the brink of financial disaster. Given these similarities, the difference between the results of the referendum in each city deserves careful consideration. Possibly the most fundamental difference between Brooklyn and Long Island City that was reflected in the referendum was that Brooklyn engendered a shared sense of identity among its residents, while Long Island City did not. Indeed, Senator Reynolds argued that the central issue in terms of consolidation was not equal taxation—which he was sure would come to pass even in the absence of a specific provision for such in the consolidation bill—but whether the residents of Brooklyn were "willing to lose their identity and become part of New York for the sake of this lowering of taxes, or do they prefer to experiment still longer in an attempt to lower them as a separate city?"[71]

A sense of place identity is made tangible by the unique physical features that define the place. In this regard, it is important to emphasize the connection between a sense of place identity in Brooklyn, the lack of such a sense of identity in Long Island City, and the physical development of these two cities. As previously discussed, at least one contemporary author recorded that the name "Long Island City" was in large part ignored because the land between the preexisting communities that had been consolidated into the city still remained undeveloped. On the other hand, infrastructural development in Brooklyn, especially the waterworks, fit into a larger booster movement that sought to define Brooklyn as a separate city from New York, with unique qualities and virtues that the larger city lacked.

If Brooklynites did view themselves as morally superior to New Yorkers, they must have found it difficult to explain the evident corruption in their city government. Still, the perennial election of reform mayors, from Kalbfleisch to Low to Schieren, suggests that there were significant forces within the community that could counterbalance a level of corruption that may have been considered standard for big cities in the nineteenth century. Brooklyn also had a tradition of being technologically progressive, as in the case of the city's sewerage system and waterworks. Even if they often served corrupt ends, public works in Brooklyn were still impressive in their own right—private motives worked in conjunction with the public good, at least as long as the city had money left to spend. By contrast, there was little evidence to show that the separate communities that formed Long Island City were able to keep even the most flagrantly corrupt politicians in check, with the result that the public good that public works could have served was sacrificed for the purpose of private gain. The residents of Long Island City appear to have weighed these problems when they voted in favor of Greater New York by a proportion far higher than voters in Brooklyn.

Infrastructural development not only played a key role in the consolidation referendum, but was also intimately connected with most of the other issues that surfaced in regard to the creation of Greater New York. For instance, Brooklyn's high tax rate and debt level were a major issue in the consolidation referendum, at least in part because Brooklyn did not have the financial means to proceed with needed public works. Likewise, Joseph Wood had supported Mount Vernon's annexation to New York because he had believed that annexation was the only means by which his small city could cope financially with its water and sewerage problems.

Ironically, the graft and corruption that came with public works in large part created the financial problems that then impeded infrastructural development. In both Brooklyn and Long Island City municipal debts and tax rates had increased dramatically, mainly because public works projects had been carried out inefficiently for the purposes of partisanship and personal gain. Because public works were central to the maintenance of a political machine, voters' perceptions of the level of political corruption in different parts of the metropolitan region were probably in large part a reflection of how they perceived that infrastructural development was carried out in those areas.

Finally, many individuals, such as those in Mount Vernon and Flushing, probably voted against consolidation in part because they felt that the suburban identity of their place of residence would be diminished if it were subsumed within a larger city. Infrastructural development could provide a sense of self-sufficiency that at least enhanced this sense of place identity. Brooklyn serves as an intermediate case, since it was both a suburb and a large city in its own right. The case of Brooklyn also suggests that only smaller suburban communities were economically viable, because a residential tax base could only support infrastructural development on a smaller scale.

The Creation of Greater New York and Later Annexation Schemes

Ultimately, local variations in the vote for consolidation were of little consequence, since the entire area originally proposed as Greater New York (with the exception of Mount Vernon) was included in the final consolidation bill that passed the legislature and was signed by Governor Levi P. Morton in May 1896. The fact that all five counties had collectively cast a majority vote in favor of consolidation in part justified the inclusion of all proposed areas in the final consolidation bill. Moreover, the state Republican boss, Thomas C. Platt, conceived that the creation of Greater New York under Republican auspices would enhance the power and prestige of his party and himself. It was even conceivable that Greater New York might turn out Republican majorities.[72]

Among other opponents of consolidation, Platt faced Mayors William Strong of New York and Frederick Wurster of Brooklyn, as well as organized groups from the towns of Flushing, Jamaica, and Hempstead in Queens. The opposition from Queens did not pose a serious hurdle, but the state charter granted the mayors of New York and Brooklyn the right to veto bills affecting their cities, a power they used against the 1896 consolidation bill. Platt, however, had enough political capital in Albany to get the votes to override the mayoral vetoes. The 1896 consolidation bill authorized nine commissioners, appointed by Governor Morton, to draft a charter for the new city, which passed in the legislature in 1897, once again over the veto of Mayor Strong.[73]

The 1897 Consolidation Act provided for equal taxation and the assumption of all municipal debts by the new city. The *Newtown Register* reported that with the knowledge that their debt was to be spread among all the residents of the new city, the "various villages and towns" in Queens County that were to become part of Greater New York were all "taking time by the forelock in the matter of public improvements." "Jamaica surpasses all her neighbors in this respect and throughout the town wherever one goes are found gangs of men building macadam roads, laying sewers or making other improvements. Newtown and Flushing have also indulged in the same line of business and all seem determined to get as many local improvements as possible before going into the Greater New York."[74]

The charter for the new city that went into effect on January 1, 1898, though flawed and quickly amended, significantly reshaped government and politics in the New York metropolitan region, not least in the area of infrastructural development.[75] More important for the discussion here, the ability of the legislature to override the wishes of communities that had voted against consolidation seriously qualifies the argument that infrastructural development was important for suburbs to remain independent from the central city. That argument assumes local control over municipal borders. By contrast, the creation of Greater New York in 1896 and 1897 demonstrates what Iowa judge John F. Dillon had made clear a generation earlier: local governments had little authority independent of their respective states.[76] Because it could create Greater New York by fiat, the New York legislature could negate local discretion over municipal boundaries, in which infrastructural development played an important role.

State legislators were beholden to local interests, however, and it is doubtful that they would have voted to create Greater New York in the face of strong opposition from their constituents. Thus while the majority vote in favor of consolidation in 1894 created no legal obligation and was ambiguous in its meaning, it probably provided the political cover for legislators to go along with Platt and vote to enlarge the city. Had a majority voted against consolidation in 1894, more state legislators would probably have been hesitant to create Greater New York. Consolidation might have then proceeded on a municipality-by-municipality basis, and local infrastructure issues would have played a larger role in the ultimate shape of New York City. Moreover, if the outlying areas examined in this and the previous chapter are any indication, the majority vote in favor of consolidation probably did reflect the fact that for most suburban residents, the services that would be extended to them as part of New York City outweighed the disadvantages of Tammany Hall.

In any case, the creation of Greater New York was a special case because it had statewide significance. A central actor in the process, Platt, was not even from the city, but from upstate Oswego. In most other instances, municipal consolidations were of only local significance, and only local actors in the legislature had any substantial interest in them. Thus the role of the legislature in the case of most municipal consolidations and annexations was to serve as an alternate arena for local politics. With the focal point of the struggle at the local level, infrastructural development would play a greater role in determining the extent of suburban autonomy in a metropolitan region.

Mount Vernon was involved in several failed attempts at consolidation that were only of local interest and in which infrastructural development did play an important role. While the residents of Mount Vernon had voted against consolidation in 1894, a new bill was introduced into the legislature in 1897 that requested authorization for a new referendum. If Mount Vernonites then voted in favor of consolidation, their city would be absorbed into Greater New York in July 1898. The Mount Vernon Board of Trade vehemently opposed the bill, and it did not pass in the legislature.[77] Another effort toward consolidation was made in 1898 when several Mount Vernon residents (described in the press as "a few representative citizens") formed an Annexation Committee and got the local state representative, Jared Sandford, to introduce a new referendum bill into the legislature. Sandford, who had served as Mount Vernon's last village president and as the interim mayor after the village became a city and who had been elected to the state assembly in 1897, declared that "he was satisfied that a large majority of our people desired annexation." The Mount Vernon Board of Trade retorted that "60 to 75 percent of our business men are opposed to annexation," and that "if it had been known that he [Sandford] intended to favor annexation to New York, he could not have carried Mount Vernon."[78]

The conflict over annexation in Mount Vernon may have involved a partisan split. The *Mount Vernon Daily Argus* reported that "fully nine tenths" of the supporters of the annexation bill were Democrats, while a similar proportion of Republicans opposed the measure. The organization most vocally opposed to annexation, the board of trade, claimed to be "non-partisan in character," although it was ready to accuse annexationists of operating in collusion with Tammany Hall. Indeed, one new argument used to promote annexation in Mount Vernon—that it "would open up positions for our young men in Police, Fire Department, City Work, and other offices in Greater New York" for which they were otherwise ineligible due to residency requirements—could be interpreted as an appeal from Tammany Hall, which was "reinstalled in almost absolute power" under the mayoralty of Robert Van Wyck.[79]

Annexation had never been an obviously partisan matter in Mount Vernon, however. In 1892, when residents voted to make their village a city—arguably also a vote against annexation to New York—the local government of Mount Vernon was controlled by Democrats. In 1894, when a majority of residents voted against consolidation, Republicans controlled Mount Vernon. In 1898 the city returned to Democratic control, and while there was apparently never another referendum on consolidation in the city, the fact that the 1898 annexation bill never passed the legislature at least suggests that there was not adequate local support for the measure.[80]

If partisanship is not a sufficient explanation, infrastructural development may serve as a useful guide to understanding support for or opposition to annexation in Mount Vernon. That Mount Vernon might benefit as part of Greater New York in terms of infrastructural development was an argument presented in 1897 and 1898, as it had been in 1892 and 1894. For instance, Mount Vernon alderman and secretary of the Annexation Committee George T. Lovell contended that annexation to New York would mean lower taxes, lower water rates, "better lighted streets," and "the settlement of our sewer question for all time."[81]

The argument that annexation to Greater New York would improve infrastructural development in Mount Vernon had failed to be convincing in 1892 and 1894 and appears to have been even less convincing later in the decade. The outspoken proponent of annexation in 1892 and 1894, Joseph S. Wood, was opposed to annexation by 1897. As Wood stated at a meeting of the board of trade (of which he was vice president) in January 1898,

> He had strongly favored annexation to New York three years ago, because he then believed that Mount Vernon could not alone provide for its water and outlet sewer; but since that time those problems have been solved. Now Mount Vernon has within its reach a larger and better water supply in proportion to population than New York, and the engineers have pointed out to us a plan for an outlet sewer that Mount Vernon can easily construct. Under

the new charter of New York all improvements must be paid for by the property holders immediately benefited. In Mount Vernon the city pays a part.[82]

If any resident knew whether or not Mount Vernon could meet its infrastructure needs on its own, it was Joseph Wood, who had played a central role in solving the water and sewer issues as they evolved in the mid-1890s. The city's water company had been brought out of receivership and reincorporated as the New York Suburban Water Company in 1895. Under the new company, the price of water rose while maintenance and service were neglected. Problems reached a high point when a pump broke and much of the city was without any water service for four days. Following Wood's advice, the legislature authorized the creation of a commission, for which Wood served as legal counsel, that would investigate and recommend a solution to the city's water problem. In response to the commission's recommendation that the city not renew the water company's contract and the threat that the city might be supplied water from another company or even New York City, the New York Suburban Water Company purchased the neighboring Mamaroneck Water Company in 1897, thereby increasing the total square miles of available watershed from three to fifteen, making several million gallons of water available to Mount Vernon residents, and improving water quality.[83]

In the area of sewerage the city's problems had increased since the early 1890s. The grand jury that in 1894 had begun to investigate Mount Vernon's dumping of wastes in local waterways had found that the city was indeed "maintaining a nuisance." Residents who lived downstream along the Hutchinson River claimed that sewage from the city had seriously damaged their property and their health, and the state board of health refused to approve further sewerage plans in the city if they increased the discharge into the Bronx or Hutchinson Rivers.[84]

Excess sewage was not a problem just for Mount Vernon but for the whole region as it urbanized and gained population. Thus in 1895 the legislature created the Bronx Valley Sewer Commission. Following the recommendations of the commission, the legislature in 1897 authorized the construction of trunk sewers through the Bronx and Hutchinson Valleys that would drain into Long Island Sound and serve both New York City and Westchester County. New York City was to pay 60 percent of the total cost of construction and Westchester County 40 percent.[85] However, for the 1897 sewer bill to become law, it also had to be approved by Mayor Strong of New York and the mayors and aldermen of Mount Vernon and Yonkers. In what the *Mount Vernon Record* referred to as "an act of political trickery," both Mayor Strong and the Mount Vernon Board of Aldermen "disapproved of the bill," but only after the end of the legislative session, so that their vetoes could not be overridden.[86]

Wood, initially a supporter of the sewer bill, had been among those most active in convincing the Mount Vernon alderman to veto it. By 1897 Wood claimed to believe that the city's sewage could be best dealt with through disposal works and chemical treatment, although this was an idea that had already been rejected by both the sewer commission and a special committee of the Mount Vernon Board of Aldermen.[87] It is actually not clear that Wood was serious about the disposal works idea, since in the summer of 1897 he and other community leaders met with Louis F. Haffen, Bronx commissioner of street improvements (and later borough president), to discuss the possibility of draining Mount Vernon's waste through sewers in New York's 23rd and 24th Wards (previously Eastchester) and into an outlet sewer that would run through Pelham Bay and out into Long Island Sound. The plan cost Mount Vernon a good deal less than the plan that had passed in the legislature and apparently resolved the sewer issue in Mount Vernon, although it left the larger regional issue of sewage pollution to be dealt with in later years.[88]

That water, sewerage, and other public works formed crucial elements within a broader sense of place identity and a pride in municipal independence is reflected in an announcement published in the *Mount Vernon Daily Argus* in January 1898, just two days after Greater New York came into existence: "Mount Vernon is better prepared to enter upon an era of enlarged usefulness and prosperity than ever before in its history . . . Few cities of its size have more miles of paved and macadamized streets and no city claims to approach it in the cleanliness of its thoroughfares . . . The water question so far as Mount Vernon is concerned, has ceased to act as a bugaboo . . . This city has five times the water per capita New York possesses . . . The sewer problem concerns no one."[89]

At least two important points can be made about the relationship among infrastructural development, municipal autonomy, and place identity in Mount Vernon. First, while Mount Vernonites evidently took pride in local public works, these achievements were made possible in large part by outside expertise. When a special committee of the board of aldermen had been considering the idea of disposal works, it had inspected the disposal works of Boston, Brockton, Worcester, South Framingham, and Lawrence in Massachusetts. Later, when the board of aldermen began to investigate the cost of building an outlet sewer, it employed an engineering firm from Providence, Shedd and Serle. Even those officials responsible for public works in Mount Vernon had gained their experience and training in other cities. For instance, the public works commissioner appointed in 1897, Harry P. McTague, a contractor, had learned his trade by laying sewer lines in Philadelphia. The public works commissioner before McTague, Frederick Odell, had trained at Cooper Union and had worked as an engineer for the city of Yonkers.[90] Thus local infrastructural development and, by extension, municipal autonomy were facilitated by the more general development of infrastructure technology and expertise that was in large part a function of earlier infrastructural development in other cities.

There was, of course, local expertise available for infrastructural development in Mount Vernon. A local directory for 1897–98 lists five civil engineers practicing in the city, including John F. Fairchild, who served as engineer of the Bronx Valley Sewer Commission.[91] The evidence, however, suggests that infrastructural development in Mount Vernon and neighboring suburbs was greatly facilitated by the resources within New York City that attracted engineering talent to the region. For instance, during consideration of the 1897 sewer bill in the legislature, interested parties employed the talents of engineers who made their businesses in New York. In his efforts to thwart the 1897 sewer bill, Joseph Wood enlisted "Mr. Loomis[,] the eminent engineer of New York city," who advised him that the outlet sewers "would cost millions upon millions of dollars." Loomis later retracted this statement when he learned that a more eminent engineer, J. James R. Croes, had endorsed lower cost estimates. Croes was a consultant to the Bronx Valley Sewer Commission; he had served as president of the American Society of Civil Engineers (located in New York City); and while Croes lived in Yonkers, his office was in Manhattan.[92] Thus Mount Vernon's proximity to New York City made a larger and more qualified pool of engineering talent available, which facilitated infrastructural development and thus municipal autonomy.

Second, the case of Mount Vernon suggests that there were internal contradictions at work within suburban infrastructural development. Waterworks, sewers, and paved, lighted streets could be used to maintain a suburban lifestyle that was free from the noise, smoke, hurry, and bustle of the city, but with all the modern amenities. Yet infrastructural development also held out the promise of growth and economic development that threatened the suburban way of life. This contradiction was evident in Mount Vernon by the late 1890s. The board of trade, which had been an active proponent of public works in the city, began to encourage the industrial development of Mount Vernon but acknowledged that "there are some who are opposed to the establishment of manufactories in our city, desiring that this shall be considered a 'city of beautiful homes.' "[93]

If Mount Vernonites' resistance to Greater New York was based largely on a fear that their suburban community and lifestyle would be threatened by annexation, then the board of trade's simultaneous endorsement of industrial development and rejection of consolidation appears contradictory. What seems likely is that Mount Vernon's businessmen did not reject consolidation out of a desire to preserve the suburban virtues of their community, but rather out of a concern that as New Yorkers, they would lose the kind of local influence that they could exercise in a small city. Certainly the board of trade was not opposed to consolidation per se. In fact, in the same year that Greater New York came into being, the board of trade proposed the creation of a "Greater Mount Vernon" through the consolidation of Mount Vernon and the town of Pelham.[94]

For Mount Vernon's businessmen, the annexation of Pelham had obvious benefits. First, if industrial development were to be encouraged, waterfront access was important. Mount Vernon was landlocked, but Pelham had a waterfront on the Long Island Sound. Second, annexing the town of Pelham posed little threat to the political power of Mount Vernon's businessmen. As a town, Pelham had only a limited governmental structure. Three villages had been incorporated into the town during the 1890s (Pelham Manor in 1891 and Pelham and North Pelham, both incorporated in 1896), but they too had only a few officials. The other conceivable option for Greater Mount Vernon would be a consolidation with the city of Yonkers, but because Yonkers was a bigger city, this would put the Mount Vernon business community at a disadvantage.[95]

For the residents of Pelham, the benefits of the Greater Mount Vernon scheme were less clear. The *Pelham Record* (actually a supplement to the *Mount Vernon Record*) made the vague claim that "there is no doubt but what Pelham would derive much good from the annexation scheme," yet advertisements in this same newspaper provide reasons to believe otherwise. Advertisements of lots for sale by the Pelham Heights Company noted that residents in the village of Pelham enjoyed "Every Municipal Improvement" (including water, gas, sewers, drains, and macadamized roads) while paying a third of the taxes and half the water rates of residents in Mount Vernon. Notably, another long-running advertisement in the same newspaper included "home rule" in a similar list of the amenities enjoyed by Pelham residents.[96]

Certainly the failure of the Greater Mount Vernon scheme could be attributed to the fact that the prospect of paying more taxes for the same services generated little excitement among the residents of Pelham. In addition, it seems likely that Greater Mount Vernon was unappealing because it represented the encroachment of an urban vision on Pelham. Although Mount Vernon's business community may have been seduced by the possibilities for economic development that infrastructural development had made possible, public works in Pelham were still used specifically to create a suburban community. At least one article in the *Pelham Record* (with the suggestive title "The Oneness of Pelham") made the connection between infrastructural development and the maintenance of a suburban identity explicit: "Pelham, with no manufacturing interests, depends upon homeseekers for its growth, and the advancement of its financial and other interests. What therefore, are the elements which will attract homeseekers? Good roads and other improvements, not in one section alone, but throughout the entire town, so that the name of Pelham is synonymous with progress, are absolutely necessary to the highest success."[97]

The failure of the Greater Mount Vernon scheme suggests at least three things. First, infrastructural development provided the means for Pelham's independence from Mount Vernon. Because Pelham residents already had infrastructure systems installed, Mount Vernon had little to offer them. Furthermore, infrastructural development in Pelham sustained a lifestyle that was threatened by annexation. Second, the consolidation of Mount Vernon and Pelham was only important to local actors. Thus the legislature did not intervene to create Greater Mount Vernon, as it had Greater New York. Third, the apparent resistance in Pelham to the idea of a Greater Mount Vernon suggests that infrastructural development enabled outlying communities to remain independent not only of New York City, but of one another as well. Thus urban infrastructural development reinforced municipal autonomy or "metropolitan fragmentation" throughout the metropolitan region.

Since there were no civil engineers practicing in Pelham in the 1890s, expertise had to come from outside. One such engineer was John Fairchild from Mount Vernon, the previously mentioned engineer of the Bronx Valley Sewer Commission, who did surveying work for the town of Pelham and also served as the engineer, and later the president, of the Pelham Heights Company.[98] Thus an engineer practicing in Mount Vernon operated the very company that advertised the benefits of living in Pelham over Mount Vernon. To the extent that infrastructural development in Pelham encouraged and provided the means for that town to remain independent of Mount Vernon, and to the extent that infrastructural development was made possible only through the availability of engineering expertise, actors outside the town, indeed from Mount Vernon, provided the means for Pelham's independence from Mount Vernon.

The influence of New York City also loomed large in the physical development of Pelham. The New York and New Jersey Globe Gas-light Company, based in New York City, had been supplying naphtha for street lighting in New York City since the late 1870s and in North Pelham since at least 1897. In 1898 the New York and New Jersey Globe Gas-light Company's bid for lighting the streets of North Pelham was once again selected over bids by the Eastchester Gas Company and the Pelham Gas Light Company.[99] By the late 1890s elevated trains had been constructed over the Harlem River, after which it appears that more contractors from New York City were making bids on infrastructure projects in Westchester County.[100]

The use of out-of-town companies and contractors for infrastructural development in Pelham was not without controversy, and there is evidence to suggest that local actors were preferred when they were available. In July 1898 the village of North Pelham awarded a contract for street and sidewalk improvements to a local contractor, Smith Brothers. In response, P. G. Hannon, a contractor from New York City, "entered a vigorous protest," charging that its bid had been lower than that of Smith Brothers, and that it should therefore be awarded the job. The village trustees dismissed P. G. Hannon's protest, noting that "the advertisement for bids distinctly stated that the Board reserved the right to reject any or all bids," and Smith Brothers remained the contractor. Similarly, in August 1898 the streets committee of the Mount Vernon Board of Aldermen decided to award a street-improvement contract to Peter Sheridan, a resident of the city, despite the fact that his bid "was $1,077 in excess of the bid of Dunn, of New York City." The decision of the streets committee prompted a "lively debate" among the aldermen, and in contrast to Pelham, Dunn was awarded the contract by a vote of 4 to 3.[101]

The willingness of the local governments of Mount Vernon and Pelham to accept local bids that were not competitive suggests that local contractors were politically connected and more generally that infrastructural development in suburban communities, as in the larger cities that they surrounded, was an inherently political process. The political nature of infrastructural development was reflected as well in Mount Vernon in 1897 when the Democratic mayor, Edwin F. Fiske, appointed as commissioner of public works Harry McTague, the previously mentioned sewer contractor from Philadelphia. The Republican *Mount Vernon Record* charged that Fiske's appointment of McTague was a blatant attempt to secure the patronage resources of the Department of Public Works for the Democratic party.[102]

While the higher bids of local contractors suggest political connections, the lower bids of New York City contractors suggest that the latter were used to a more competitive market. The extent to which outlying communities such as Mount Vernon and Pelham benefited from the low bids by New York City contractors is of course lessened by the extent to which contracts went to politically connected locals who offered higher bids. But to the extent that suburban communities did benefit from low bids of New York City contractors, and to the extent that these lower bids were an outcome of more competitive markets generated by a greater level of infrastructural development in the central city, central city infrastructural development facilitated suburban infrastructural development and thus suburban autonomy.

The physical development of Pelham also provides evidence of national markets of supplies for public works. For street pavement, the village of North Pelham used the Barber Asphalt Company, which was based in New York City, with a plant in Long Island City and eight branch offices throughout the United States. By 1894 the Barber Company's asphalt had been used in the streets of thirty-nine cities throughout the country, including Yonkers and Mount Vernon, as well as the village of Pelham Manor.

The relationship between infrastructural development and municipal autonomy after the creation of Greater New York can be seen in other communities in Westchester County and on Long Island besides Pelham and Mount Vernon. For instance, one of the primary motivations behind the incorporation of Bronxville (located in Eastchester) as an independent village in 1898 (approved 24 to 8 in a village referendum) was to remain independent of Mount Vernon, Tuckahoe, and New York City, all of which had wanted to annex the community at different points. Incorporation as an independent village coincided with significant increases in infrastructural development in Bronxville, such as the introduction of water supplied by the New Rochelle Water Company in 1896 and a growing movement to build a sewerage system for the village, starting in 1899.[103]

On Long Island the eastern towns of Queens County that were not annexed to New York in 1898 (Hempstead, North Hempstead, and Oyster
Bay) separated to form Nassau County in 1899. These eastern towns were
still largely agricultural in the 1890s, and there is little indication that they
were ever seriously considered for inclusion in Greater New York, although
at least one "dissident" made that suggestion during the meetings at which
the creation of Nassau County was discussed. Alexander Stewart's Garden
City, located in Hempstead, could conceivably have had an interest in consolidation, since it was nonagricultural and had a high population density
compared with that of the surrounding area. However, Garden City was
a planned, progressive community, developed in the 1870s with all the
modern amenities installed, such as water supplied by a Holly pump and
paved streets, and there was no evident interest among its residents to be included in Greater New York.[104] Since Garden City and Bronxville were much
smaller communities than either Mount Vernon or Pelham, there seems
little doubt that they used outside personnel and materials to develop their
infrastructure systems and thus probably can be said to have relied on the
larger, more urbanized communities that surrounded them to maintain
their municipal independence.

Infrastructure Politics and Urban Growth in and around New York City

Figure 10 repeats Figure 5 from Chapter 1, including the evidence provided
for the general argument in this and the preceding two chapters. As the figure
indicates, the municipalities of the New York metropolitan region do not
break down neatly into cities and suburbs. While New York City was clearly
the center of the metropolis, Brooklyn, Long Island City, Yonkers, and Mount
Vernon, to a limited degree, all possessed some "central city" characteristics.
As we move from left to right in the diagram, we fade from central cities into
municipalities that are more clearly suburban, such as Pelham and Flushing.

One thing that I have claimed distinguished central city infrastructure
politics was the presence of political machines. Yet in at least two outlying
communities—Long Island City and Brooklyn—there were also political
machines that relied for resources on public works. Especially in the case of
Long Island City, political corruption, centered on infrastructural development, compelled residents to approve the annexation of their community to
New York, thereby reversing the expected relationship between suburban

infrastructural development and suburban autonomy. I have indicated with an asterisk in Figure 10 those outlying communities that had political machines, and in which public works would thus not be expected to reinforce suburban autonomy.

The arrows in Figure 10 have been dashed to indicate that there are not causal links between all of the municipalities within different categories. For instance, there were political machines in Brooklyn, Long Island City, and New York City, but only the political machine in New York City raised fears of higher taxes in Flushing, Yonkers, and Mount Vernon. Likewise, infrastructural development in Brooklyn proceeded at least in part with the aid of engineering expertise from New York City. Infrastructural development did not lead to an autonomous Brooklyn, however, nor is there evidence to suggest that infrastructural development in Brooklyn led to municipal autonomy in

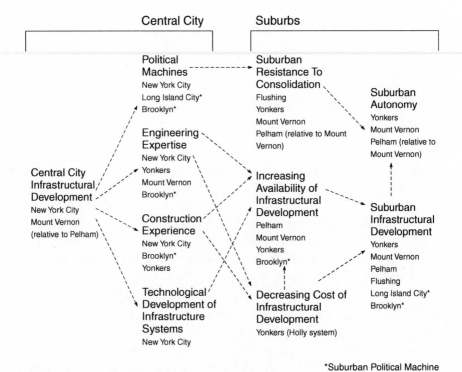

Figure 10. Relationship between central city public works in New York City and suburban autonomy in surrounding counties

Mount Vernon or Pelham. Yet there is some evidence to suggest that Brooklyn served as an example for public works, and thus for suburban autonomy, in Yonkers. There is not enough evidence to draw a continuous causal path from central city infrastructural development to suburban autonomy. Instead, each of the separate case studies can be used to provide evidence for different parts of the general argument. Put together, the case studies then provide a relatively comprehensive picture of the relationship between infrastructural development and fragmented metropolitan growth.

The arrow between the technological development of infrastructure systems and the decreasing cost of infrastructure systems has been eliminated in Figure 10. As discussed in Chapter 2, the technological development of infrastructure systems was primarily a national and even international process, involving the successive development of infrastructure systems in different cities. The contributions to the technological development of urban infrastructure made in New York City (primarily through the Croton and New Croton Aqueducts) may have contributed indirectly to the development of the relatively affordable Holly pumping system and thus to the creation of an independent waterworks in Yonkers, but there is certainly no direct connection.

The case study in Chapter 2 indicated that politics and infrastructural development in New York City were closely related to each other. Fernando Wood, William Tweed, and later political bosses could bolster their organizations through the patronage resources of large public works projects. Their ability to gain control over public works in the city was in large part determined by state legislation. While the legislature was an external actor in the politics of New York City, it was frequently used as an arena through which local actors such as Tweed could more effectively gain political power in the city. Because the use of public works projects for the pursuit of political power could result in large expenditures, infrastructural development could create a countervailing reform movement. The case of New York City, however, indicates that in the event of a successful reform movement and calls for fiscal retrenchment, public works would proceed at prereform levels, at least in part because of institutional arrangements that granted engineers significant control over public works in the city.

Infrastructural development served similar purposes in many of the smaller communities that surrounded New York. For instance, in Long Island City, Brooklyn, and possibly Mount Vernon as well, public works solidified political alliances through patronage. But by using infrastructural development as a source of patronage, politicians opened themselves to charges of corruption. Voters probably used perceived levels of corruption to determine the relative costs and benefits of consolidation. With regard to New York City's geographic expansion, infrastructural development was thus a two-edged sword. On the one hand, with expanded infrastructure systems, New York City presented an incentive for residents in outlying municipalities to desire consolidation. On the other hand, to the extent that larger infrastructure systems provided greater opportunities for graft, perceived levels of corruption in New York City would be higher, thus making consolidation less desirable to the residents in outlying communities.

In outlying municipalities the relationship between infrastructural development and corruption had the opposite effect on municipal consolidation to the effect it had in the central city. All else being equal, residents in outlying municipalities supplied with independent infrastructure systems would be less likely to desire consolidation to the central city. As we have seen, infrastructural development in Yonkers and Mount Vernon provided these cities with the means to supply residents with essential services without the help of New York City's infrastructure. In towns that had relatively little infrastructure, such as Kingsbridge, West Farms, and Morrisania, there were greater perceived benefits from annexation to New York City. However, if infrastructure systems in the outlying municipality had been built at great expense as a vehicle for patronage, residents might actually prefer consolidation to municipal independence. Thus in Long Island City infrastructural development was carried out in such an inefficient and even harmful manner that annexation to New York City was the preferred option among residents.

There is good reason to believe that infrastructural development in smaller communities would be less likely to be characterized by political corruption than infrastructural development in larger cities. First, because smaller communities such as Pelham did not have enough local infrastructure suppliers, they had to rely on outside contractors. With few local recipients for the patronage made available from infrastructural development, there was little opportunity to use public works for nefarious purposes. Certainly local officials in Pelham and Mount Vernon were eager to provide patronage to local contractors, but the evidence suggests that local suburban contractors were small in numbers and often more expensive than contractors from New York. Second, smaller communities relied to a greater extent on private utility companies, especially for their water. Moreover, in the case of Westchester County at least, we have seen that municipalities such as Mount Vernon could choose between water companies. Because private companies had to make profits in a competitive environment, they probably could not afford to assume the costs of political patronage in the same way that a local government could. If it was thus characterized by lower levels of corruption, infrastructural development in smaller communities more likely contributed to desires among residents for municipal independence from the central city.

Infrastructural development in outlying communities also encouraged municipal independence because it served to define those communities as suburbs and "cities of homes" that were culturally distinct from New York City. Water supply, sewerage, street lighting, and street paving in Mount Vernon, Pelham, Flushing, Bronxville, and Garden City were not used to facilitate unprecedented increases in population and population density, as they were in New York City, but were meant instead to provide modern amenities for middle- to upper-class homeowners and buyers.[105]

Infrastructural development in outlying communities not only contributed to a distinctly suburban sense of place identity but also played a significant role in determining the substance of that identity. First, suburban infrastructural development was only possible because suburbs were of a relatively small scale. Second, infrastructural development could only be afforded on a residential tax base if the residents were relatively wealthy. Thus suburban infrastructural development was closely tied to the development of suburbs that were small enclaves for the affluent. These suburbs were also culturally more predisposed to municipal independence. For instance, the main opposition to consolidation in Brooklyn came from the "Protestant social elite," who saw their "city of homes" as a place of moral virtue that would be defiled by a closer association with New York City.[106] This cultural difference between New York City and its suburbs may explain in part the apparent aversion that suburban residents had to Tammany Hall and New York City politics in general.

While suburban infrastructural development contributed to a distinct sense of place identity and provided the means to remain independent from New York City, outlying communities also depended on New York City for infrastructural development. Three possible ways in which central city infrastructural development facilitated suburban infrastructural development were discussed in the Introduction and Chapter 1. First, through central city infrastructural development, a pool of engineering talent was created that outlying communities could rely on in building their infrastructure systems. Second, as central city infrastructural development advanced the technology of infrastructural development, infrastructure systems could be mass-produced for a national market and sold to smaller communities at comparatively low prices. Finally, central city infrastructural development created competitive markets of contractors that would lower the cost of infrastructural development for surrounding communities.

In regard to labor and contractors, the scanty available evidence suggests that suburban communities could use contractors from New York City at less cost than local contractors, but political considerations often favored local contractors. The case studies provide more evidence for the transfer of infrastructure technology from central cities to suburbs through the medium of the engineering profession. The expert opinion and advice of engineers from New York City was used in Yonkers, Mount Vernon, and Brooklyn and possibly in Pelham. Of course, New York City was not the only center for engineering talent. Mount Vernon hired engineers from Providence to advise that city on a plan for a sewer outlet, Mount Vernon's first commissioner of public works, Frederick Odell, brought to that city his experience as an engineer for the city of Yonkers, and the second public works commissioner, Harry McTague, brought to the city his experience from public works in Philadelphia. The city of Yonkers relied on the advice of engineers in both New York City and Brooklyn in developing its sewerage system and looked to cities throughout the United States and Europe in developing its waterworks. Similarly, Mount Vernon relied on the experience of several communities in Massachusetts in considering the feasibility of a disposal works. Finally, Brooklyn relied on advice from engineers in Jersey City, as well as New York, concerning the construction of its sewerage system, and in Pelham the engineer most obviously responsible for infrastructural development was from Mount Vernon. Despite the proliferation of sources of advice, it appears that the flow of information and especially of expert opinion most often moved from larger to smaller cities. For instance, Pelham relied on engineering talent from Mount Vernon; Mount Vernon relied on the development of expertise in Yonkers; and Yonkers took advice from Brooklyn, as did Brooklyn from New York City.

There is also evidence to suggest that infrastructural development in the suburbs of New York was made possible by the availability of mass-produced infrastructure systems and materials; the best example is the Holly pump, used in Yonkers, Long Island City, and Garden City, as well as other cities throughout the northeastern United States. The example of the Holly pump does not completely fit with the argument made here, however, since it does not serve as an example of technology transfer of infrastructure from a large central city to smaller suburban communities. That a company based in Lockport, a small city in upstate New York, sold water pumps throughout an entire region of the United States suggests that by the mid- to late nineteenth century, water infrastructure technology was no longer confined to central cities but had become truly national. Similarly, while the Barber Asphalt Company did have its headquarters in New York City, it also had branch offices throughout the country and had only sold asphalt to New York City a decade after the company was founded.[107] Still, the nationalization of infrastructure technology may have depended on infrastructural development in large central cities such as New York.

In short, the case study of the New York metropolitan region in this and the preceding chapter suggests that the political process of infrastructural development in New York City created resources that encouraged infrastructural development in surrounding communities. Consequently, these surrounding communities were able to maintain their municipal independence in the face of New York City's territorial expansion. Because infrastructural development opened up opportunities in New York City for extensive graft and corruption, it helped to lower the desire for consolidation among suburban communities. Central city infrastructural development then also provided the means for outlying communities to remain independent. It remains to be seen whether this process of infrastructural development and metropolitan growth was unique to New York City and its suburbs, or whether the same process existed in and around other central cities. The following two chapters on the municipalities of northeastern New Jersey address this final question.

CHAPTER 4

Expansionist Jersey City
and Its Discontents

Our story now moves across the Hudson River to Hudson County, New Jersey, where, on Tuesday, October 5, 1869, residents in eleven towns, townships, and cities cast votes either for or against the consolidation of their respective municipalities into an expanded Jersey City. The *New York Evening Post* noted at the time that if each municipality approved consolidation, Jersey City would have a "territory somewhat larger than the city of New York," with "a water front available for commercial purposes more extensive and valuable than any other city in the United States."[1] Rather than reaching for urban greatness, however, residents in Hoboken, Bayonne, Greenville, Weehawken, West Hoboken, and North Bergen voted by majorities against consolidation. The residents of Jersey City, Hudson City, Bergen City, the town of Union, and Union Township voted by majorities in favor of consolidation (Table 1 and Figure 11). A state restriction that allowed only contiguous municipalities to consolidate meant that only Hudson and Bergen Cities actually became parts of Jersey City. Greenville residents reversed themselves in a referendum three years later, and their township was annexed to Jersey City in 1873.[2]

In the geographic expansion of Jersey City, we can discern a reflection and elaboration of the general process that was also evident on the New York side of the Hudson, by which infrastructural development provided city officials with the motivations for annexation and split suburban communities between those that would fuse with the central city and those that had the means and motivation to remain independent. To maintain and increase their power, central city political machines needed new territory in which they could control infrastructural development and thereby control jobs, contracts, and real estate speculation. Suburban communities might welcome their annexation to the central city, since it meant the

Table 1. Results of the referendum on a city charter that would annex outlying municipalities to Jersey City

	Charter	No Charter
Jersey City	2,220	911
Hudson City	1,320	220
Bergen	815	108
Hoboken	176	893
Bayonne	100	250
Greenville	24	174
Weehawken	0	44
Town of Union	123	105
West Hoboken	95	256
North Bergen	80	225
Union Township	140	65

Source: William H. Shaw, *History of Essex and Hudson Counties, New Jersey* vol. 2 (Philadelphia: Everts and Peck, 1884), p. 1142.

introduction of new municipal services that came with infrastructural development. Yet those infrastructure systems that promised new services could also be perceived by suburban residents as the tentacles of fiscally reckless political machines that were seeking new sources of plunder. Thus many suburban communities, if they could, sought to maintain their

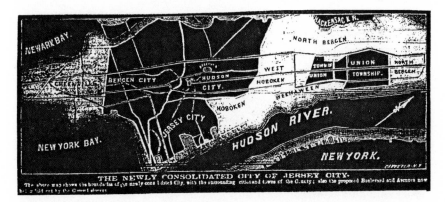

Figure 11 Map of the municipalities of Hudson County from the *Evening Journal*, October 7, 1869. The municipalities in black are those that voted in favor of consolidation. Because of a contiguity provision in the consolidation act, the town of Union and Union Township did not become part of Jersey City.

municipal independence by building their own water and sewerage systems and by paving their own streets. In doing so, suburban communities borrowed from the base of knowledge that had accumulated and the technological advances that had been made as a result of central city infrastructural development. Engineers, who had gained visibility, power, and knowledge by building central city infrastructure systems, provided suburban communities with the expertise that they needed to build their own public works and remain independent of the central city. Thus infrastructural development facilitated suburban autonomy and metropolitan fragmentation and laid the groundwork for the "urban crisis" of the twentieth century.

In conformity with this general account, the most prominent issues surrounding the Jersey City consolidation vote were the related topics of taxation, corruption, and infrastructural development. On the one hand, residents would support the consolidation of their municipality to Jersey City if it meant that they would be supplied with new and better services. On the other hand, the expectation that an enlarged Jersey City would be characterized by political corruption and high tax rates made residents wary of consolidation. Suburban residents could entertain the idea of independence from Jersey City to the extent that their own municipalities could supply them with adequate water, sewerage, and street pavements at a reasonable cost. Suburban municipalities in Hudson County that had supplied themselves with these urban services were likely to have done so with the assistance of Jersey City engineers. Thus infrastructural development in Jersey City facilitated suburban autonomy and diminished the likelihood that there would ever be a rival city to match New York on the New Jersey side of the Hudson River.

The nature of suburban residents' resistance to annexation differed, depending on the specific circumstances of their respective communities. In Hoboken resistance to consolidation found its greatest support in the city's largest landowner, the Hoboken Land and Improvement Company. Infrastructural development in Hoboken involved a struggle between the city government, which promoted public works, and the Land and Improvement Company, which resisted policies that would increase the local tax burden. As a result, public works in Hoboken proceeded cautiously, under relatively stringent economic constraints, and were not characterized by the sort of excessive spending that ultimately compelled cities such as Bergen and Hudson to approve consolidation. Infrastructural development would probably have proceeded at a quicker pace in Hoboken had residents approved consolidation. Instead, taking their lead from the Land and Improvement Company, residents appear to have voted by a majority against consolidation because of concerns about political corruption and taxation.

In contrast to Hoboken, apparent political corruption related to infrastructural development in Greenville ultimately made residents more amenable to consolidation. Suspect practices by the township's street commissioners that resulted in a significant tax increase provoked much of the impetus for residents to vote in favor of consolidation in 1872. As in the case of Long Island City in Chapter 3, outlying communities with their own particularly nefarious political machines might view consolidation with the central city as an anticorruption measure. Unlike Long Island City, however, Greenville was a small, almost wholly residential community. The example of Greenville thus serves to refine our understanding of local infrastructure politics by identifying a type of "corruption" more characteristic of smaller communities.

As in Hoboken, the residents of Bayonne feared that consolidation would bring corruption and high taxes, although a vocal minority did believe that the street improvements that would be extended to them as a part of Jersey City outweighed these possible disadvantages. An especially distinctive circumstance in Bayonne was that much of the resistance to consolidation was based on an understanding among residents that their city was a suburb of New York and thus shared little in common with Jersey City. Infrastructural development in Bayonne contributed to an explicitly suburban sense of place identity. Yet although Bayonne residents conceived of their community as a suburb of New York, engineers from Jersey City assisted in the physical development of Bayonne, which contributed to residents' majority vote against consolidation.

In this chapter I discuss infrastructural development in Jersey City leading up to the 1869 consolidation vote; I then examine the majority decisions against consolidation in Hoboken and Bayonne and Greenville residents' 1872 reversal in favor of consolidation. If there was any rival to Jersey City's status as the preeminent city in Hudson County after the Civil War, it was Hoboken. By contrast, Bayonne was in many respects a rural hinterland even after its incorporation as a city in 1869. Put together, Hoboken and Bayonne thus provide a broad definition of what it meant to be a suburban municipality in Hudson County in the years after the Civil War. In addition, the vastly different outcomes of the 1869 and 1872 votes in Greenville present the opportunity to examine reasons for variation in the consolidation vote within a single municipality.

From Paulus Hook to Jersey City

Jane Jacobs has pointed out that there was no inherent or "natural" reason why the New York side of the Hudson River, rather than the New Jersey side, became the center of the metropolitan region around New York Bay. The New Jersey shores of the Hudson had the advantage of being part of the mainland, not an island, as on the New York side. Certainly the founders of Jersey City—a group of prominent New York Federalists incorporated as the Associates of the Jersey Company in 1804—were aware of the potential advantages of building a city on the New Jersey side of the Hudson. The Associates of the Jersey Company (known simply as "the Associates") conceived that the grid they laid out on Paulus Hook—nineteen streets that formed forty-five blocks, with 1,344 separate lots, on what was then a "series of sand hills, jutting out into the river"—would expand to become the Federalist metropolis of the world, eclipsing Republican New York.[3]

Several impediments stood in the way of the Associates' dream of a Federalist metropolis—or, for that matter, their desire to make money on their investment. First, the purchase agreement between the Associates and the Van Vorst family, which had owned Paulus Hook since 1698, impeded the sale of lots. The Associates purchased Paulus Hook "for a perpetual annuity of six thousand Spanish milled dollars . . . secured by an irredeemable mortgage" and then stipulated that each lot owner had to pay an "annual rent" that would cover the mortgage payments to the Van Vorsts. This was, in effect, a property tax levied by a private corporation, with the additional risk that if the Associates defaulted on their mortgage, the property would revert back to the Van Vorsts. The second impediment to growth was the city of New York, which claimed ownership of the Hudson River up to the low-water mark of the New Jersey shore and challenged the right of the Associates to build docks or operate a ferry service beyond that point. It is not clear if New York's claim ever impeded ferry service or the building of docks—indeed, the Van Vorsts had been running a ferry from Paulus Hook to Manhattan since 1764—but the "uncertainty engendered by New York pretensions" made potential investors wary. The end result was that of the 1,344 lots for sale at Paulus Hook, 7 were sold at the first auction.[4]

More than fifteen years after the first auction, the streets of Paulus Hook had still not been graded, the sidewalks were unpaved, "and the buildings [were] few and inconsequential."[5] In an effort to improve the condition of their settlement, the Associates petitioned the legislature to grant a city charter creating a municipal government for Jersey City in 1820. The Associates faced the dilemma of wanting to establish a city, yet not wanting to relinquish control to a city government, probably in large part because they were concerned about meeting the mortgage payments to the Van Vorsts when residents were also subject to a municipal property tax. Thus the 1820 charter authorized only a weak government, limited to levying taxes that could bring in a maximum of $100 annually, of which $18.45 was collected in 1825 and $39.87 was collected in 1828. A new charter, adopted in 1829, expanded the tax levy to $300, although, as the previous figures indicate, it is doubtful that that amount was ever collected. Neither of the two charters allowed the government to charge special assessments on property owners affected by specific improvement projects.[6]

In 1830 the mortgage on Paulus Hook was transferred to the Associates, removing the threat that the property might revert to the Van Vorsts through a default. Moreover, in 1834, pursuant to a treaty agreement between the two states, New York abandoned its claim to ownership of the New Jersey side of the Hudson River. Yet there were new developments that brought the Associates and the city government into conflict. In 1836 the Morris Canal was extended through Jersey City, and the New Jersey Rail Road and Transportation Company established rail service between Jersey City and New Brunswick.[7] These new means of transportation, combined with interlocking directorates between the Associates and the railroad company, gave the Associates the motivation to use their rights over the waterfront, granted to them in their 1804 charter, to make Jersey City a rail terminus in the service of imports and exports coming in and out of New York. In the opinion of many residents, the Associates' use of the waterfront for the railroad "delayed, if not prevented, other improvements that might possibly have hastened the development of the city." The issue of the Associates' right over the waterfront served as the primary local political issue, dividing the monolithically Whig city into pro- and anti-Associates factions.[8]

The Associates' power lay in their large property holdings and in their corporate charter, which granted them control over the use of streets and other public spaces, including the waterfront, on the land purchased from the Van Vorsts. Yet Jersey City's growing population required an increasingly powerful municipal government that would expand the city into territories that were beyond the Associates' control.[9] In 1804 the population on Paulus Hook had "numbered fifteen including boatmen." By 1829, the population of Jersey City was 1,025, and it increased rapidly, to 1,439 by 1834—a rate of growth probably greater than that experienced by Newark during the same years.[10]

Residential demands for street improvements, combined with dramatically increasing land values, provided the political pressure and justification to increase the municipal government's authority. In 1835 the board of selectmen began to erect oil street lamps at the request of residents and was receiving petitions from residents requesting that their streets be regulated and paved. To accommodate these requests, the legislature in 1836 amended the city charter to allow the municipal government to charge special assessments for street improvements. Under the amended charter, the *Jersey City Gazette* reported that "the Board of Selectmen are steadily performing their duty in providing for the regulation and grading the streets and paving all the principal ones." Revealing that its city was still not much more than a prospective suburb, the *Gazette* speculated with excitement that "ere another year Jersey City will be one of the neatest and best regulated . . . places of residence in the vicinity of New York." Yet the government was still hamstrung by its limited authority to levy general property taxes, with the result that much of the money collected for special assessments had to be "used for current expenses."[11] A new city charter, passed by the legislature in 1838, granted greater powers of taxation for the purposes of constructing common sewers, for paving streets, and for "supplying the city with water for the extinguishment of fires and other purposes." To go along with these increased powers, the number of aldermen was increased from seven to ten, and the elective office of mayor was created.[12]

Within a year under the new charter, the city government began paving at least six streets, and those that were not being paved were "ordered graded." Grand Street, which served as the east-west axis of the city, "was sewered and repaved by the city at the expense of J. P. Hill, the sewer contractor, who had neglected to do it." In 1839, the city began to increase the amount of usable land by filling in various "swamps and creeks." Between 1841 and 1855 the municipal government extended the city into the Hudson River by an additional block, filled in Harsimus Bay to create approximately eighty new blocks that abutted the southern end of Hoboken, and brought the mud flats at its southern end to grade to create an additional forty city blocks.[13]

Despite its impressive growth, Jersey City still had somewhat less than 7,000 residents by 1850.[14] A small, undoubtedly close-knit local community provided the context for a civic-minded elite to pursue the physical and technological development of their city out of the combined motives of boosterism, progressivism, and pursuit of profit. As Alexander McLean, a local historian and resident of Jersey City himself, wrote in the 1890s, "The well-to-do citizens lived in the section south of Grand Street and east of Washington. It was the habit of the men to call at David Smith's store on the northwest corner of Grand and Greene streets. This was a common meeting place for those who had no taste for sitting in drinking places. During the informal talks around the stove in this store the needs of the town were freely discussed, and from them came the gas-works and, later, the water-works.[15]

The regulars at David Smith's store no doubt included Peter McMartin, Peter Bentley, Benjamin Edge, Andrew Clerk, and Erastus Randall, the founders of the Jersey City Gas Light Company, incorporated in 1849. McMartin and Bentley had both served as mayors of Jersey City, in 1840 and 1843, respectively. Edge was serving as commissioner of appeal at the time of the gas company's incorporation and had previously shown his public spirit by lending the city $1,000 in the penurious times prior to the 1838 charter. Clerk was a civil engineer, city surveyor, and partner in a firm with Robert C. Bacot, who was also a city surveyor and prominent engineer. Edge, Clerk, and Randall would all later serve on the Jersey City Board of Water Commissioners—an entity created in 1851, whose members were variously described as "men in whom every citizen had confidence" and "very much in the overlord class."[16] Another resident who could probably often be found around the stove at David Smith's store was John D. Ward, another of the original water commissioners and "an engineer of some note"; he was also later a partner with Bacot and a "prominent figure in the early history of the city," who developed a plan for a city waterworks that he submitted to the city council in both 1844 and 1845, but with no luck.[17]

As previously noted, the 1838 charter had granted the common council the authority to raise taxes for the purposes of supplying water, but council committees organized to examine the possibilities for building a waterworks proved consistently inconclusive. It may have been that Jersey City, while growing rapidly, was simply too small to justify a waterworks, since the commission that was finally authorized by the legislature in 1851 to "examine and consider all matters relative to supplying . . . a sufficient quantity of pure and wholesome water" was to do so not just for Jersey City, but for the neighboring municipalities of Van Vorst and Hoboken as well.[18]

The establishment of a commission that was to explore a collective water supply for the three municipalities was clearly connected to an interest among at least some residents and officials that they be consolidated into a single city. In the same month in which it created the board of water commissioners, the legislature passed a new charter for Jersey City that expanded the city's boundaries to include Van Vorst, subject to referendums in both municipalities. Residents in both Jersey City and Van Vorst voted overwhelmingly in favor of consolidation, 489 to 3 and 426 to 49, respectively.[19] Two days before the legislature created the board of water commissioners, the Jersey City *Sentinel and Advertiser* reported that "Hoboken is not so far off but what we can see her . . . We predict, that before many years, a ferry will be started from the Long Dock. Then our streets running North South, will be continued on to this dock, from thence we expect our Hoboken friends to continue the lines. It would seem by glancing over the Maps of the two places that, the streets of each were laid out with the view eventually of uniting them both in one, and we venture to say, that in less than ten years it will be done."[20] As it turned out, Hoboken had other plans, which will be discussed later.

Part of the desire in Jersey City to annex Hoboken probably derived from a wish to add waterfront to the city that was not controlled by the Associates and the railroad, although there was certainly more widespread support for the measure. The *Sentinel and Advertiser* was, in fact, the pro-Associates newspaper. Similarly, although there was clearly widespread support for the annexation of Van Vorst (advocated, again, by the *Sentinel and Advertiser*), the anti-Associates *Daily Telegraph* reported that consolidation would "break down the central organizations of certain pot-house politicians who have uniformly endeavored . . . to drag our citizens into the net of the Monopolies—not the least of which are the New Jersey Railroad and Transportation Company, and the Jersey Associates." For their part, Van Vorst residents and officials clearly expected that annexation would facilitate infrastructural development in their community.[21]

The annexation of Van Vorst nearly doubled the population of Jersey City, to approximately 12,000. Work on supplying the newly enlarged city with water started almost immediately. In 1852 the legislature authorized the financing and construction of a water supply and sewerage system that would serve Jersey City and parts of surrounding municipalities. The plan for the waterworks was that adopted by the water commissioners of 1851, which was based in large part on the recommendation of an engineer from Boston, William S. Whitwell, but was also very similar to the plan proposed earlier by Ward, calling for reservoirs at Belleville and Bergen Hill, to be filled by water pumped from the Passaic River. The legislation received only cursory coverage in the local press, a fact that suggests unanimity of opinion in favor of a public water supply system, befitting a developmental policy. Reflecting the general trend that authority over infrastructural development followed municipal borders, Hoboken had dropped out as a participant in the water-works project by 1852. One of the most innovative measures in the legislation authorizing the planning and construction of the Jersey City water-works was the additional provision for the development of a comprehensive sewerage system. In 1851 no major city had yet implemented a comprehensive sewerage plan. By the end of 1853 the Jersey City Common Council had approved a comprehensive sewerage plan prepared by the water commissioners, with which all sewer projects thereafter had to comply.[22]

For almost twenty years the board of water commissioners played the primary role in infrastructural development in Jersey City, excepting street paving, which was the responsibility of the common council, and street lighting, which was contracted to the Jersey City Gas Light Company. By 1853 construction of the Belleville reservoir had begun and nearly eight miles of distributing pipe had been laid. In 1854 the waterworks began delivering water to the city. In 1856 the first sewer was built in accordance with the comprehensive plan, and the water commissioners reported that the reduction of property damage from fire "since the introduction of Passaic water" had lowered insurance rates in the city. By 1857 the revenues from water rents were sufficient to meet the interest payments on their bonds "without having recourse, as heretofore, to borrowing, in anticipation of water rents becoming due." In 1861, when the population had increased to more than 29,000, the water commissioners received authorization from the legislature to increase the water supply of their system more than fourfold through the construction of a new main between their two reservoirs. Between 1855 and 1870, judging from the available data, it appears that the board of water commissioners laid, on average, a bit more than two miles of sewer pipe (main and lateral) per year.[23] By the time of the consolidation vote, Jersey City was supplying water not only to itself, but to several surrounding municipalities as well, including Hoboken and Hudson City. As we will see, the control that Jersey City had over the water supply in Hudson County would play a key role in the consolidation debates.

Consolidation: Hudson, Bergen, and Jersey Cities

In 1869 Jersey City was described by one local newspaper as "a compact completed city."[24] On the one hand, Jersey City officials may have felt pleased with the progress that they had made. On the other hand, they may have worried that without the construction jobs and contracts that came with infrastructural development, they would begin to lose their power. That the latter is more likely is suggested by the fact that as soon as Jersey City had been declared "completed," Jersey City officials and others set about enlarging the city to bring in land that still needed improving.

In fact, the motivations behind the Jersey City consolidation scheme are obscure and were no doubt multifaceted. The idea of enlarging Jersey City had been contemplated for decades—the "ambitious little city" had attempted to annex Van Vorst as early as 1825—but the specific plan for consolidating all of the municipalities in Hudson County was first brought to the county governing body, the board of chosen freeholders, in 1868, by Robert Gilchrist and William Brinckerhoff. Gilchrist had probably found himself around the stove at David Smith's store in the early years of Jersey City; he was a long-standing alderman and had served as president of the city council from 1835 to 1836 and as mayor of the city from 1850 to 1852. Brinckerhoff had been the mayor of Bergen City, which was primarily a middle-class suburb of New York and Jersey City.[25]

Gilchrist and Brinckerhoff were Republicans, former Whigs, who were probably interested in consolidating their two cities in order to maintain the dominance of the native-born, Republican elite against the Democrats, who found much of their political strength in the Irish working class. Yet Jersey City annexed not only Bergen City, but also Hudson City, which was composed largely of Irish and German immigrants who worked in the local railroad stockyards and granite quarry. It appears that consolidation ultimately benefited the Democrats over the Republicans, as will be discussed later.[26]

The residents of both Bergen and Hudson had good reasons for wanting to join with Jersey City that transcended issues of ethnicity or class. No matter how different the two cities were in terms of the socioeconomic characteristics of their respective populations, both Hudson and Bergen were in debt, yet lacked adequate infrastructure systems.[27] As one Jersey City resident, highly critical of the consolidation scheme, noted, "Hudson has not one square foot of paving" and "Bergen has the part of a street half done." Moreover, residents in both Hudson and Bergen defended consolidation as an anticorruption measure that would dilute the power of local political bosses and "rings" whose corrupt practices had created the burdensome municipal debts.[28]

For the residents of Jersey City, the advantages of consolidation were not necessarily clear. One evident concern of the city's residents was that through consolidation, Jersey City would simply foot the bill for developing outlying areas. One oft-repeated complaint was that newly annexed territories would be served by a water supply system on which a good deal of the debt had already been paid off; the conclusion was that Jersey City was "giving away" its waterworks. Against this claim, one pro-consolidationist argued that consolidation would provide more people who would share in paying off the waterworks debt that remained and the debt that would be incurred in extending the system. Jersey City would benefit along with all the other cities in systematizing its sewerage, street, policing, and schooling systems over a larger area, which, it was argued, would have a beneficial effect on the area as a whole.[29]

Many Jersey City residents may have also believed that expanding municipal boundaries would break the monopoly of the local gas company. By the 1860s the Jersey City Gas Light Company was widely criticized in the local press for supplying inadequate lighting. The *Evening Journal* claimed in 1869, on the day of the consolidation referendum, that Jersey City was the "poorest lighted city of its size in the country" and had been so for some time.[30] If Jersey City residents had access to the gas companies that supplied neighboring municipalities—and they would ostensibly have access to those gas companies once the municipalities they served became part of Jersey City— then they might be provided with better lighting. As the *Evening Journal* had noted earlier in the year, "Companies have formed in the adjoining cities, and can easily connect with this city, unless our monopoly acts better toward the people than it has done for some years past." Indeed, there were four gas companies in addition to the Jersey City Gas Light Company in Hudson County by 1869.[31]

With eleven municipalities each deciding whether or not to consolidate, no one in Hudson County could have had a good idea of what Jersey City would ultimately look like. It may therefore be safe to assume that much of the pro-consolidation sentiment relied on a nebulous "booster spirit," during a period of relative prosperity, that equated geographic expansion with progress and growth. It does seem likely, however, that many residents had at least a sense that those municipalities deepest in debt were most likely to approve consolidation; even pro-consolidationists had to concede that this would increase costs for the municipal government and thereby increase taxes. As one Jersey City resident who was in favor of consolidation felt compelled to argue, "If Jersey City is called upon to give more than her neighbors, may we not urge that, as the oldest, the richest, the strongest, she can best afford to give?"[32]

As it turned out, Jersey City would be expected to give. After the results of the referendum, city officials in Bergen and Hudson notably increased expenditures on public works, obviously with the expectation that they would not have to shoulder the costs after consolidation. Charles H. O'Neill, the first mayor of the consolidated city, noted in his first address to the common council that while every department of the Jersey City government had ended 1869 with a surplus, in Hudson City "almost every department has exceeded its appropriations, thus making a deficiency . . . equal to one-third of the whole tax ordinance of last year." For Bergen, while most of the city departments had not spent more than they had been appropriated, "the Committee [*sic*] on Salaries, Fire and Water, Finance and Lamps, have exceeded their appropriation, some of them to a very large amount." Bergen had the most debt of any of the three cities, despite the fact that Jersey City had had a larger population than both Bergen and Hudson combined. As McLean noted twenty-five years later, "For years afterwards the city was paying for work ordered in the month preceding passage of the charter."[33]

Given that Hudson and Bergen Cities were well known to be in debt, residents throughout Hudson County probably expected those two municipalities to vote in favor of consolidation. In Jersey City residents perceived that the benefits of living in a much larger city outweighed the costs of taking in two heavily indebted cities. Residents in other surrounding municipalities, such as Hoboken and Bayonne, thought otherwise. I first turn to Hoboken to understand why suburban residents might resist annexation.

A Suburban Company Town

What most likely explains the majority vote against consolidation in Hoboken is that the city's financial condition was far better than that in Bergen and Hudson. Hoboken mayor Hazen Kimball pronounced proudly in 1869, six months before the consolidation referendum, that "Hoboken keeps pace at least, if it does not go beyond, our sister cities in rapid increase of population and wealth."[34] Fifteen years later one prominent resident claimed of Hoboken

that "no city of its size has better credit."[35] Without entering into ruinous municipal debt, Hoboken had managed to supply many public improvements to
its residents that were lacking in Hudson and Bergen. If the differences
in these cities' finances can explain the majority vote against consolidation in
Hoboken, they also raise the further question of why Hoboken had such an
enviable financial condition. There are no doubt structural explanations,
such as Hoboken's advantageous location on the Hudson River, but the
answer also lies in the specific development of Hoboken as a suburb and
pleasure resort.

Colonel John Stevens (more famous as an inventor and railroad engineer)
purchased the "tract known as Hoboken" from the state of New Jersey in
1784, and in 1804 he advertised the sale of "about 800 lots of ground" on his
land. In contrast to the Associates of the Jersey Company, who were intent
on establishing a city that would rival New York, Stevens promoted Hoboken
as a suburban location where one could escape the trials of the big city, such
as yellow fever and "heavy taxes."[36] The different intentions of Stevens and
the Associates are reflected in the fact that Hoboken legally became a city
only in reaction to population growth, when its residents numbered in the
thousands, and two decades after Stevens's death. By contrast, the Associates
got a city charter for Jersey City from the legislature in anticipation of
growth only sixteen years after they had purchased Paulus Hook, and when
the population of their settlement numbered less than 1,000. Stevens's innovations in transportation across the Hudson River—he introduced steam
ferry service in 1811 and even proposed an underground tunnel to Manhattan—speak not only to his engineering talents but also to his emphasis
on creating Hoboken as a suburb of New York.[37] Moreover, Stevens did
not promote the commercial potential of Hoboken's location along the
Hudson River but created park grounds along the waterfront, called the
Elysian Fields. As late as 1855 Hoboken's mayor said of his city that "its
tasty walks and shady groves, combine to render it a place of general resort in the summer. The pleasure-seeker, and the toil-worn mechanic,
alike desire to wander among the fields, and breathe our pure and bracing
atmosphere."[38]

In 1838 Stevens died, and his land was transferred to his sons and other
associates in the form of the Hoboken Land and Improvement Company
(HLIC), incorporated by the legislature in the same year.[39] Early on, HLIC
officials appear to have found themselves caught between Stevens's suburban legacy and a desire to boost Hoboken's potential as a growing city.

For instance, HLIC advertisements promoted Hoboken as a residential enclave, noting that it provided a more healthy and attractive atmosphere, with lower taxes, than New York, while three ferry lines provided easy transit to the big city. HLIC president Edwin F. Johnson noted in 1840 that "as a place of residence for persons engaged in business in New York City, Hoboken presents many advantages." However, HLIC officials were also aware that Hoboken's location along the Hudson River, combined with ready access to railroad and canal transportation, portended more than simply a suburban future for the square-mile city. Indeed, Johnson also claimed that "Hoboken is not dependent solely upon the advantages which it offers as a place of residence" and that it was "destined to become something more than a mere appendage" to New York. The HLIC president estimated that one-third of the approximately 4,200 lots at that point owned by the company would eventually be used for "stores, shops, warehouses, offices & c.," and the remaining two-thirds of the lots would be used for "dwellings," each with an average of seven inhabitants. Thus at a time when it had less than 1,000 inhabitants, Johnson predicted that Hoboken's population would grow to 19,131 in the "not very distant" future, thereby placing it among the fifteen largest cities in the country.[40]

While it seems obvious enough that the HLIC would want to see the city grow, the company was actually in a contradictory position. Urban growth required public expenditures, which were for a long time the responsibility of the HLIC, defined in its charter as "a body politic and corporate" and granted significant powers over land use for such public purposes as "laying out . . . lots, streets, squares, lanes, alleys."[41] Yet the HLIC was also a private company with extensive commercial interests; it owned and operated the ferries that went across the Hudson, the railroad that went to Newark, and the local streetcar company.[42] As a private company, the HLIC had little incentive to divert its capital to the construction of public works. Even if the HLIC were empowered to charge residents special assessments for street improvements (which it was not), this would be a one-time sale that would be unlikely to generate much in the way of profit. Residents could hardly be charged each time they used a paved street or a sewer, but they could be charged for every ride on a ferry or a train.

Indeed, at the time of its creation, it appears that residents and the HLIC itself were aware that there was a problem with granting municipal powers and responsibilities to a private company. In 1841 "numerous residents of Hoboken" presented a petition to the legislature requesting that the HLIC's charter be repealed. The minutes of the HLIC directors' meetings from the same period also reveal that at least one major shareholder, Joshua R. Sands, wanted to dissolve the corporation, conceivably because the HLIC's subsidiary companies—the Hoboken Ferry Company, the Hoboken Railroad Warehouse and Steamship Connecting Company, the Hoboken and Hudson City Horse Car Railroad Company, and the Hoboken and Newark Railroad Company—would be more profitable without the drain of a charter that saddled the company with municipal responsibilities.[43]

Evidence that the HLIC had been neglecting its public duties in favor of private gain can be found in a growing political movement to improve the physical condition of Hoboken. The movement for infrastructural development led to the incorporation of Hoboken as a city in 1855 and was spearheaded by the man who would serve as the first mayor, Cornelius V. Clickener. This is the message of the extant campaign material from Clickener's run for a state senate seat in 1856—a laudatory article in the *New York Atlas*. Indicating the extent to which public works must have been of concern to Hoboken residents, Clickener's political career was described almost entirely in terms of infrastructural development. Clickener was first elected to the Hoboken Town Committee in either the late 1840s or early 1850s, and his first accomplishment was to get the streets paved, "which greatly enhanced the value of property in Hoboken." Alluding to the period when the city's streets were under the control of the HLIC, the *Atlas* article noted that "they who remember the horrible condition of the streets in Hoboken five years ago, especially during the wet months of the cold season, can easily appreciate the advantage of good pavements." During Clickener's second term on the town committee, he made a "liberal arrangement" with the Jersey City Gas Light Company that "secur[ed] to the citizens well-lighted streets" and also "advanced the value of property."[44]

Clickener also saved Hoboken's first city charter from "considerable opposition" in the legislature by inserting a clause in the legislation providing that the charter would be subject to approval in a special election. Hoboken residents approved the charter by a vote of 237 to 185 in 1855 and elected Clickener mayor in the same year.[45] It is not clear who opposed the city charter, although there would seem to be two likely candidates: other cities and towns in Hudson County, who were concerned about Hoboken's growing power, or the HLIC, which would lose much of its control over the area and would be subject to higher taxes. Indeed, into the 1880s the HLIC was by far the largest single taxpayer in the city.[46]

Further evidence that the HLIC probably opposed the 1855 charter comes from the company's later struggles with the municipal government over control of infrastructural development, most notably in regard to the city's water supply. In his first annual message to the city council, Clickener declared that

> arrangements should be entered into as early as practicable, for the introduction of a sufficient supply of pure and wholesome water. I cannot conceive why, when the Passaic water was introduced into Jersey City, Hoboken failed to secure a portion of it. Such, however, is the lamentable fact. It behooves you then to ascertain upon what terms it may be afforded to our citizens. It is needless to expatiate upon the important advantages it would secure, both in the prevention of fires and in offering to our citizens the luxury of universal comfort, cleanliness and health.[47]

Indeed, why had Hoboken not "secured a portion" of the Passaic water when it was introduced to Jersey City? We have already seen that the legislation authorizing the Jersey City waterworks initially included Hoboken as an equal partner in the plan. Yet within a year new legislation indicated that the waterworks would serve "the inhabitants of Jersey City," but only *parts* of the townships, of Bergen, North Bergen, and Hoboken." Moreover, while the five water commissioners named in the 1851 act included one resident of Hoboken, the 1852 act named three water commissioners who were all residents of Jersey City and further stipulated that the two remaining commissioners were to be "the president of the board of aldermen of Jersey City for the time being, and one person to be elected at the next charter election held in Jersey City."[48]

The decision not to participate in the development of a water supply system was most likely made by the HLIC. The company was in a position to play the lead role in developing Hoboken's water supply. In its 1838 corporate charter the HLIC was granted the authority to construct, on its own land, "aqueducts or reservoirs, for conveying, collecting and providing pure and wholesome water." Moreover, the one water commissioner named in the 1851 act who was a resident of Hoboken was Edwin A. Stevens, a son of Colonel John Stevens and a director of the HLIC.[49] Company officials had already shown a disdain for public waterworks on account of the resulting tax burden. In explaining why residents of Hoboken enjoyed lower taxes than the residents of New York City, HLIC president Johnson explained in 1840 that New Yorkers had to pay the expense of their waterworks. "The construction of the Croton Works alone will require from the inhabitants of that city more than one million of dollars annually to pay the interest and redeem the principal in the time specified."[50]

The notion that American cities should be supplied with water by aqueduct was certainly novel in 1840, and thus Johnson's disparaging comments about the Croton system, while not progressive, were not necessarily reactionary either. Yet the fact that the HLIC was still resisting the idea of a waterworks by the 1850s suggests that there may have been something more to Johnson's comment. Recall from Chapter 2 that the construction of the Croton Aqueduct was characterized by patronage and political corruption, which contributed to its cost. Thus Johnson's comments may have been aimed not at waterworks per se, but specifically at public works, which must have seemed to have inevitably become the vehicles for graft.

HLIC officials were clearly aware that significant powers were vested in the organization that controlled a city's waterworks, and the company was hardly prepared to cede such control to a municipal government. Eleven days before the legislature granted Hoboken a city charter, the state governing body also passed a supplement to the HLIC's corporate charter giving the company the authority to "take and hold any lands or other real estate necessary for the construction" of a waterworks that would supply "the inhabitants of Hoboken with pure and wholesome water." While the company was thus granted broad authority to construct a waterworks, the municipal government was only authorized to "make all necessary arrangements for a full and copious supply of good and wholesome water for public and private use." HLIC officials may have planned to construct a waterworks and sell water to the city. Spending restrictions in the city charter, however, suggest that the HLIC was possibly more concerned that the city's water have a minimal effect on the tax rate, no matter who supplied it. City officials were restricted to spending only a maximum of "one dollar per annum, per capita, for every actual resident in the city" for water. The charter also established an absolute ceiling of $20,000 that could be paid to a company annually. The city was authorized to sell bonds for financing a public water system only if it did not enter into a contract with a water company within a year, and then only if the bond issue was approved in a referendum by a two-thirds majority vote.[51]

In short, the intent of the city charter was clearly to minimize the possibility that Hoboken officials would finance and construct a public water system and to ensure that they would instead purchase water from a private supplier. The 1855 charter thus followed in the HLIC's tradition of antipathy toward public waterworks and probably public works in general. By opting for a private water system, the city of Hoboken distinguished itself from growing cities in the region that had adopted public waterworks during the 1850s, such as Jersey City and Brooklyn. By favoring a private over a public water system, Hoboken looked more like a suburban community, along the lines of those in Westchester County (see Chapter 3), than a city. Furthermore, HLIC officials may have planned that their company would supply Hoboken with water, as the amendments to the company's corporate charter suggest. Mayor Clickener's evident desire for Jersey City water may therefore have been not only a desire to supply Hoboken with water, but also to diminish, or at least check, the power that the HLIC had over city services.

Clickener's comments also indicate that the demand for water in Hoboken, which had more than 6,700 residents by 1855, was probably great enough to require "pure and wholesome" water more immediately than the HLIC could provide it. That it was never the intent of the Hoboken city charter that the city be supplied with Jersey City water is evident from the fact that the charter had to be amended twice, in both 1856 and 1857, before the city of Hoboken was authorized to enter into an agreement to purchase water from Jersey City.[52]

Thus, probably despite the intentions of the HLIC, Hoboken was by 1857 being supplied with both its gas and water from Jersey City, the former from a private company and the latter from the municipal government. This was a significant difference. The Jersey City Gas Light Company was apparently content to extend its works into Hoboken in return for money.[53] The municipal government in Jersey City would not be satisfied simply with money in return for water, however, even though Hoboken residents who subscribed for Passaic water paid 10 percent more than subscribers in Jersey City. Jersey City officials clearly conceived of water as a source of municipal power. Only four years after it began supplying Hoboken with water, the Jersey City Board of Water Commissioners noted that its plan to increase the capacity of the waterworks in 1861 would give it "a command of water adequate . . . to supply all suburban places which will ultimately be embraced within the extended boundaries of our future city."[54]

More striking evidence that water was conceived of in terms of municipal power was provided by an article in Jersey City's *Evening Journal* published immediately before the 1869 consolidation vote:

> In case Hoboken votes against consolidation and the other portions of the county are consolidated, the water works will pass into the possession of

the new-formed city, and Hoboken, of course, will have no voice in their management, and at the will of the authorities of the new city they can, having a larger territory to supply with water, refuse to supply Hoboken, and at once cut that city off from receiving any water from our works. No greater catastrophe could happen to Hoboken than this, and it is almost certain to follow if the people of that city reject consolidation. Our Commissioners take this view of the matter and the people generally, and it behooves the people of Hoboken to consider it well before they decide to cast their votes in the interest of rings and pot house politicians . . . The question to be voted upon in Hoboken is really, water or no water, and is one of greater importance to that city than to other places, for the reason that it is now enjoying the blessing while the other places have never had it.[55]

The HLIC and other Hoboken residents evidently did not find the threat of being denied water very credible. W. W. Shippen, HLIC president at the time of the consolidation vote, addressed an anticonsolidation meeting in Hoboken where, the *Evening Journal* reported, "there was a large attendance of the property holders of the city, who evinced the utmost enthusiasm during the proceedings." Shippen, who "was received with great cheering," argued that the "real question" regarding consolidation "was one of dollars and cents," and Hoboken had a lower tax rate than either Jersey, Hudson, or Bergen Cities.[56] That Shippen compared Hoboken's tax rate not only to the tax rate in Jersey City but also to those in Hudson and Bergen suggests that there was a general expectation that Hudson and Bergen would approve consolidation. Shippen was evidently not concerned by the prospect that Hoboken might lose its access to water, and he was in a good position to know, having been elected to the Hoboken Board of Water Commissioners from 1857 to 1867 and having served as the board's president from 1860 to 1867.[57]

The *Evening Journal* was hardly sympathetic to the HLIC, and thus the newspaper's report that Shippen was greeted with "great cheering" by Hoboken's property owners is most likely an understatement. Indeed, on the very same day (and on the same page, no less), a "correspondent writing from the borough of Hoboken" for the *Evening Journal* strongly suggested that the HLIC's opposition to consolidation was a distinctly undemocratic attempt to avoid paying taxes. The issue of taxes again centered on the issue of infrastructural development. The *Evening Journal* correspondent singled out the issue of a proposed trunk sewer for Hoboken's

Fourth Ward, which would have run through waterfront property owned by the HLIC. The company had apparently put a stop to the sewer "by threats of injunctions and interminable lawsuits. In short, they would not pay their part of the tax for the sewer, and the people had to empty it into a place where the outlet is encumbered by mud, and not half so effective as if going direct to the river." In another devious plot to avoid paying taxes—a plan the correspondent noted was "so ingenious that Mr. Shippen should have it patented"—the HLIC used its influence in the legislature in 1859 to have a portion of Hoboken incorporated separately as the town of Weehawken. Included in the new town was a narrow strip of land, wholly owned by the Stevens estate, "which cuts nearly the whole of the splendid waterfront away and exempts them from Hoboken city taxation, and prohibits the latter city from running its streets to the river."[58]

The case of the Fourth Ward trunk sewer was yet another example, like the water supply or street pavements in the 1850s, of the HLIC's resistance to public works for the sake of minimizing its tax burden. Yet by 1869 Hoboken was a much different city than it had been in the 1850s. Despite the separation of Weehawken in 1859, Hoboken's population had increased to 9,659 by 1860, and by the time of the consolidation vote the city probably had some 20,000 residents.[59] Moreover, Hoboken was becoming more of a commercial community; Mayor Hazen Kimball commented in 1869 that "a number of useful and extensive manufactories have been put in successful operation."[60] Class divisions had no doubt become clearer in Hoboken, as indicated by the account in the *Evening Journal* that the HLIC president was cheered by other "property owners," while "the people" of the Fourth Ward were denied adequate sewerage.

The establishment of a municipal government in the 1850s had evidently been a movement on the part of Hoboken residents to gain power apart from the HLIC in order to promote public works and thereby increase property values. By the 1860s and 1870s, no doubt as a reflection of growing class divisions, the HLIC and other taxpayers had joined together against the municipal government, which was accused of engaging in wasteful public works projects for the benefit of certain well-connected contractors and engineers.[61] The *Evening Journal* correspondent noted of Hoboken that "like all similar places, it is governed by a lot of lazy, ignorant loafers who study their own interests alone, and care as little as possible for the people."[62] The fact that Shippen had been consistently elected to the board of water commissioners for ten years is also evidence that the HLIC had the popular support of Hoboken residents.

The residents of Hoboken, Bergen, and Hudson all complained about the operation of "rings" that had taken over their respective local governments, yet apparently only enough residents in Bergen and Hudson believed that consolidation to Jersey City was a viable solution to municipal corruption. The Hoboken Tax-payers' and Citizens' Association in 1873 provided one explanation as to why consolidation was not a solution to municipal corruption for its city:

> The cowardly desertion of the leaky ship may result in drowning. For instance a resident of Hoboken may decide to . . . remove to a neighboring municipality, under whose care he will place his effects, which may soon be swallowed up, the disease *ringology* or *ringgold* prevailing there, without the counteracting influence of a Tax-payers' Association. A wise policy is to remain and resolve that the leak *shall and must be stopped*, and that a vigorous effort *shall and must be made* to catch and punish the *rats* that caused the leak by gnawing the hull.[63]

As the *Evening Journal* correspondent had suggested as well, corruption was inherent to municipal government. The best citizens could do was battle the negative symptoms of "ringology or ringgold" with a powerful counterorganization. Hoboken residents, unlike those in Hudson or Bergen, were blessed with the HLIC, which, while it might slow the pace of infrastructural development, would also protect against excessive municipal spending. If this was in fact what many residents were thinking at the time they voted for or against consolidation, their belief followed the classic American political tradition of the *Federalist Papers*. The presence of both a municipal government and a private company that operated in many respects as a municipal government provided at least a rough system of checks and balances in Hoboken. Because there was no effective check against municipal spending in Hudson and Bergen, residents in these two cities sought, in James Madison's words, to "extend the sphere" through consolidation in order to "take in a greater variety of parties and interests" that might provide effective protection against the tyranny of excessive municipal spending.[64]

Another reason that Hoboken residents probably rejected consolidation was that they followed in the long tradition of understanding themselves to be part of a suburban community. In Jersey City the Associates were reviled and rebuked by many residents because they had impeded the commercial development of the city. Hoboken residents were probably less concerned with commercial progress, because this had never been a primary goal of the settlement, as it had been on Paulus Hook. It does not seem likely, for instance, that the separation of Weehawken from Hoboken impeded commercial development any more than the establishment of the Elysian Fields. Even Mayor Clickener's criticisms of the HLIC in the 1850s centered on the suburban qualities of Hoboken. The mayor complained that the company charged too much for ferry rides to Manhattan, noting that this was "a fruitful cause of injury to the growth of this city." But clearly "growth" in this context meant an increasing residential population that commuted daily to New York. Similarly, Clickener defended a general tax rather than a special assessment for gas streetlights around the waterfront because they benefited the general commuter population by illuminating their respective paths "from the ferry homeward."[65]

Guided by the HLIC, Hoboken would continue along the suburban trajectory of growth well after consolidation, as indicated again by the water supply. During the 1870s, as it became increasingly evident that water from the Passaic was not fit for drinking, and as the city's population grew to more than 40,000, still Hoboken produced no public waterworks, as did other cities of similar size during the decade, such as Yonkers and Long Island City. Instead, the city switched to a new private water supplier, the Hackensack Water Company Reorganized ("Reorganized" because it had gone bankrupt in 1879). The HLIC was a major shareholder and enjoyed an interlocking directorate with the new company.[66]

The story of the Hackensack Water Company Reorganized is a telling one in terms of how infrastructure technology diffused across northern New Jersey. The Hackensack Water Company was founded in 1869. The company's waterworks had been designed by the estimable Jersey City engineering firm Bacot and Ward, which purchased the company after it went bankrupt. Bacot and Ward quickly entered into a ten-year contract to supply the city of Hoboken with water. Here is an example of the diffusion of infrastructure technology from Jersey City to its outlying suburbs. The plan for using the Hackensack Water Company to supply Hoboken with water, however, was originally conceived by a professor at the Stevens Institute of Technology, which was the engineering school in Hoboken, founded in 1871 from the bequest of Edwin Stevens, who died in 1868 and left money and land in his will to establish the school.[67]

Although it was founded after the consolidation vote, the Stevens Institute clearly put Hoboken in a unique position of being a small city that was a center of regional engineering talent. For instance, the chief engineer and superintendent of the Hackensack Water Company Reorganized was Hoboken engineer Charles B. Brush. Brush also served as a city surveyor and was a partner in the Hoboken firm of Speelman and Brush. Hoboken had no city engineers, but instead appointed city surveyors for life. In 1893 the city surveyors were Brush, Beyer and McCann, and Tivy and Smith. The information that exists about these Hoboken engineers suggests that they were trained on larger infrastructure projects in the metropolitan region. For instance, before T. H. McCann formed a partnership with Albert Beyer, he had worked on the engineering staff of the Croton Aqueduct Board, serving directly under chief engineers Alfred Craven and George Green.[68] Thus the case of Hoboken provides some evidence of a causal path from central city infrastructural development to suburban infrastructural development. Engineering expertise within Hoboken was at least in part developed through training on larger infrastructure projects in larger cities in the metropolitan region.

Most contractors who worked on infrastructure projects in Hoboken were probably also residents. Of those contractors who worked on street improvements and whose names are still known—John McDermott, Dennis Eagan, James Coughlin, and Michael Callahan—only McDermott appears to have come from a neighboring municipality, probably either Jersey City or Bergen City.[69] As in engineering, it appears that Hoboken had some assistance from Jersey City but had an ample local labor pool upon which it could draw for the purposes of infrastructural development.

In sum, the case of Hoboken provides some evidence that central city infrastructural development created both the motivation and means for suburban autonomy. The relationship between Jersey City and Hoboken was not strictly that between a central city and its suburb, but Hoboken was a smaller city and at least more suburban in character than Jersey City. In weighing consolidation in 1869, Hoboken residents probably considered not only the present state of Jersey City politics and finances but also the politics and finances of those municipalities that were thought most likely to vote in favor of consolidation. The fact that such fiscally reckless municipalities as Hudson and Bergen Cities appeared likely to consolidate with the city could not have made consolidation more enticing. One of the guiding principles of the HLIC and other property owners was that political corruption accompanied infrastructural development and resulted in higher taxes. Thus Hobokenites' apparent fear of higher taxes were they to become residents of Jersey City probably indicates as well a fear of political corruption in the larger city. At the same time, Hobokenites could only seriously consider municipal autonomy from Jersey City if they were supplied with basic urban services from public works. Unwilling to pursue infrastructural development and thus foster corruption, Hoboken relied on Jersey City's infrastructure systems, which, ironically, endangered Hoboken's municipal autonomy. In securing the services of infrastructure systems that were not controlled by Jersey City, most notably in the case of water supply, Hoboken relied on the work of engineers from Jersey City. As a midsize city with an engineering school, however, Hoboken obviously had local expertise relevant to infrastructural development. In the case of Bayonne, we will see that a less populated outlying community had to depend to a greater extent on neighboring communities in order to pursue local infrastructural development.

Invasion of the New Yorkers

While Hoboken was by 1869 a suburban community that was beginning to look more like a city, Bayonne was a rural hinterland that was beginning to look more like a suburb. In 1850 approximately 500 people lived in four distinct villages on the peninsula between New York and Newark Bays—Centerville, Constable Hook, Bergen Point, and Pamrapo (otherwise known as Salterville). The peninsula experienced rapid population growth in the decades prior to the consolidation vote, reaching approximately 1,300 in 1861 (when the four villages became the township of Bayonne) and 3,834 in 1869 (when the township became a city).[70] Despite this rapid growth, the population of Bayonne was still much smaller than that of Hoboken prior to 1870 and was spread out among communities that were still very separate. The local paper, the *Bayonne Herald,* admonished its readers in 1869 that "we shall object in future to publish . . . such names as *Bergen Point, Centerville* and *Pamrapo.* This is the City of Bayonne, which is divided into the First, Second and Third Wards. Let us live in the present, not in the past."[71]

Probably at the behest of some of the more politically active landowners of the peninsula, in 1857 the legislature took the first step in unifying the various communities that would later become Bayonne by creating a map and grade commission, whose responsibility was to "survey and map" the area south of the Morris Canal and to design a system of "streets, avenues and squares, of such width, extent and direction as . . . shall seem most conducive to the public good." All "streets, avenues and highways" that were opened were then required to conform to the plan approved by the commissioners. The result of the map and grade commission was the "Ryan Map," a grid system named after James Ryan, a surveyor from Elizabeth hired by the commissioners.[72]

The Ryan Map soon faced resistance, especially in the area just south of the Morris Canal, known as Salterville, a real estate development founded by the Salter family in the 1830s. The Salters and their compatriots would become the most outspoken critics of the Bayonne city government, claiming that it was controlled by residents from Bergen Point and Centreville, and these lower villages were thus disproportionately benefited, while Salterville was neglected.[73] The Salters' criticisms of Bayonne city government would figure prominently in later debates over consolidation with Jersey City.

As a result of numerous lawsuits regarding the Ryan Map, mostly dealing with street openings in and around Salterville, the map and grade commission was disbanded in the early 1860s and replaced by a decentralized system whereby residents applied to the Hudson County court for authority to open individual streets.[74] The decentralized system clearly impeded the opening of streets and thus the development of a functioning street grid. At the same time, new means of transportation that drew Bayonne into closer contact with outlying areas created a greater need for better streets. In the 1850s Bayonne was, by at least one account, two hours from Jersey City by stagecoach.[75] In 1860 the Jersey City and Bergen Rail Road Company began to lay a streetcar line that started at the ferry dock in Jersey City and then went south "through the woods and the fields" of Bayonne to Bergen Point. The line (known as the "Dummy Railroad" because it used steam engines instead of horses) was completed and began to take passengers near the end of 1863. In the following year the Central Railroad completed a rail line that ran from Elizabeth to Jersey City, going the entire distance of Bayonne. By 1869, according to one real estate circular, there were "over fifty regular communications daily by the Central Railroad . . . two steamboats, and a dummy railroad, which communicates with Jersey City every hour." The new means of transportation both attracted "a commuting population to Bayonne" and created new jobs on the peninsula, many of which were associated with the coal docks built by the Central Railroad in 1866.[76]

Despite new means of transportation and a growing population, the only paved street in Bayonne was a toll road with wooden planks, known as the Plank Road, running the distance of the peninsula. The proprietors of the

Plank Road had counted on the planks lasting ten years, but, resting on the moist ground of the peninsula, the wood rotted and had to be replaced within five years. The widest street, later known as Avenue C, was a dirt road. The Dummy Railroad ran between Avenue C and the Plank Road, and its "light iron rails were laid on wooden cross-ties set directly in the spongy soil . . . In rainy weather the mud oozed up between the ties and the tracks sank on one side or the other," causing the steam cars to derail on a regular basis. The weekly editions of the *Bayonne Herald* from 1869 are filled with complaints about the conditions of the roads and the lack of drainage in various parts of the new city. In September, for instance, the local paper declared that the "new missionary hymn" of the city council was "From Greenville's muddy mountains to Corktown's marshy strands."[77]

Bayonne's newer residents, increasingly suburbanites who commuted to New York, were not about to stand for such conditions. In a telling passage, well worth quoting at length, the city's newspaper (whose editor and founder had come from New York) outlined the struggle that these "New Yorkers" faced in their new home:

> In 1853 there were only four or five New York families in Bergen Point, and the lower portion of the plank road . . . was occupied entirely by oystermen and boatmen who had but limited ideas of improvement. In fact many of them were bitterly opposed to all innovation, and evinced an antagonistic feeling to the "foreigner" as they styled New Yorkers. As an instance of this strange conduct on the part of them, almost pagan aborigines, one gentleman from the metropolis, after grading and regulating a new sidewalk, was much mortified on the following morning to find that some iconoclast had ploughed it down and made a ditch in front of his residence. After numerous inquiries he found that this piece of destructive wasteness had been perpetrated by the roadmaster, who gave as his only excuse, "I'm going to show these New Yorkers and foreignors [sic] they can't have things just as they want them." . . . The old element, however, has disappeared before the light of metropolitan civilization, and the Rip Van Winkles, like their prototype, the Red Indians, have been annihilated.[78]

We see here a new variant on the diffusion of infrastructure technology from central cities to suburbs in the New York metropolitan region: as part of a larger cultural diffusion of "New York" values that would displace the primitive folkways of the "almost pagan aborigines." The reference to "Red Indians" suggests the role that infrastructural development played in the development of a "progressive," technologically advanced, and distinctly nonethnic society. Infrastructural development worked in tandem with a nativism that would define suburbanization well into the twentieth century.

By the late 1860s the New Yorkers were clearly having their way in the physical development of Bayonne. By an act of the legislature in 1868, the map and grade commission was reestablished to meet "the need for streets and avenues for the growing community in the new industrial era." Toward this end the new commission was granted greater financial means, being authorized to issue up to $50,000 worth of bonds for opening and grading streets. To avoid the constant "trouble, expense and litigation" that had plagued the previous commission, the legislature made it substantially harder for residents to challenge the street plan, specifying that no "changes, alterations and improvements" could be made unless they were "requested in writing" by property owners representing at least five-eights of the value of properties on the affected streets.[79]

An indication of the influence that New Yorkers had in the physical development of Bayonne is their prominence as officials in the new city government, the charter for which was authorized by the legislature in 1869 and approved in a public referendum, 225 to 34, in the same year.[80] The city's first mayor, who also served as a map and grade commissioner, Henry Meigs Jr., had lived and worked as a banker in New York City until the age of forty-eight, when he and his family moved to Bergen Point in 1857. After moving to Bergen Point, Meigs still worked in New York City as a stockbroker and remained a member of the New York Stock Exchange throughout his ten-year mayoralty. The *Bayonne Herald* mentioned in September 1869 that several of the members of the new city council were New Yorkers who had been elected because residents on the peninsula "expected more metropolitan enterprise and less of the proverbial dilitariousness which has retarded the growth of this favored city." Other local elite institutions besides the city government were also run by people who had only recently come from Manhattan Island, such as John Stephen, formerly "a New York journalist," who founded the *Bayonne Herald* in 1869, and J. G. Armour, the proprietor of the Latourette House, a hotel in Bergen Point that was the social center of Bayonne high society as well as "the abiding place of guests of National celebrity."[81]

The New Yorkers conceived of infrastructural development as a way to attract yet more New Yorkers to Bayonne. In his inaugural address to the common council, Mayor Meigs warned that "without improvements to roads, education and postal service . . . Bayonne would not reap the benefits of the city's proximity to New York, nor attract its working people looking to live in a nearby New Jersey community." Likewise, the *Herald* noted that the population of New York had increased from 60,000 in 1800 to 1.2 million in 1869, creating a "problem of locating this increasing mass of humanity" that was "well nigh insolvable . . . the middle classes . . . must seek homes in the many rural towns and cities which cluster around the metropolis and are vitalized by its proximity." The best way to make sure that the "mass of humanity" chose to reside in Bayonne was "by making necessary improvements, by grading and paving the streets and sidewalks, by opening sewers, by tidal drainage, by school houses, by equalization of taxation, and by enforcing the laws in regard to order and propriety."[82]

Not only was infrastructural development necessary for making Bayonne a suburb, but infrastructural development itself was to be of a uniquely suburban type, as in the *Herald*'s admonishment to use the more expensive Nicholson pavement instead of Belgian block on one of the city's main thoroughfares, Avenue S. The smoothness of the Nicholson pavement would keep the noise from street traffic to a minimum, which was important to the growth of the city because "New Yorkers come to the country for repose and tranquility, but if Avenue S has a Belgian pavement then good-bye to rural calm and rustic repose, and high-ho for the silence that, like a poultice, comes to heal the wound of sound." By contrast, with Nicholson pavement, "Villa residences . . . would spring up by the stroke of the enchanters [sic] wand," thereby guaranteeing that Bayonne's "popularity would be such as to make it a household word in the great metropolis."[83]

The minutes of the common council printed in the *Herald* indicate that one of its primary pieces of business every week was approving grades for various streets, assessments, and awarding contracts and approving the payment of contractors for grading the streets. Before the consolidation vote in October, the council had entered into discussions with the Central Railroad over a proposed plan to build a tidal sewer to drain the First Ward.[84] Progress was also being made on lighting the streets. In July 1869 the *Herald* reported that subscriptions for the stock of a Bergen Point Gas-light Company had gone on sale. The founders of the new gas company— Henry Meigs Jr., Hiram Van Buskirck, Jacob R. Schuyler, Solon Humphreys, and Erastus Randall (possibly the same man who was also a founder of the Jersey City Gas Light Company)—included the mayor of the city and four of the five map and grade commissioners. An Indication of the extent to which infrastructural development was understood as an element of municipal autonomy is that the only map and grade commissioner who did not take part in the establishment of a gas company for the new city was also the only map and grade commissioner who had been publicly opposed to the city charter.[85]

Despite the reestablishment of the map and grade commission and the establishment of a city government, there were still impediments to the rapid development of Bayonne. Applications for street improvements were published in the local press for ten days, then had to be approved not only by the common council and the map and grade commission, but also by affected property owners. Proposed assessments had to be determined and then published for twenty days, presenting another opportunity for property owners to protest.[86] As before, much of the resistance to new street improvements came from Salterville. In his second address to the city council, Mayor Meigs noted of Salterville's streets that they were "laid in . . . an unreasonable and irregular manner" with "scarcely a right angle in the district." The new street map called for straightening and right-angling the streets in the area, and the map and grade commission had "endeavored to obtain the approval of the property owners," but had been rebuffed. Indeed, Mayor Meigs lamented that were it not for the streets in Salterville, the work of the map and grade commission would "now be drawing to a close."[87] The *Herald* described the situation in a comical fashion that captured the role that street improvements played in establishing local power and autonomy: "If the Map and Grade Commissioners are not a little more active in Salterville, their occupation will be gone . . . That redoubtable Falstaff Smith Salter, was discovered the other day surveying and grading the street . . . His line was perfectly correct, and he boldly declares that if the Map and Grade Commission won't do anything for the Third Ward, *he* will."[88]

Reversing the standard suburban argument that public works in the central city were more expensive because they were used to support machine politics, residents in Salterville complained that they already received inadequate services for the taxes they paid and would do better as residents of Jersey City. The *Herald*, once again poking fun in a telling fashion, blamed the dissatisfaction among Salterville residents on "some artful intriguers from Jersey City" who had succeeded in representing the map and grade commission "as an arbitrary and expensive institution, that was doing the property owners great injury in right-angling the streets." It seems likely, however, that the agitation for annexation in Salterville was actually homegrown, since it continued in fits and starts throughout the 1870s.[89]

As for Bayonne residents as a whole, they indicated their preference for an independent Bayonne by voting by a majority against consolidation, 250 to 100. In a disingenuous display of objectivity, the *Herald* declined to state an opinion about consolidation prior to the referendum, although it did publish an article weighing the possible costs and benefits. On the positive side, the *Herald* provided only the vague speculation that "a stronger government might be better for Bayonne." On the negative side, the newspaper warned that consolidation would mean assuming "responsibility for the bonded debt of Jersey City" and therefore accepting "the imposition of new taxes" that would "check investment in real estate in Bayonne in proportion of that additional charge imposed upon the lands."[90]

Perhaps emboldened after the majority vote against consolidation, the *Herald* was later more strident in denouncing Jersey City. Only weeks after the consolidation referendum, the legislature briefly considered a new bill that called for another vote on annexation. With the knowledge that such profligate cities as Bergen and Hudson were now to become part of Jersey City, the *Herald* argued that if Bayonne were to be annexed, "every improvement would degenerate into a job, and only those streets would be opened for which the ring received the most money." Taxes would increase, primarily to "fill the pockets of 'patriotic' place hunters and political thieves." Furthermore, the *Herald* argued, there was no common identity between Bayonne and Jersey City that justified their consolidation. "Few if any of our citizens ever go to Jersey City, as their business places are in New York, and the entire trade of this city is with that metropolis, from which we not only receive supplies, but also the additions to our population." Although New York City had been unified by "continuous lines of bricks and mortar" that ran for "seven or eight miles," Hudson County was "made up wholly of independent cities having their own retail stores, with no identity of interests."[91] The next logical step in this analysis would have been that if continuous lines of bricks and mortar had served to unify municipal government on Manhattan Island, then the independent cities of Hudson County maintained their separate identities of interest in large part by maintaining separate physical plants.

In intimating that separate municipal identities, abetted by independent infrastructural development, justified municipal fragmentation in Hudson County, the *Herald* conveniently overlooked Salterville, which was itself physically distinct from the rest of Bayonne and clearly had its own identity, yet had been subsumed into the peninsular city over repeated protests. If

Jersey City could attempt a municipal imperialism, using its water supply and other essential services to expand its territory, so could Bayonne attempt to subdue the northern colony of Salterville by straightening its streets and bringing it into the city's grid. Infrastructural development in Bayonne can be distinguished from that in Jersey City because it was used in the former city to create a suburban enclave for New Yorkers, yet in both places infrastructural development also served to reinforce municipal power.

Bayonne was probably in a good position to maintain its independence because it did not rely on Jersey City for water in 1869. Bayonne's relative geographic isolation, combined with a smaller population, probably allowed residents there to rely on wells for a longer period. Indeed, water (purchased from Jersey City) was only introduced by aqueduct to Bayonne in 1881, and then largely for the purposes of fire protection. In other areas as well, Bayonne appears to have had natural advantages that reduced the costs of infrastructural development. The *Herald* commented in 1869, for instance, that "the improvements to be made in Bayonne are comparatively inexpensive to those in Hudson and Jersey Cities, where marshes are to be filled, and long cuttings for drains made through the solid rock."[92]

While the evidence is scarce, what does exist suggests that the physical development of Bayonne was facilitated by outside expertise that came mostly from Jersey City. As previously noted, the author of the Ryan Map, who later did other surveying work for the city, came from Elizabeth. In the same year that the Ryan Map was completed, another map was completed for Bayonne by John Fouquet, then the city surveyor of Jersey City. The Fouquet Map was drawn for a planned residential development around the middle of the peninsula that influenced the later pattern of "deep lots and wide streets" that is still evident today. The street plan for Bayonne was "thoroughly revised" by Emmet Smith, who was in 1868 appointed as the Bayonne city surveyor and then as city engineer, a position he held until his death in the second decade of the twentieth century. Smith was trained at the Jersey City firm of Mallory and Muller.[93]

Given its small population, Bayonne may have relied to a great extent on outside contractors as well, though there is hardly enough evidence even for conjecture. There is evidence of only two contractors having worked on infrastructure projects in Bayonne in 1869—John H. Vanburkick (probably a misspelling of Van Buskirck) and the partnership of Hutchinson and Roke. Vanburkick (or Van Buskirck) was likely a resident of Bayonne, but there is no record of either a Hutchinson or a Roke having lived in Bayonne in the

1860s or 1870s, although there is also no record of either of them in Jersey City or Hoboken during this same period.[94]

Resistance to consolidation in Bayonne was apparently based on two main considerations. First, as suburbanites of New York City, the residents of Bayonne (at least those for whom the *Bayonne Herald* spoke) did not perceive that they had interests similar to those of the residents of Jersey City. Second, the residents of Bayonne voted against consolidation at least in part because they feared that infrastructural development in their area under the auspices of Jersey City would be carried forward in a corrupt fashion. If Bayonne residents were wary of corruption from Jersey City, however, they also depended on expertise from Jersey City to supply themselves with essential urban services. Infrastructural development in Jersey City served to create both resources upon which Bayonne could rely—expertise and, later, water—and an antipathy to Jersey City politics. As the *Bayonne Herald* suggested, the fear that Jersey City politicians would profit disproportionately from building infrastructure systems at the expense of Bayonne residents was probably in large part responsible for the majority vote against consolidation in the southernmost city in Hudson County.

If the majority of residents in Bayonne were resistant to Jersey City because they believed that the larger city was a seat of corruption, then Salterville served as a local alter ego where residents desired consolidation to Jersey City because they were resistant to what they perceived as municipal corruption in Bayonne. Representing a small minority, drawn into Bayonne probably only on account of the Morris Canal having served as a convenient municipal boundary, Salterville could be conveniently disregarded by the residents who lived in the more southern regions of the city. Into the 1870s the *Herald,* published at the southern tip of the city, in Bergen Point, continued to dismiss the noises coming from Salterville. Greenville residents' majority vote in favor of joining Jersey City at the end of 1872 once again raised the prospect to Salterville residents (who lived immediately adjacent to Greenville) that they too might join Jersey City—ultimately a vain hope. In response, the *Herald* provided only patronizing commentary: "Salterville has got on another fit for annexation to Jersey City."[95]

The Bumsted Ring and the Greenville Tax War

Why did Greenville residents reverse themselves and vote in favor of consolidation to Jersey City in 1872 after they had voted by a majority against the same measure in 1869? The evidence suggests that changes in both Greenville and Jersey City since the initial referendum led to the Greenville reversal. When Greenville residents voted on the consolidation issue a second time, Jersey City was in a reform period, but Greenville's local government was mired in corruption and feuding. Thus the roles had reversed themselves: suburban residents voted to join the reformed city as an anti-corruption effort.

The expanded version of Jersey City that resulted from the consolidation vote was clearly a Democratic metropolis. The Republican and nativist *Evening Journal* noted of the new city charter being considered in the Democratic-controlled legislature in 1870 that "things are fixed generally with a very special regard to the interests of the Democratic small politicians."[96] Yet not just the new charter would help Democratic politicians in the city. Jersey City voters also tended to elect Democrats. Thus in 1871, when Republicans gained control of the legislature, they passed a new charter for Jersey City that created three five-person commissions, appointed by the legislature, each of which had broad authority over certain policy areas, while the popularly elected city council, in the words of one contemporary observer, was "divested . . . of every public function, except that possibly of granting licenses to saloon-keepers."[97]

One of the three commissions created by the legislature in 1871 was the board of public works, which was given authority to lay sewers and water pipes, pave streets, and charge special assessments for improvements regardless of the wishes of the owners of the affected properties. Moreover, the mayor had no veto authority over the board of public works. Two of the five members of the board of finance were to be drawn from the board of public works, thus making the board of finance, as the *Jersey City Times* proclaimed, "THE INSTRUMENT through which the Board of Works are to raise all the money by the sale of . . . untold and unlimited . . . bonds that the Board of Works are empowered to spend."[98]

One of the original supporters of the charter, who may have had a hand in its design, was William H. Bumsted, a well-connected Republican who had followed his father into the general contracting business, specializing in sewers and street repairs. In the 1850s Bumsted had lived in Jersey City, and his name appears throughout the minutes of the common council as a contractor for the city. Bumsted later moved to Bergen, where he was alleged to be the leader of the local "ring" and was frequently under suspicion of corrupt dealings in his multiple positions as alderman, water commissioner, sewer inspector, partner in a general contracting firm, and a shareholder in a local gas company and street-paving firm.[99]

Bumsted was elected an alderman in the consolidated city and was appointed president of the board of public works, and under his direction infrastructural development proceeded at a brisk pace. In 1871 and 1872 more than twenty miles of water pipe were laid, expanding the existing pipe network by approximately 25 percent, and approximately six miles of sewer pipe were laid, an amount that, although not a tremendous increase, was greater than the average rate at which sewers had been laid in Jersey City for the preceding two decades. Although some of this construction may have been due to the contracts awarded by Hudson and Bergen prior to consolidation, twenty-nine contracts for sewers were awarded by the board of public works in 1871 alone. In addition, work on a third water reservoir began in 1871.[100]

A rising tax rate and municipal debt, brought about in large part by the increased rate of infrastructural development under the board of public works, provided the appropriate public mood for Democrats to strike back against the 1871 charter through a county grand jury, which managed to indict "every appointed official on one charge or another." As the president of the board of public works and a long-suspected ringleader, Bumsted served as a convenient target for those intent on discrediting the 1871 charter, and he was, by most accounts, singled out for especially harsh treatment. Bumsted was indicted and then found guilty of having informed a real estate speculator about land that the board of public works was planning to purchase for the purposes of building its third reservoir and then having split the $60,000 profit that the speculator had made by buying the property and reselling it to the city within a space of two months. Although he was later granted a pardon, Bumsted served his full jail term of nine months and, according to one author, died as a result of his "disgrace."[101]

Bumsted's ordeal is probably significant for understanding the dramatic reversal in Greenville, where voters rejected consolidation in 1869 by a vote of 174 to 24 but in 1872 voted in favor of consolidation to Jersey City by 291 to 55. Like Bayonne, Greenville was a rural farming community that began to experience significant suburban population growth with the introduction of the Central Railroad and the dummy line. Population growth of course raised the related issues of street improvements and greater local control. Thus the independent township of Greenville was created by the legislature in 1863, and a board of street commissioners was established for the area in 1865. Right from the beginning, it appears, street improvements were politically motivated. In 1868 "a change in the political sentiment of the Legislature" enabled one local group to oust the sitting street commissioners and have themselves installed in their place.[102]

The feud over control of the street commission entered prominently into the debates over consolidation in 1869. At one citizens' meeting in Greenville, the principal reason given in favor of being annexed to Jersey City was that the street commission would then be disbanded.[103] Yet consolidation was not the appropriate solution to Greenville's problem, which was that the street commission had been captured by a local faction and did not represent the interests of most residents. As the *Bayonne Herald* reported, a month after the consolidation vote, "The Map Commissioners are doing things all in their own way, and their labors are not appreciated by many. Jerseymen do not relish the system of legislating men into office. An effort will be made to have the bill appointing the Commission repealed at the next session of the Legislature. Elect your public officers and they will be more solicitous to accommodate you."[104] Being annexed to a larger city would only dilute the ability of Greenville residents to have their interests represented in the local government, a fact reflected in their vote against consolidation. Instead, in 1872 the office of street commissioner in Greenville was made elective.[105]

Ironically, the elected board of street commissioners generated even more hostility than the appointed one, probably because of its enhanced ability to levy taxes for street improvements.[106] In response to a large tax increase in the township that was a result of the activities of the board, disgruntled residents organized into the Committee of 27. Operating under the authority of a writ of certiorari issued by the state supreme court, the Committee of 27 proceeded to copy, with the help of two stenographers, "in full the minutes and proceedings" of the street commission and discovered $20,000 of unexplained expenditures (out of total expenditures of $62,000) in the process. The committee presented the commissioners with a written request that they resign. The commissioners, who were reported to have "surrounded themselves that evening with a gang of roughs," rejected the committee's request "with silent contempt."[107]

What actually transpired in the process of Greenville's "tax war" is difficult to determine. The *Bayonne Herald and Greenville Register* (formerly the *Bayonne Herald*) reported that the excessive tax revenues had resulted from "errors" that were "more or less explainable, but in some points inexcusable." In the following week two of the street commissioners, J. O. Seymour and John A.

Cadmus, along with the treasurer of the township, John Morrell, were arrested "on the affidavit of Judge Dilloway," given a bail of $6,000, and ordered to appear before a grand jury at the beginning of January 1873. Shortly thereafter Judge Dilloway himself was arrested for perjury. The entire situation was characterized in the *Herald* as a "moral Epizootic, which has now become epidemic . . . each party bringing one or the other before some of the half dozen Hudson County Justices, and . . . taking preliminary steps to bring each other before the Grand Jury."[108]

Resolution of the "tax war" came quickly with a state supreme court ruling that lowered the tax rate and thus provided some relief to the taxpayers of Greenville, although the Committee of 27 was apparently still pursuing a further reduction. Further resolution to the dispute was sought by reopening the question of consolidation with Jersey City. The General Consolidation Act of 1868 included a provision that if any of the municipalities voted against consolidation in 1869, they could vote on the matter again at a later date.[109]

What group or groups of Greenville residents actually initiated the new consolidation referendum is unclear.[110] Despite a claim made in the *Herald* that "the people of Greenville are in much of a mixed up mind on this subject," the overwhelming vote in favor of consolidation in 1872 as well as the higher turnout (346 total votes in 1872 versus 198 in 1869) suggests a general public disgust with the tax war. The combatants themselves do not appear to have favored consolidation, although accounts in the *Herald* are unclear on this point. Judge Dilloway and the street commissioners, despite their past differences, were reported as being united in their opposition to consolidation, "although the Commissioners pretend to be in favor of it." Another article written after the referendum reported that "a few of the leading members of 'the Committee of 27,' took quite a feeble-active part against consolidation." Two of the street commissioners were known to have not voted in the referendum; of the other three, "one is supposed to have voted 'No Charter,' and the others, with the officials and the Town Committee, voted, if at all [,] in favor of consolidation."[111]

There were undoubtedly many issues that led voters in Greenville to accept consolidation with Jersey City. The issue that stands out, however, is the street commission and its excessive tax levy in 1872. Debate regarding the 1869 consolidation vote indicates that the street commission was an issue even before the tax war. What thus seems likely is that the tax hike of 1872 was the precipitating event that brought existing issues concerning the physical development of the township to the surface. Factional splits that arose concerning who had control over infrastructural development, which might have assumed less importance in the context of a large city, rendered the government of a small township inoperable. Thus paralyzed in their attempts to provide themselves with physical improvements, the residents of Greenville gave up hope and threw in their lot with the big city.[112]

Jersey City probably looked like a more hospitable city to join by the end of 1872. In April of that year, in an effort to appease public outrage and to move beyond the Bumsted scandals, the Jersey City Board of Works voted to halt "new construction in the following year," except in certain circumstances, and to "improve streets" only upon "approval of the frontage owners." Possibly also as a response to public criticism, the board of public works created a bureau of civil engineering and surveying in 1872, consisting of the board's chief engineer and "as many assistants as may be necessary." The bureau was given broad authority to "take charge of all public works now in progress in this city," so long as total annual expenses did not exceed $50,000. The bureau of civil engineering obviously raised the status of engineers, notably the chief engineer, and as a result provoked resistance. As the chief engineer in 1872, John Culver, noted, somewhat cryptically, "In starting a system whereby the method of superintending public improvements was to be revolutionized, antagonistic interests were naturally arrayed against it, and failing to defeat its attempt, endeavored to hamper its execution." Nevertheless, Culver was able to report in that same year that under the bureau of civil engineering, property owners were being assessed for street improvements at rates 75 percent lower than before the bureau's creation.[113]

Because so many contracts had been awarded in 1871 and in the beginning of 1872, no significant decrease in infrastructural development was apparent until 1874. In 1873 another 8.9 miles of water pipe were laid, although only eight contracts were awarded for sewers. In 1874, probably in response to the panic of 1873 and the subsequent depression, the miles of sewer pipe laid dropped to 2.5, and only three sewer contracts were awarded. Even after the depression of the 1870s, however, infrastructural development showed a notable decline in Jersey City. For instance, only 5.6 miles of sewers, both brick and pipe, were laid between 1879 and 1886, far less than previous annual averages. From 1879 to 1882 less than one mile of street pavement was laid. By 1882 only approximately 44 of the city's 200 miles of streets were paved, and within those streets only 54 miles of sewers had been laid by 1885. As Figure 12 indicates, the miles of water pipe laid in the city also declined after the highs of 1871–73, reaching especially low points in 1881, 1883, and 1884, although picking up again in 1885. In Greenville only approximately half the streets had been graded (much less paved), and no sewers had been laid as late as 1880.[114] The water supply system was extended to Greenville by the 1880s, although Jersey City's continued use of the Passaic River made the benefits of this service questionable by that time.

If Jersey City had been successful in annexing outlying territories because it could offer essential services through the extension of its infrastructure systems, the decline in infrastructural development in the 1870s, which extended into the 1880s, may explain why Jersey City annexed no new territory after 1873. Even after the depression of the 1870s, political conflicts among the public works commissioners, resulting in large part from the commission being made elective in 1877, impeded public works in the city. Engineers were unable to establish the board of public works as an institution through which they could attain power in the city government. For instance, individuals rotated rapidly through the position of chief engineer until 1884, suggesting that they were in large part political appointments (Table 2).[115]

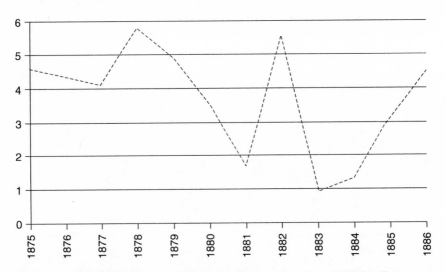

Figure 12. Miles of water pipe laid annually in Jersey City, 1875–86. *Data source:* Board of Public Works of Jersey City, *Reports of the Chief Engineer, 1871–1887* (n.p., n.d.).

Table 2. Chief engineers, Jersey City Board of Public Works, 1871–98

Year	Chief Engineer
1871	John P. Culver
1872	John P. Culver
1873	S. B. Dougherty
1874	John P. Culver
1875	?
1876	Levi W. Post
1877	Levi W. Post
1878	Levi W. Post
1879	W. W. Ruggles
1880	W. W. Ruggles
1881	W. W. C. Sites
1882	W. W. C. Sites
1883	?
1884–1898	W. W. Ruggles

Sources: Board of Public Works of Jersey City, *Reports of the Chief Engineer, 1871–1887* (n.p., n.d.); *Manual of the Board of Street and Water Commissioners, of Jersey City* (published annually by Noland Brothers, New York and Jersey City, 1887–1907).

The conditions that contributed to the decline in infrastructural development had apparently changed by 1884, when W. W. Ruggles became the chief engineer of the board of public works and stayed in that position until 1898, when he was replaced by Charles A. Van Keuren, who served as the city engineer into the 1920s. Under a new city charter in 1889, the six public works commissioners were replaced by three street and water commissioners, appointed by the mayor for one-, two-, on three-year terms. Only one of the six public works commissioners was appointed as a street and water commissioner. Jersey City kept no detailed statistics regarding infrastructural development after 1887. If the numbers of pages of official proceedings of the board of street and water commissioners are any indication, however, it appears that infrastructural development increased notably in 1895. Certainly at some point between 1887 and 1905 infrastructural development increased markedly, since by this latter date the city had approximately 139 miles of paved streets and 116 miles of sewers.[116]

By the turn of the twentieth century, Jersey City was clearly maturing. Its population increased steadily after the Civil War, reaching 206,433 in 1900, by which time it "loomed as a strong competitor for Newark's industrial prominence."[117] The Jersey City Board of Trade became an influential advocate for a new water supply and other public improvements after it was formed in 1888. In 1895 Jersey City finally abandoned the Passaic River and signed a contract for water to be supplied from the Pequannock watershed by the East Jersey Water Company—a company that played a significant role in the physical development of Newark, as we will see in the following chapter. In 1899 the city entered into negotiations with a private contractor to develop a waterworks that used the Rockaway watershed. Ownership of the Rockaway waterworks was transferred to the municipality in the first decade of the twentieth century.[118]

Despite all of these improvements to Jersey City's physical plants, the city did not increase in territory after 1873. As we will see in the case of Newark as well, the opportunity for cities to annex outlying territory was shrinking by the turn of the twentieth century. National markets for engineers, infrastructure systems, and materials made outlying communities less and less dependent on surrounding central cities. Thus if residents in Hoboken and Bayonne were not willing to join their property and communities to Jersey City in the 1860s and 1870s, they were even less likely to do so by the 1900s.

Conclusion

Much of the organizational structure that would facilitate infrastructural development in Jersey City into the twentieth century was in place, at least in rough form, prior to the consolidation of 1870. While the 1871 charter centralized infrastructural development under a board of public works, the development of the city's water supply and sewerage systems had proceeded since 1852 through a similarly organized board of water commissioners. Engineers, starting at least with John Ward, had played a central role in infrastructural development in Jersey City prior to 1870 as well. Central planning of physical development had begun at the very outset of the city through the 1804 street grid, which set a pattern for outlying areas to follow and build upon as they were developed. Ironically, if this early development set the broad outline for later development, it also enabled the political convulsions and sluggishness in infrastructural development experienced during the 1870s and 1880s. It was, after all, in large part specifically because Jersey City was a leader in infrastructural development in Hudson County that surrounding communities were interested in consolidation.

As we have already seen in the case of New York City, politicians and engineers could work in tandem within city government because they both stood to benefit from large-scale infrastructure projects. In pursuing the benefits that infrastructural development offered, politicians often brought their careers to an end through scandal, while engineers more often expanded their power in city government. The exposure of political scandal in the central city provided much of the motivation for surrounding suburban communities to resist annexation. At the same time, the development of a pool of engineering talent within the central city was a resource that suburban communities could rely upon to maintain their municipal independence.

In various ways, both Hoboken and Bayonne relied on engineering expertise from Jersey City to build independent infrastructure systems and thus become more independent municipalities. Engineers from Jersey City developed the water supply system used by Hoboken after that city ended its reliance on the Jersey City waterworks, and the long-standing engineer of the city of Bayonne had been trained by engineers in Jersey City. Hoboken and Bayonne could have most likely built infrastructure systems with engineers from other places, but the presence of a relatively large pool of engineering talent in Jersey City that was knowledgeable about local resources must certainly have made infrastructural development easier for surrounding communities and thus facilitated their municipal independence.

Many of the residents of Hoboken, Bayonne, and Greenville probably had some form of infrastructural development on their minds when they voted either for or against consolidation with Jersey City. Many voters in Hoboken must have been aware that the 1869 referendum could have a significant impact on the future water supply of their city. Possibly those residents in the Fourth Ward imagined that they might get the trunk sewer that had been denied them if they voted in favor of consolidation. In Bayonne many residents in Salterville apparently voted in favor of consolidation because they believed that their area would be better supplied with infrastructure as a part of Jersey City. At the same time, the possibility of increased infrastructural development as a result of consolidation raised fears among many residents in Hoboken and Bayonne of increased taxes and political machines. By contrast, Greenville residents probably voted in favor of consolidation in 1872 in large part because they believed that as residents of Jersey City, they would receive physical improvements at a lower tax rate and with less contention.

The evidence suggests that political corruption in Jersey City did not play as large a role in the vote on consolidation in Hudson County in 1869 as did Tammany Hall in the annexation of lower Westchester County in 1874 or in the vote on Greater New York in 1894. Timing was possibly the most important difference between perceived levels of corruption in New York City and Jersey City. New York City's efforts to expand its jurisdiction in the early 1870s coincided with the exposure of the Tweed Ring, and the 1894 referendum on Greater New York coincided with the exposure of political corruption by the Lexow committee. By contrast, the 1869 referendum on the Jersey City consolidation preceded the scandals of William Bumsted and his associates. Hudson and Bergen Cities, however, were known to have politically corrupt "rings" in government before the consolidation vote. Indeed, Bumsted came from Bergen City. The expectation that residents in Hudson and Bergen were likely to approve consolidation (possibly as part of an anticorruption movement) undoubtedly suggested to many residents in Hoboken and Bayonne that the enlarged version of Jersey City would be characterized by machine politics and thus expensive infrastructural development and higher taxes.

If an expectation of increased political corruption from consolidation with Jersey City contributed to the motivation for municipal independence in Bayonne, so did a suburban identity. Articles in the *Bayonne Herald* were explicit in identifying Bayonne as a suburb of New York City, which for that reason shared little in common with Jersey City that would justify the consolidation of the two municipalities. The residents of Bayonne (at least those whose interests were represented in the *Herald*) perceived that the growth of their city was dependent on the growth of the population that commuted daily to Manhattan Island, not on the expanding jurisdiction of Jersey City. Infrastructural development in Bayonne was thus pursued for the purposes of creating a suburb, not a city. The same argument can be applied, although to a lesser degree, in the case of Hoboken under the control of the HLIC. In the case of Greenville, I have argued that the consolidation vote also hinged on issues particular to a small town, although in that case the nonurban context favored consolidation.

It is possibly an important point that the relationship between central cities and suburbs on either side of the Hudson River was not the same. Suburban communities in New York perceived themselves to be suburbs of New York City. Suburban communities in Hudson County also perceived themselves to be suburbs of New York City, not Jersey City. In Chapter 3

I suggested that the suburban identities of municipalities such as Mount Vernon and Flushing provided at least some of the motivation for residents wanting to remain independent of New York City. If New York City's ability to expand its jurisdiction was thus impeded by suburban identities in surrounding municipalities, Jersey City faced the additional problem that residents in outlying municipalities had rejected it as a central city and identified themselves as suburbanites of New York, a city that could never threaten them with annexation.

If Jersey City was less of a central city because it had no suburbs that it could call its own, the same cannot be said of Newark. At least at the turn of the twentieth century, most of the suburban communities surrounding Newark were not within commuting distance of New York City. Moreover, Newark was larger than Jersey City. It therefore resembled New York City more than Jersey City. At the same time, as I will argue in the following chapter, Jersey City was actually more similar to New York City than was Newark in terms of infrastructural development. Compared with New York City and Jersey City, Newark was slow to pursue infrastructural development. Thus Newark provides a new and different perspective on the relationship between central city infrastructural development and suburban autonomy than the cases that have been examined so far.

CHAPTER **5**

The Rise and Fall
of Greater Newark

In his annual message to the common council in January 1905, Newark mayor Henry Doremus boasted that "our streets are nearly all paved and sewered and no added expense need be feared here except to keep pace with the natural growth of a healthy municipality."[1] Doremus's comments are indicative of the history of infrastructural development in Newark. While the city's public works were a source of pride, their expense was a source of fear. The city had achieved a level of physical completion, but it had only done so reluctantly. It was not in the nature of the political culture of Newark, as it was in New York City, to take pride in such monumental public works projects as the Croton Aqueduct despite the fact that they ran millions of dollars over their projected costs. It was more in the spirit of Newark to be proud if the city managed to "keep pace" with "natural growth." A civic leader who dared to push a monumental infrastructure project, no matter how necessary, was likely to face public scorn and political ruin.

In previous chapters I have argued that the personal benefits and political power city officials gained through public works gave them the incentive to pursue suburban annexation at the same time that the public works provided suburbanites with an incentive to stay independent of the city. The case of Newark provides an important qualification to this argument. In Newark public works proceeded with relatively little graft and corruption because powerful business leaders, organized into a board of trade, effectively limited public expenditures. If suburbanites used the presence or absence of political machines as a proxy for the expected costs and benefits of annexation, we would expect suburbanites living around Newark to be more accepting of annexation than suburbanites living around New York or Jersey City. Yet suburban communities around Newark showed just as much, if not more, resistance to being annexed.

What made Newark unique among central cities in the New York metropolitan region was that the dominance of business interests limited graft but also fundamentally altered the incentive structure of infrastructural development and annexation. In the cases of both New York and Jersey City, public officials supported the annexation of relatively undeveloped land because they stood to profit personally through the construction of new public works. Because Newark officials stood to profit less from infrastructural development, they were slow to pursue annexation. When annexation did become an official policy of both the city and the board of trade in the form of the "Greater Newark" movement in the early twentieth century, public officials and business leaders supported only the annexation of communities that had already been developed, such as Bloomfield, Irvington, Montclair, and the Oranges. Yet these were the very communities that had the least incentive to join the city, since they had already supplied themselves with essential services. The only communities successfully annexed were townships that were relatively undeveloped, such as Clinton (parts of which were annexed in 1869, 1897, and 1902), Woodside (annexed in 1871), and the Ivy Hill section of Maplewood (annexed in 1927), or those in which development had been characterized by flagrant waste and corruption, as in the borough of Vailsburg, annexed in 1905 (see Figures 1–3 in the Introduction).[2]

The specific process by which Newark established an adequate water supply also hindered the city's ability to annex outlying areas. As early as the 1880s, the Passaic River had clearly become an inadequate and even dangerous source of drinking water, yet Newark officials were reluctant to establish a more adequate water supply until the 1890s. Officials' intransigence gave speculators the opportunity to buy up land in the Pequannock watershed and establish the East Jersey Water Company, from which Newark was compelled to buy water after it had finally abandoned the Passaic. Because Newark officials lost control over their water, they lost an important asset that might have compelled more suburban communities to accept annexation. Instead, suburban communities could buy water directly from the East Jersey Water Company.

Finally, by the time of the Greater Newark movement, wider markets for urban infrastructure systems and services facilitated infrastructural development in the suburbs of Essex County. As we have already seen, municipalities throughout the New York metropolitan region during the late nineteenth century were relying increasingly on water pumps and street pavements produced for regional and national markets. Combined with growing local markets of engineers and contractors, the nationalization of infrastructural development rendered municipal consolidations less likely by the turn of the century, the point at which the Greater Newark movement had only begun.

The Puritan City

Unlike New York and Jersey City, Newark's founders were little concerned with the growth of the community that they established along the Passaic River. The sixty-four Puritan families who founded Newark in 1666 chose their site because of its "splendid isolation." Trade between Philadelphia and New York City largely bypassed the Puritan town in favor of Perth Amboy. While New York City's population exceeded 20,000 before the American Revolution, Newark's did not exceed 1,000. A fairly equal distribution of wealth and an inclusive local governing structure—the town meeting— further differentiated Newark from the burgeoning metropolis on Manhattan Island.[3]

In contrast to either New York City or Jersey City, Newark Township experienced a net loss in land size until it was incorporated as a city in 1836. The original tract settled by the Puritans ran along the Passaic River for approximately fifteen miles and stretched westward to "the foot of the great Mountaine called Watchung," according to the 1667 purchase agreement. Before the close of the seventeenth century, Newark had expanded westward past Watchung Mountain so that the Passaic River bordered it on both the east and the west. Newark then remained unchanged until the late eighteenth century, at which point the western parts of the township began to split off, starting with Springfield Township in 1794, Caldwell Township in 1798, Orange Township in 1806, Bloomfield Township in 1812, and Clinton Township in 1836.[4]

The urbanization of Newark began with industrialization. By the turn of the nineteenth century, shoemakers and carriage makers in the town were producing for a market "wider than the local farm population." Production for larger markets, especially in the South, was facilitated by expanding means of transportation, starting in 1794 with the construction of a road to Paulus Hook and bridges that crossed the Passaic and Hackensack Rivers and continuing with the introduction in 1821 of a stagecoach that made daily trips to Jersey City, the completion of the Morris Canal in 1832, and the introduction of rail lines that put Newark along the transportation route that covered Philadelphia, Trenton, and New York City.[5]

According to historian Susan Hirsch, Newark was by 1860 "the leading industrial city in the nation. It was the eleventh largest city, with 74 percent of its labor force employed in manufacturing, and sixth in the nation in the value of its manufactured product."[6] Industrialism was especially pronounced in Newark because its reliance on New York City's capital markets probably retarded the growth of a local commercial sector.[7] Industrialization could proceed, of course, only with a cheap and plentiful supply of labor. In 1830, with a population of 10,953, Newark was significantly smaller than the mean size of cities (those with populations greater than 2,500) in the Northeast. Ten years later, with a population of 17,290, Newark was only 360 people short of the mean size of cities in the Northeast, and by 1850, with a population of 38,894, it was practically twice the average size. While New York City's population grew by approximately 300 percent between 1830 and 1860, Newark's increased by approximately 560 percent in this same period.[8]

With population growth came the organizational elaboration of local government. As Isaac Andruss, chairman of a committee created to study the reorganization of Newark's government, noted at a special town meeting in June 1832, owing to the town's increasing population, "a division of the Township into two or more districts . . . would be a great public convenience by affording an opportunity to a greater proportion of the Inhabitants to assemble and take a part in the Township business." In 1833, following Andruss's recommendation, Newark was divided into four separate wards that functioned as independent townships. Interward rivalries impeded the proper functioning of the local government, and thus in 1836 the legislature passed a city charter for Newark that was approved by a majority vote of 85 percent in a referendum held in April of that year. The municipal form of government was obviously less participatory than the town meeting, but the overwhelming majority vote in favor of the city charter suggests little public resistance, although some property owners did express fears in the local press of increasing taxes.[9]

The establishment of city government was clearly connected to the increasing necessity for public works. In 1831 an estimate for "McAdamizing the streets in the Town Plott" was read at the annual town meeting, though there is no record of any action being taken. The form of government established in 1833 was apparently inadequate because, as one contemporary state legislator put it, "the people could not in four distinct meetings harmonize upon any plan for repairing and improving the streets and highways." The city charter of 1836 gave the common council power "for causing common sewers, drains or vaults to be made . . . ; for the paving, flagging, or gravelling the streets of said city, and for lighting the same"; and for "preserving acqueducts [sic] . . . and sinking and regulating wells, pumps, and cisterns in the streets thereof."[10] Even before the city charter, the town street commissioners announced in the local press that any residents "desirous of having any sidewalk or other part of a street graded, for the purpose of paving" should apply to the street commissioner for their ward "in order that a proper survey can be made, and directions given." Despite these obvious efforts at establishing public works, the first known street pavement in Newark was not laid until 1853, which was also the year in which the first underground sewer of record was completed.[11]

Comparison with New York and Jersey City provides an important perspective on infrastructural development in Newark. In New York City streets had been paved and sewers had been laid by the turn of the eighteenth century, at which point the population on Manhattan Island was approximately 5,000.[12] Newark only began paving streets and laying sewers at a point when its population had probably exceeded 40,000. Similarly, Newark's population was more than five times that of Jersey City in the 1840s, yet Newark's streets remained unpaved and without sewers during that entire decade, while Jersey City had paved streets and at least one sewer before 1840.[13] By the time the first sewer was completed in Newark, Jersey City was actively engaged in unifying its sewers into a comprehensive system. By 1870 Jersey City had twice as many miles of sewers as Newark.[14] Likewise, Newark commenced building its waterworks when its population was probably close to 90,000, while Jersey City began construction on its waterworks before its population exceeded 20,000.

There were undoubtedly many reasons for variations between the three cities in terms of when different infrastructure systems were installed. For instance, the construction of sewers in Newark may have been delayed because the city's location at the base of the Orange Mountains provided it with good natural drainage.[15] Yet the sizes of the variances between the three cities, both in terms of the date and the population at which infrastructural development began, and the fact that Newark differed in similar ways from both New York and Jersey City—themselves two very dissimilar cities—suggests that factors beyond topography made Newark unique.

Early infrastructural development in New York City was undertaken primarily to facilitate commercial activity—the flow of commodities within the city.[16] In Newark, where commercial activity was not the sine qua non of urbanism that it was in New York City, infrastructural development had to wait for another motive force, namely, the pressure of massive population growth that accompanied industrialization. The relationship between population and infrastructural development in Jersey City seems to have followed the pattern of New York City rather than that of Newark, even though Newark and Jersey City were responding to the same growth stimuli at approximately the same time. Both, for example, gained access to rail lines and the Morris Canal within a few years of each other.

There are at least two probable explanations for the different relationships between population and infrastructural development in Newark and Jersey City. First, unlike Newark, the development on Paulus Hook was planned as a city. In Jersey City urban infrastructural development required no reconceptualization of the settlement from a Puritan village to a center of industry and trade. Jersey City's early commitment to growth makes it similar to New York City in the seventeenth and eighteenth centuries, which may in part explain the similar points of population growth at which these two cities paved streets and laid sewers, even though the commitment to growth derived from different sources in each city—in New York, from the fact that it was a colonial center for trade, and in Jersey City, from the fact that it was a residential real estate development.

Second, because Jersey City was a residential real estate development, the exchange value of land was most probably a central concern in its planning, and thus development was probably aimed at a higher class of clientele that would expect such amenities as streetlights, paved streets, and sewers. One author notes, for instance, that the Associates of the Jersey Company made a concerted effort "to attract men of means and enterprise."[17] By contrast, in Newark, where urbanization was in large part a product of industrialization, if any concerted effort was ever made to attract a population, it was probably to attract low-wage workers.[18] The fact that the Associates actively tried to attract an upscale clientele to Jersey City may explain why oil streetlights were installed when the city's population was less than 2,000, while both Newark and New York City were lit by oil only when their respective populations were well over 10,000. Streetlights were an obvious and highly visible indication of urbanization, and their primary function—to protect against street crime—was probably of more concern to those with more wealth.[19] .

Newark introduced oil lamps to its streets when its population was approximately 14,500, while New York City introduced oil street lighting when its population was approximately 18,000—very similar figures, especially compared to the wide disparity in population levels at the time of the introduction of sewers and street pavements in each city. The fact that oil street lighting was introduced in quite different time periods in both cities—1836 in Newark and 1761 in New York City—may also indicate that population level alone was the driving force behind street lighting. Both cities thus probably introduced oil street lighting at similar levels of population because the importance, if not the prevalence, of street crime was in large part a function of population growth and the attendant increase in public anonymity.[20]

If the introduction of oil streetlights was more closely associated with population level than with any specific time period, the introduction of gas street lighting appears to have been related more to a specific time period than to general population levels. Gas companies were first granted charters to supply lighting in New York City and Newark in 1823 and 1845, respectively—a time differential that is less than half of that for oil street lighting, approximately a tenth of that for street paving, and approximately an eighth of that for sewers. Tellingly, what distinguishes gas lighting from sewers, street pavement, or oil street lamps is a profit motive. Among an electorate that had never experienced the benefits of modern infrastructure systems, city officials might not find any benefit from supplying public works and may have been concerned about raising the ire of taxpayers. Gas companies did not have to worry about angering taxpayers and had the incentive of profits to seek a franchise and lay down gas lines.

One contemporary of Newark's first gas company, the Newark Gas Light Company, recalled that it was at first "looked upon by many as a chimerical scheme, and they not only stood aloof from the enterprise, but dissuaded others from embarking on it."[21] Indeed, the company faced no competition for twenty-three years, but this may have had more to do with the fact that five out of the ten original officers of the company served on the common council, and one, Beach Vanderpool, served as mayor in 1846.[22] City officials with a stake in the company may have been inclined not to grant a franchise to a competitor. Furthermore, the legislature was at the time reluctant to grant charters to utility companies that would compete with those already established. When the Citizens' Gas Light Company was granted a charter and franchise in 1868 that put it in direct competition with the Newark Gas Light Company, the two companies quickly came to an agreement that they would supply gas in mutually exclusive territories.[23] The establishment of an additional gas company had a beneficial effect on street lighting, however. In 1872 there were ninety-two people for every gas streetlight in Newark, but only fifty-six people per gas streetlight in New York City. By 1883 Newark had surpassed New York in gas street lighting. By 1884 it had one gas streetlight for every forty-four residents; New York had one for every fifty-four.[24]

The private supply of water did not have as beneficial an effect on the city as the private supply of gas. The Newark Aqueduct Company, granted a corporate charter in 1800, was described by one Newark historian as "a patriotic enterprise, like all the other movements for public benefit at the time." Indeed, although it was apparently never mentioned in the town meetings, all but one of the original officers were prominent in that governing body. Stock in the new company was offered at $20 a share on February 5, 1800, and each family was limited to one share. The company supplied water from a variety of local sources, which was piped to the subscribers' homes through wooden conduits.[25]

The Newark Aqueduct Company competed against nature for subscribers; wells and springs in the town still provided a clean and sufficient supply of water at the turn of the nineteenth century. But an ample supply of clean water delivered by aqueduct increasingly became a necessity as industrialization and population growth increased the frequency of large, devastating fires and disease epidemics, and the accumulation of human and industrial wastes polluted local water supplies. Yet the very urban growth that created new demands for water appears to have stifled any motivation on behalf of the Newark Aqueduct Company to increase its supply. Urbanization not only brought new demands concerning public health and safety but also created a society more anonymous and heterogeneous and less bound by the communal ties by which order had been maintained in the Puritan town.[26] Although the Newark Aqueduct Company was only nominally a private company in the context of a small town, the spirit of privatism inherent within its institutional form grew more prominent in the urban context, and the company was increasingly incapable and unwilling to meet the needs of the city that had grown up around it. The company refused to provide fire hydrants, and although it served only a small proportion of city residents, it used its influence in the legislature to assure that should the city of Newark decide to create a municipal water supply system, it would have to purchase the company's waterworks.[27]

The proviso that the city had to buy out the Newark Aqueduct Company effectively ended plans for a municipal water supply in 1838. Yet it would be too much to say that the Newark Aqueduct Company denied an adequate water supply to the city of Newark. Certainly there were other factors, as various authors have suggested. To reiterate a point made in previous chapters, public water supplies were only beginning to become commonplace, and only in the largest cities, in the 1830s. More important, what appears to have most impeded infrastructural development in Newark, including water supply, was what Susan Hirsch has called the "mechanics' ideology," which espoused limited government action and promoted private enterprise. The mechanics' ideology, "however archaic, was the major point of consensus in Newark's political arena"; it maintained its role in the city's politics because most incipient working-class activity, especially in the craft unions, was considered apolitical. To the extent that journeymen and other laborers participated in local politics, the major issues centered on ethnic and cultural issues. The mechanics' ideology served the purposes of the city's elite, who wanted a minimal local government that kept taxes and public debt low through limited spending.[28]

The constraints imposed by the mechanics' ideology consistently served as impediments to large public works. For instance, in 1855 the common council created the first of two committees that worked for more than a year to devise a plan for a public waterworks that would pump water into the city from the Passaic River below Paterson. Just as the plan was being completed, the panic of 1857 and the subsequent depression convinced the common council that it should hold off on a waterworks for the sake of economy. At the same time, in New York City the local government actively pursued public works as a form of unemployment relief during the depression. In Newark the city refused to finance infrastructural development despite large rallies by workers during the winter of 1857–58 demanding that they be given employment on public works projects. In 1860 the legislature created a semi-independent agency, the Newark Aqueduct Board, that was authorized to purchase the "property and rights" of the Newark Aqueduct Company and then to construct a new waterworks along the lines of the original common council plan. Financing and construction of the waterworks were stalled by the Civil War, and the new public waterworks were finally completed in 1870, at which point the Passaic was already badly polluted and becoming more so. As one historian has described the sad situation, "The city found itself owning a water supply insufficient for the city's needs and one which became the cause of regular typhoid epidemics."[29]

At approximately the same time as the completion of the new waterworks, a new organization that exemplified the mechanics' ideology, the Newark Board of Trade—"a pressure group *par excellence* of Newark's business community"—was founded in 1868.[30] The influence of the mechanics' ideology in both the business community and the municipal government is evident from a passage in the board's *Annual Report* for 1874: "What we have said of the conservative characteristics of our businessmen, is equally true of the municipal government of our city . . . Their foresight and their wisdom cannot be too highly commended. We should all remember, however we may differ as to the policy of expenditures for improvements, that debt means taxes; and that in the ratio in which taxes increase or diminish, so will manufactures which are the life of our city, be encouraged or driven from us."[31]

Even as they complimented the city's public officers for their "foresight" and "wisdom," members of the board of trade had to admit that "the great majority of our citizens" found the city's water to be of a less-than-desirable quality. Yet the board of trade offered no solutions, nor were public agencies very responsive to what was clearly an emerging public health crisis. Only in "response to public pressure" in 1874 did the Newark Aqueduct Board consider purchasing the Morris Canal, the water from which tested pure as late as 1873. The recession of the mid-1870s provided a rationale for abandoning the plan, however. The Newark Aqueduct Board also refused to endorse a plan proposed in 1879 by Croes and Howell, an engineering firm employed by the board, that recommended the Pequannock watershed as a source for the city's water.[32] In 1881 Mayor Henry Lang acknowledged that "a new water-supply is needed; yet on account of the great expense involved, and on account of the fact that the usual health of the city has been maintained and compares favorably with the health of any other city, we can afford to make haste slowly in this matter, and examine each step carefully as we proceed."[33]

Contrary to Mayor Lang's statement, the Newark Board of Health had declared in 1880 that contaminated water from the Passaic had "unquestionably added to the mortality of the city"; in 1881 a paper mill upstream from Newark's intake was found to be dumping carbolic acid into the Passaic; and in this same year Hoboken switched from the Passaic to the Hackensack as its water source. In 1881 the Newark Aqueduct Board and Jersey City's boards of public works and finance created a board of inspection of the pollution of the Passaic River and its tributaries, which showed some initial success in reducing industrial pollutants in the river but proved itself largely ineffectual by 1886. As late as 1885, however, the Newark Aqueduct Board was claiming in regard to the development of a new water supply system "that the initiatory step should be taken by the citizens and tax-payers, who have to carry the burden."[34]

An emphasis on economy may not have precluded the development of infrastructure systems adequate for Newark's needs, but it certainly seems to have made that outcome less likely. It is notable in this regard that the person often given primary credit for ultimately providing Newark with a water supply from the Pequannock, Joseph E. Haynes, did not emphasize economic considerations to the extent that others had. Haynes, who was mayor of Newark from 1883 to 1893, noted in his annual address to the common council in 1886 that "the importance of an abundant supply of pure water for domestic purposes, as well as for the manufacturing interests of any city, cannot be over estimated." At the annual dinner of the board of trade in 1886, Haynes declared that the expenditure of $5 million—an amount greater than the city's bonded debt and annual revenues combined—would be justified to secure a water supply from the Pequannock.[35]

Haynes's mayoralty represents a turning point in the social, political, and physical development of the city. As Newark developed into a large, diverse city with a vibrant financial sector, especially in insurance, it began to outgrow the mechanics' ideology and Republicanism that had their roots in the manufacturing and Puritan traditions of the town. Haynes was a Democrat who made explicit appeals to the working class.[36] Under his mayoralty, work began on the construction of an intercepting sewer in 1884 that was the first step in unifying the sewerage of the entire city. Unlike previous sewer projects, which had been paid for through special assessments on affected property owners, this first intercepting sewer was paid for through bonds, and its cost thus fell on the city as a whole. Under Haynes the city also entered into its first major contract with Edward Weston's Newark Electric Light and Power Company for electric streetlights, of which there were 150 by 1887.[37]

The significance of shifting the city's water supply from the Passaic to the Pequannock under Haynes is indicated in an answer by the board of street and water commissioners to a communication from the board of trade in regard to a new proposed reservoir. Noting that Jersey City had "depended entirely for many years" on a single, small reservoir, the board of trade questioned whether it was necessary for Newark to spend more money on a new reservoir. Newark had lagged far behind Jersey City in developing a municipal water supply system and had in fact followed the smaller city's lead in using the Passaic. By 1895, however, the Newark Board of Street and Water Commissioners could answer the board of trade with the comment that "we do not think Jersey City has either a proper water supply, or a proper system of distribution. We do not think it wise to follow the example of Jersey City in either respect."[38]

Ironically, infrastructural development under Haynes, especially the water supply system for which he is given so much credit, also contributed to his political decline. When the city of Newark was finally compelled to search for a new water supply beyond the Passaic, it confronted the claims of speculators who had been buying up land in the Pequannock watershed ever since publication of the Croes and Howell report in 1879. Thus in 1889 the city entered into a contract with the East Jersey Water Company (organized by the previously mentioned land speculators) by which the company would build an aqueduct that could supply Newark with 50 million gallons of Pequannock water a day. The city was given the option of purchasing the waterworks after they were built for $6 million. The Republican press was critical of the terms of the contract and of Haynes, who had apparently been secretly negotiating with the East Jersey Water Company even though his public statements had indicated that he was "unalterably opposed to dealing with land speculators." Haynes was specifically attacked for having supported the contract with the East Jersey Water Company in order to get the support of the two "bosses" of the Democratic Party in northern New Jersey, James Smith Jr. and Gottfried Kruegel. Smith expected to profit from lucrative construction contracts with the East Jersey Water Company, and Kruegel wanted a new water supply on account of his extensive interests in Newark's beer industry. Haynes needed the support of Kruegel and Smith in order to win reelection in 1889.[39]

For Newark's Republican press, the water contract signified the corruption of Haynes at the hands of New Jersey's Democratic political machine. The *Newark Sunday Call* called Haynes a "suppliant, who, to retain office, abandoned principle and reversed his record." This was a theme that could be repeated with each new issue. Thus prior to the 1891 mayoral election, the *Sunday Call* took issue with the newly created board of street and water commissioners, known more informally as the board of works.[40]

Like similar agencies created in New York and Jersey City, the Newark Board of Works shifted the functions and responsibilities of the common council's committees of sewers and streets and the Newark Aqueduct Board to a body governed by five commissioners, all of whom were appointed by the mayor for five-year terms. Centralizing authority for city services in the executive branch could be justified as a functional response to the increasing needs of a growing city, although it was not lost on contemporaries that the board of works also took patronage resources away from the Republican-controlled common council. The board of works was probably not meant to increase the patronage resources of Haynes, but of Governor Leon Abbett, who was centralizing patronage resources in all New Jersey cities in order to build up support for his intended run for the U.S. Senate. Indeed, commissioners on the board could only be removed upon approval by the governor. The *Sunday Call* noted, "Mr. Haynes is neither more nor less than a tool," as indicated by "his connection with the Board of Works, his selection of Commissioners, and by his other appointments." The newspaper was no doubt making reference, among other things, to Haynes's appointment of James Smith Jr. as president of the board of works. Smith was reported as saying that the board of works would only hire Democrats, a highly unpopular statement that may have had something to do with Haynes's razor-thin majority of approximately 200 votes in the mayoral election of 1891. Haynes was either not nominated or declined to run again for mayor in 1893, and the board of works was made elective in 1894.[41]

By the end of the nineteenth century, Newark had found the "ring" against which it could promote economy, efficiency, and local rule. Haynes's downfall, while hardly as dramatic, has some notable similarities to those of the Tweed Ring in New York City and Bumsted in Jersey City. Put together, these three instances of perceived political corruption suggest a more general relationship between infrastructural development and city politics. In each instance, state legislation provided the organizational means to centralize power within executive agencies at the local level. Each purported ringleader—Tweed in New York, Bumstead in Jersey City, and Smith in Newark—took personal authority over the key patronage resource, public works. In each instance, public works were purportedly carried out as sources for graft. In Newark the *Sunday Call* made obscure reference to an "intercepting sewer scandal" and an "asphalt scandal," though whether any of these charges were ever substantiated is unclear. Haynes did make mention of financial irregularities in the Newark Aqueduct Board in his annual address to the common council in 1890, and in 1894, Haynes's successor, J. A. Lebkuecher, made mention of "unusual expenditures" by the "former" board of street and water commissioners.[42]

The fact that there was never a scandal in Newark such as those that surrounded Tweed and Bumsted suggests that there was a lower threshold in Newark for the graft that almost necessarily went along with public works in big cities. Like the Land and Improvement Company and the Tax-payers' and Citizens' Association in Hoboken, Newark's business community, organized into the board of trade, was effective at keeping city officials in check and keeping municipal expenditures, and thus infrastructural development, to a minimum. Yet if Newark's business community eliminated the private benefits that public officials might accrue through public works, they also eliminated those officials' interest in annexing undeveloped territory, a fact that would become obvious within a decade of Haynes's political demise.

As with the creation of the department of public works in New York, the creation of the board of street and water commissioners in Newark served not only as a vehicle for graft, but also as the organizational means by which to carry forward the physical development of the city at an unprecedented pace long after the mayoralty of Haynes. Infrastructural development empowered those agencies that performed the work of building Newark, and those agencies were then able to lobby for more resources. The long tenures of civil engineers in Newark's municipal government suggest that their expertise placed them outside the sphere of patronage politics and made them effective lobbyists for their departments.[43] Between 1891 and 1903 the miles of paved streets (mostly granite block and asphalt) in Newark increased by approximately 190 percent.[44] The increase in street pavements was made possible by an act of the legislature in 1894 that permitted property owners on streets to pay off the assessments for paving "in five year instalments [sic], with a low rate of interest." In 1897, in response to widespread opinion that at least 25 to 30 percent of street pavements should be paid out of the general revenues of the city, the common council authorized the board of street and water commissioners to spend up to $100,000 for new street pavements in a single year. Along with street pavements, the sixteen years between 1894 and 1910 marked the "greatest era of sewer construction in Newark."[45]

The Reluctantly Expanding City

The turn of the twentieth century also saw the first fleeting attempt to annex outlying communities to Newark, starting with Irvington. Annexation began to interest Irvington residents late in 1896, but the movement "suddenly ceased" early in 1897. The *Newark Sunday Call* speculated that Irvington residents had not yet felt the pressures of urbanization and were thus not yet ready for annexation. "Not until the expense of 'modern improvements,' such as sewerage, water, public lighting, police and fire protection becomes a heavier burden than the smaller community can bear does the annexation fever take hold." In fact, Irvington was already supplied with at least some urban services. Gas streetlights had lined "some of the principal streets" of the town by 1879, and water had been introduced under the auspices of the Irvington Water Company in 1893.[46]

In any case, Newark had less to offer its suburbs in terms of infrastructural development than neighboring central cities and thus less leverage to compel annexations. As we have seen in the previous chapters, New York's and Jersey City's respective water supplies were crucial resources that had compelled suburban residents to approve annexation. In Newark, by contrast, resistance on the part of city officials and business interests to assuming the necessary costs for a sufficient water supply system gave speculators the opportunity to buy land in the Pequannock watershed. Where Newark officials had not acted, private actors had stepped into the breach. Thus the city was dependent on the East Jersey Water Company for its water supply. Newark did not gain title to its waterworks until 1900, by which time the East Jersey Water Company was supplying water to various other municipalities and water companies, including the Irvington Water Company.[47] In New York City and Jersey City the development of municipal water supply systems had provided training grounds for engineers who then went on to sell their expertise as consultants to suburban communities. In Newark not only engineering expertise but the water supply itself could be sold by private interests to surrounding communities, thereby providing them with services without the threat of annexation and reinforcing suburban autonomy.

If Newark can be distinguished from Jersey City and New York City by its reluctance to take on the expense of developing an adequate water supply, it can also be distinguished by its reluctance to take on the expense of geographic expansion. For instance, not only Irvington had lost interest in the idea of consolidation in 1897; as the *Sunday Call* reported of Newark, "We do not understand that this city is in any mood to compel the union."[48] There was a long tradition in Newark of resistance to annexing outlying territory. In 1874, after New York and Jersey City had both significantly expanded their municipal boundaries through annexation, the Newark Common Council organized a citizens' committee that was to consider the annexation of various Essex County townships. The citizens' committee, reflecting the prevailing mechanics' ideology, reported that annexation was "impracticable and uncalled for." That this expressed resistance to geographic expansion was also a resistance to expanding the city's existing infrastructure systems is suggested by the argument made in the board of trade's annual report for 1875 that "the improvements in our suburbs should be stopped, or, if carried on, let them be done by those who wish to improve their property and bring it into market."[49]

The reluctance of a city to annex outlying land in 1874 may of course have been due more to the prevailing economic slump than to any general resistance to geographic expansion. However, both Jersey City and New York City annexed relatively undeveloped outlying territories in 1873 and 1874, respectively. Moreover, the resistance to geographic expansion in Newark was not restricted to periods of economic depression. The towns of Kearny and Harrison, lying across the Passaic River from Newark in Hudson County, "asked for annexation to Newark" in 1886, but the city's fiscal watchdog, the board of trade, "was instrumental at the time in frustrating the move."[50]

Those annexations that did occur in nineteenth-century Newark were mostly instigated by the communities that were annexed. For instance, one account from 1909 (which should probably be taken with at least a grain of salt) of Woodside's annexation to Newark in 1871 explains that the project was "engineered" by three Woodside residents, one who "longed to be sheriff, but must live in Newark to secure the nomination, and did not wish to remove from this pleasant land," and two who believed that their large property holdings would increase in value if they were part of Newark. Likewise, at a meeting of the Newark Common Council in 1897, when the proposed annexation of Irvington was being discussed, "A number of residents from Clinton township were present and advanced reasons why portions of Clinton township should be annexed to the city."[51] A portion of Clinton Township, rather than Irvington, was annexed to Newark in that year.

In terms of infrastructural development, the residents of Clinton and Woodside had a greater motivation to be annexed to Newark than did the citizens of Irvington. In 1897 Irvington was supplied with gas and water systems, while Clinton Township was almost entirely without any "modern improvements." The extant minutes of the town committee of Clinton from 1872 to 1888 record only one minor instance of infrastructural development, in October 1887, when property owners along "the public road known as

Clinton Avenue" petitioned the town committee to have the sidewalk and crosswalks on one side of the avenue paved with "first quality blue stone flagging." Likewise, there is little evidence to suggest any substantial physical development of Woodside before it was annexed to Newark in 1871. According to one local author, Woodside was "purely agricultural district, except for the factories along Second river, and contained but four roads of any moment."[52]

The portion of Clinton Township annexed to Newark in 1897 was relatively undeveloped. Newark mayor James Seymour, in his annual message to the common council in May 1897, noted of the newly annexed area that "ten years from now its admission seems certain to be financially a good investment, but for some time as a purely business enterprise its annexation will be expensive." Seymour noted that the tax revenues that would come from the annexed part of Clinton "will not more than pay the salaries of the policemen and for the fire protection of the district. Lighting, school facilities and all other expenses incidental to its government will be, until it is more thickly populated, a net annual charge on the old wards." In the future, Seymour contended that "we ought to consider the wants of citizens who have been paying taxes for years, before we admit considerable quantities of unimproved property now forming a part of the townships." Sizable communities that were already substantially developed, such as "Vailsburg, Belleville, East Orange, Harrison and Kearny[,] may be entitled . . . to admission, but I do not think we would be justified in running our municipal line around nearly uninhabited territory or other large sections which have few improvements other than rail fences."[53]

Seymour continued to object to the annexation of undeveloped territories throughout the rest of his mayoralty. For instance, in his address to the common council in 1900, the mayor contended that "we should acquire contiguous territory, if possible, as fast as it is built up and obtains rudimentary improvements." He warned, however, that "townships such as Franklin and parts of Clinton would necessitate vast expenditures out of the municipal treasury without any compensating income." In his final annual address to the common council in 1902, the mayor elaborated that "where towns are built up and have schools, sewers, fire protection, pavements & c., they should, if they desire it, be annexed, but I shall oppose the indiscriminate extension of our municipal lines round farms, rail fences and county roads."[54]

Mayor Seymour's contention that Newark should only annex outlying territories that had already been supplied with modern systems of service delivery may have made sense from a conservative financial standpoint, but it made little sense as an expansionist policy. It was precisely those outlying communities that already had infrastructure systems installed that had no reason to consolidate with Newark. Only those communities that would expect to benefit from annexation, especially in terms of infrastructural development, had a motivation to be annexed. Thus despite Seymour's annual refrain against annexing undeveloped territories, the next area that was annexed to Newark after the portion of Clinton in 1897 was another portion of Clinton Township in 1902.

Several factory owners in Clinton who wanted fire and police protection instigated the annexation of 1902. The *Sunday Call* reported that "there was not great enthusiasm over this addition, because the territory is so largely of strictly rural character, and does not require city government at present."[55] In Clinton, at least, the desire for annexation was not aimed at achieving economies of scale. Instead, influential interests in undeveloped Clinton pursued annexation as a way to gain access to city services.

In contrast to Clinton Township, an attempt to annex one of the more developed suburban areas surrounding Newark, the town of Bloomfield, notably failed in 1902. Bloomfield had been one of the original townships to separate from Newark Township in 1812. Over the next century various communities within the township broke away, including Montclair, Glen Ridge, Belleville, and Woodside, ultimately reducing the size of Bloomfield from approximately twenty-one to six square miles. Despite the loss in territory, Bloomfield steadily gained in population after 1850, largely because of the introduction of railroads to the township in 1856. With rail service, Bloomfield became a commuting suburb. Descriptions of the town's "wide streets, magnificent elms, and comfortable old homesteads" suggest that residents did not see themselves as city dwellers. Indeed, Bloomfield was described by one resident in 1902 as "attractive to business men seeking a country home, near enough to the city for them to attend business each day without spending too much time in travel." Although a number of industries were located in the town, it was still "notably a community of homes."[56]

After the Civil War several real estate developers began building houses in Bloomfield, and with them came "the demand for public improvements." In 1873 the legislature passed the Bloomfield Street Improvement Act, which authorized the township committee "to map out existing streets, to open new ones, to establish grades, to curb, gutter and pave streets upon petition, and to issue improvement bonds." The result was that "some of the streets were macadamized, the expense met by a general road appropriation." It was also in 1873 that the Montclair Gas and Water Company established gas service in Bloomfield, at least for residences along the "principal streets" of the township. Water was first introduced into Bloomfield in 1884 when "a system of water pipes was laid throughout the more densely populated sections of the township, and connected with the Orange Water Works." The water supply was followed by a sewerage system, developed in conjunction with Montclair and the city of Orange. The three municipalities participated in constructing a union sewer, finished in 1893, that started in Bloomfield and drained into the Second River. Construction began in 1898 on a more comprehensive "system of sewers," and "macadamized road construction on a large scale" began in 1899.[57]

Despite the obvious physical improvements in Bloomfield, the *Sunday Call* characterized the township as undeveloped. At the same time, however, the newspaper also endorsed the township's annexation to Newark, thus reflecting a new view toward the geographic expansion of the city: "Of all the suburban towns of Essex, Bloomfield seems to have advanced least in the last twenty years, although it possesses many attractions. Unquestionably, it would make rapid strides if annexed to Newark, and the bill permitting this should be passed by the Legislature. The city of Newark needs more territory, and the welfare of both communities would be served by the union."[58]

An indignant response to this characterization of the town appeared in a letter of a Bloomfield resident to the editor of the *Sunday Call* the following week. The response clearly indicates that infrastructural development in Bloomfield provided the means for the town to remain independent of Newark and also defined the town as suburban, possessing a character different from that of the city:

> We have all the modern improvements, water, gas, electric lights, sewers . . . We fail to see what we would gain by giving up housekeeping for ourselves and becoming only a lodger. A good many of us came away from big cities and have no desire to be forced back into one again. If must be then let us have a union of all the townships of Essex county, which would be an ideal city because the people are all suburban in their tastes, and desires, and we could build up a beautiful city that would delight the eyes of you Newarkers.[59]

The Bloomfield annexation bill, introduced in the legislature first by Senator Thomas N. McCarter of Newark, provided that if the residents of Bloomfield voted in favor of annexation, their town would then become a part of the city of Newark. The two chief groups opposed to consolidation (at least as identified by the *Sunday Call*) were Bloomfield business and religious interests. Religious groups opposed annexation because it would mean "fewer schools and more saloons," while a delegation of "business men" went to Trenton to urge Senator McCarter and Assemblyman Robert M. Boyd Jr. from Montclair not to support the annexation bill. Assemblyman Boyd consequently let the bill die in the Assembly Committee on Towns and Townships, of which he was chairman.[60]

One explanation for the resistance of Bloomfield business interests to annexation is suggested by the fact that at the same time as they were organizing against annexation to Newark, they were also organizing a Bloomfield Board of Trade, which, one author noted, "had a large influence in the development of the town." Indeed, the board of trade provided town authorities with "material assistance . . . in making a favorable contract in 1905 for a supply of water."[61] Thus business opposition to annexation was associated with business support of infrastructural development in Bloomfield, yet another example that public works and suburban autonomy went hand in hand.

Embracing Expansion: Greater Newark

The attempt to annex Bloomfield was an indication that the traditional resistance to geographic expansion in Newark was evidently giving way by 1902. Indeed, while the board of trade had lobbied against the annexation of Harrison and Kearny in the 1880s, in 1899 it requested that the legislature annex the two towns to Essex County "in order to facilitate public affairs, to promote business interests, to develop property values and to enjoy natural social conditions."[62] By 1902 the Newark Board of Trade was calling for the creation of a vastly expanded "Greater Newark" and proposed two possibilities. The first, more ambitious scheme proposed a new city that would include the existing city of Newark, as well as Jersey City, Elizabeth, East Orange, Orange, Harrison, and Kearny, to create a city that would be larger than Boston by 17,000 people. The second scheme, which included only Newark, the Oranges, Harrison, Kearny, Montclair, and Bloomfield, would create a city that would at least be larger than Buffalo by 8,000 people. The *Sunday Call*, echoing the board of trade, proclaimed in January 1903 that Newark "should have more room, and this can only be obtained by annexing some of the towns about it."[63]

The Greater Newark movement may have motivated the renewed effort to annex Irvington in 1903. In Irvington property owners actively supported annexation. When Assemblyman Edward Gnichtel introduced a bill into the legislature "under which the people of Irvington may vote on the question of annexation to Newark," he attached to it a petition that had been signed by "66 percent of the property owners and 25 percent of the voters of Irvington." The bill passed in the Assembly, in spite of "opposition from some of the Essex members," and then passed in the Senate. If Irvington residents had voted in favor of annexation to Newark at the special election authorized by the act (which they did not), then a vote on the same subject would have been held in Newark in November of the same year.[64]

The fact that the Irvington annexation bill passed in the legislature suggests that there was greater support for annexation in Irvington in 1903 than in Bloomfield in 1902. There were several differences between the two towns that probably had a significant impact on the degree of support for annexation within them. Irvington was approximately half the geographic size of Bloomfield and had a smaller population. Also, Irvington still had no rail service at the beginning of 1903, although the town committee was negotiating with two companies for trolley service. Finally, Irvington was not as physically developed as Bloomfield. According to one author, there was only "one paved street in the borough" by 1909. In fact, as late as 1923, "nearly a third" of Irvington's "three square mile area was undeveloped vacant land." While the town was supplied with gas and water, there may very well have been problems with the Irvington Water Company, because the company had tried, "on several occasions" and with no success, "to sell its holdings to the town at less than cost."[65]

A brief comparison between Irvington and Bloomfield suggests that a greater need for infrastructural development in Irvington may have created a greater demand for annexation to Newark, but the issue of infrastructural development in Irvington in 1903 actually appears to have worked against annexation. For instance, at least one local group, the West End Improvement Association, formed in Irvington in 1902, believed that public works could best be carried out if the town remained an independent municipality.[66] Moreover, in 1901 Irvington, Vailsburg, Newark, Millburn, Summit, South Orange Village, and West Orange entered into an agreement to build a joint sewerage system that would drain into Newark Bay. Construction was completed in 1904. At a town meeting in Irvington in February 1903, the *Sunday Call* reported that "several of the Irvington property owners who had signed the petition to the Legislature for the annexation of the town to Newark had decided to withdraw their signatures." The reason for this change, according to one of the property owners, was that "if Irvington was annexed to Newark many small property owners would have to pay in one single assessment for the sewer."[67] Thus infrastructure projects Irvington engaged in as an independent municipality served to differentiate the interests of the town from the interests of Newark and conceivably diminished the demand among Irvington residents for annexation.

The failure to capture Irvington did not seem to faze the new expansionist spirit in Newark. The city had a new mayor, Henry Doremus, who had a more liberal attitude about annexation than his predecessor, Mayor Seymour. In his first annual address to the common council in 1903, Doremus noted that because "we are constantly enlarging our boundaries," the city should assume a greater responsibility for infrastructural development in the newly annexed territories. Doremus noted that there was a need to extend the city's sewerage to "the outlying sections of the city" that were "being improved largely by the homes of our artisan, mechanics and working population." He argued that the cost of the homes constructed by these residents was burden enough, and that the city should help them in the cost of laying sewers in their streets by lowering the interest rate charged on the deferred payment of assessments.[68] The new attitude of the city government under Doremus appears to have revived the possibility of annexing Bloomfield, as previously espoused by the *Sunday Call*, and Vailsburg, which had been on the previous mayor's list of municipalities whose internal improvements were sufficient to warrant annexation.

The first significant movement toward annexation in Vailsburg was a meeting of "about twenty-five citizens," including several officials of the borough, held early in January 1904. From the meeting a committee was selected "to look after the annexation bill to be presented to the Legislature by Assemblyman [Edward] Duffield." Duffield's bill called for annexation to be approved by a referendum in Vailsburg and was introduced into the legislature in January 1904. By early February the bill had made it through the Assembly "without a hitch." Amended to allow for approval by the Newark Common Council after a positive vote in Vailsburg, the bill passed in both chambers of the legislature in March, and a vote on annexation was scheduled in Vailsburg for April 12, where residents voted by a majority in favor of the measure.[69]

The annexation issue served to further differentiate Vailsburg's two local political parties, the Citizens' Association and the Taxpayers' Association. Both parties supported local infrastructural development but were divided on the issue of whether baseball playing, bicycle racing, and public beer drinking should be allowed on Sundays, with the Taxpayers' Association being more "antagonistic" to these activities. The Taxpayers' Association won the vast majority of local offices in the 1903 elections, but the Citizens' Association came back in 1904 to capture majority control of the borough. By the time of its electoral defeat in 1904, the Taxpayers' Association had come out in favor of annexation, while the Citizens' Association was opposed.[70]

Possibly even more important for annexation than the local political divisions in Vailsburg was the role of Thomas N. McCarter, the previously mentioned state senator from Newark who had introduced a bill in the legislature to have Bloomfield annexed to Newark in 1902. McCarter was also the president of the Public Service Corporation, which provided streetcar service in Vailsburg through its subsidiary, the North Jersey Street Railway Company. McCarter announced that his company would provide more extensive streetcar service in Vailsburg and the "transfer privilege on both east and westbound travel," but only if borough residents voted in favor of annexation.[71]

The increased streetcar service through Vailsburg promised by McCarter presents an interesting and somewhat unique case where the prospect of increased transportation between the city and the suburb provided an incentive for annexation. Changes in the suburbs wrought by the streetcar and the electric trolley were not always welcome. Many suburbanites living around Newark saw the "trolley revolution" as a threat to their privileged isolation because it would shorten the distance between them and the urban masses. One Montclair resident noted that trolley service would bring "the usual and wretched surroundings which always follow in its train—'the half-way house,' the beer saloon, Sunday picnics, loafers, and other riff-raff."[72] If suburban communities around Newark resisted the trolley because it threatened to blur class distinctions between the cities and the suburbs, they probably resisted annexation to Newark for the same reasons.

Class distinctions between cities and suburbs cannot explain resistance to annexation in Vailsburg, however. In contrast to Montclair, the local political party in Vailsburg that was opposed to such supposedly nefarious Sunday activities as beer drinking and picnics also supported annexation and thus assimilation with the "riff-raff" and "wretched surroundings" of

Newark. The differences between Vailsburg and such suburbs as Montclair were probably in large part ones of culture and class. Montclair was an affluent suburb, but Vailsburg, largely an Irish and German settlement, already shared more of the socioeconomic characteristics of the central city and was thus less threatened by annexation.[73]

Possibly class and ethnic affinities with Newark's population made Vailsburg residents more receptive to annexation. However, Vailsburg's inability to supply itself with infrastructure systems at a reasonable cost was evidently the more pressing local issue with which residents concerned themselves. Vailsburg mayor Alexander Maybaum, elected on the Taxpayers' ticket in 1903, lamented in his inaugural address to the council that most of the borough's physical infrastructure was a financial liability. The water department was "not self-supporting but is maintained at a loss"; "considerable money" had been "devoured by the borough electric lighting system"; and the borough's sewerage had cost "considerably more than first estimated by the engineer." One Vailsburg resident in favor of annexation mentioned at a "mass meeting" on the subject in early April 1904 that his local taxes had increased more than twofold over the previous several years, with little increase in municipal services. During Maybaum's mayoralty there had been a plot among some of the council members and one of the two local water companies to get the borough to purchase the facilities from the company at an excessive cost. Maybaum was able to stop the proposed sale, but it was brought up during the annexation debates in the borough as a reason to support annexation, since the city of Newark would then purchase the water plant through eminent domain at a significantly reduced price.[74] While Vailsburg had been able to supply itself with infrastructure systems, in doing so it also revealed that the existing political system within the borough could not sustain municipal independence.

Mayor Doremus, clearly pleased with the decision of Vailsburg residents to consolidate their borough to Newark, spoke of annexation in his annual message to the common council in 1905 as a part of the Greater Newark plan: "My views in regard to greater Newark are known. I believe that this city will eventually again come into possession of its own; that is, that at some not far distant future time the boundaries of our city will be again as they were in the days when the first settlers landed in the shores of the Passaic River, giving the name of Newark to all that territory lying east of the Watchung Mountains and west of the Passaic River."[75] Despite Mayor

Doremus's optimism, a vote against annexation by Bloomfield residents in 1904 suggested a less grandiose future for the central city. The annexation issue arose in Bloomfield in conjunction with the township's decision to purchase the waterworks of the Orange Water Company. The decision to purchase the water system had been rejected in a referendum the previous year, when the water company had offered it for $220,000. Early in 1904, however, the water company accepted an offer of $90,000 made by the township, and the purchase was approved in a referendum by a vote of 272 to 160. The township entered into a contract to be supplied with "filtered water from the Upper Passaic" by the Montclair Water Company, which was itself a subsidiary of the East Jersey Water Company.[76]

One author noted of the water system purchase that "Bloomfield . . . embarked upon the unknown sea of municipal ownership with many misgivings on the part of the conservative element of the community." Soon after residents had approved the purchase in the referendum, the *Sunday Call* reported a rumor that before any bonds could be issued to pay for the water system, "the most prominent citizens of the town" would seek to have a court declare the election illegal "because no registry day was held." Furthermore, a bill that would provide for annexing Bloomfield to Newark was to be introduced into the legislature, according to unreported sources.[77]

Possibly because they were not able to get the courts to declare the water system referendum illegal, the "prominent citizens" continued to agitate for Bloomfield's annexation to Newark, starting with "a meeting of about twenty-five of the leading taxpayers" of the town in March 1904 in which it was decided that an annexation bill would be drafted and sent to the legislature. While the taxpayers at the meeting all favored annexation, approximately fifteen people who had also been invited did not attend, suggesting at least some resistance to the idea of annexation among the wealthier members of the community. The fact that only six of the taxpayers who attended the meeting supported an annexation bill that would require a referendum on the subject in Bloomfield implies that they were aware of a possibly significant level of resistance to the proposal in the town at large.[78]

At least some Bloomfield residents believed that annexation to Newark would bring them better water. Thomas Oakes, one of the residents who attended the first annexation meeting, stated that "the water question . . . is the main question which now confronts the people of Bloomfield. If . . . we annex to Newark, we will get a supply of good Pequannock water, while if we do not we will have to be content with the water from the Passaic."[79] Yet Bloomfield was already being supplied with water from a subsidiary of the East Jersey Water Company, which was also supplying Newark with water. This suggests that Bloomfield would have gotten the same Passaic water after annexation as it had been getting before. At the very least, the fact that the city of Newark did not own the Pequannock watershed made the connection between annexation and water supply unclear. For instance, at a later meeting on the annexation issue, with "more than 500 persons" in attendance, one antiannexationist, Samuel Ellor, "asked if anyone could guarantee that they would get Pequannock water. He declared that he had been informed that if they went to Newark they would get Passaic water."[80] Once again it appears that Newark's earlier reluctance to secure an adequate water supply later compromised the city's ability to annex outlying land.

Water was not the only point of contention (and confusion) in the annexation debates in Bloomfield in 1904. Another matter discussed at length, but with little clarity, was taxation. While the taxpayers who attended the first annexation meeting declared that "annexation will mean a lower tax rate," one prominent antiannexationist, Godlove Seibert, claimed at a later meeting that "by comparison of taxation rates those of Newark were higher than those of Bloomfield. They were likely to be higher still." Although annexationists still claimed that taxes would be lower, one did equivocate, noting that "it is no mean thing . . . to be a citizen of Newark, and I am in favor of going there even at a sacrifice." The taxation issue was made unclear by the relationship between tax rates and valuations, with annexationists denying apparent claims that Newark would substantially increase property valuations in Bloomfield were the town to be annexed. At one of the final meetings on the annexation issue in Bloomfield, an antiannexationist declared that "no one knew what the tax rate would be."[81]

The issue of taxes appears to have differentiated Bloomfield from Vailsburg. In Vailsburg infrastructural development had proceeded at such a high cost that annexation could be expected to lower taxes. Moreover, the fact that government officials had attempted to purchase a water system at inflated prices to line their own pockets suggests that much of the cost of infrastructural development in Vailsburg went to supporting corrupt politicians who squandered the public trust. By contrast, Bloomfield officials showed themselves to be responsible public servants by bargaining down the sale price of the Orange Water Company from $220,000 to $90,000. Even if the cost of infrastructural development did not actually differ much between Vailsburg and Bloomfield (and there is no way to know if it did), the evidence suggests that Bloomfield residents had greater faith that their local government was supplying infrastructure systems at the lowest possible cost, and they could do no better as a part of Newark. In these two suburban towns that were already supplied with infrastructure systems, the financing of those infrastructure systems and the perceived level of corruption among government officials thus likely played important roles in annexation decisions.

Nativism may have also played an important role in the annexation votes in both Bloomfield and Vailsburg. As has already been noted, Vailsburg was split politically over the issue of Sunday beer gardens, bicycle racing, and baseball playing. In Bloomfield the connection between these Sunday activities and annexation was more apparent. Antiannexationists at one of the last meetings in Bloomfield noted several times that annexation would mean "beer gardens and Sunday baseball galore." The specter of beer gardens no doubt referred to Newark's large German population and the presence of German breweries, whose power was evident in the career of political leader Gottfried Kruegel. As one article in the *Sunday Call* in 1898 claimed of Newark politics, "It is the saloon-keeper . . . that the politician of the Board of Works is afraid of."[82]

If suburban communities around Newark, Jersey City, and New York City did not want to be annexed to the central city because they wanted to maintain a greater separation between themselves and more recently arrived immigrants, they had to achieve the physical and financial means to maintain their independence. Suburban infrastructural development was vital to the physical separation between city and suburb. The costs incurred in infrastructural development might prove that a suburban municipality was in fact unable to maintain its independence, and suburbanites could thus not afford to express their nativism through municipal boundaries.

There is also evidence to suggest that infrastructural development could reinforce municipal independence in the suburbs of Newark even in the absence of ethnic and class differences. In 1903 the city of Orange was promoting the creation of a Greater Orange through its consolidation with East Orange, West Orange, and South Orange. The idea of a Greater Orange may have originated in the New England Society, a civic association located in Orange and described by the *Sunday Call* as "more thoroughly representative

than any similar organization in the community . . . its decisions are therefore regarded as voicing the public sentiment as accurately as could be."
Members of the New England Society had been discussing the consolidation
of the Oranges since early in January 1903 and by early February had
adopted a resolution favoring the measure, in conjunction with a consolidation bill introduced into the legislature by Assemblyman William A. Lord, a
resident of Orange.[83]

Unlike the various proposals to annex outlying communities to Newark,
the consolidation of the Oranges presented little threat to the suburban
identities of those communities and in fact was seen by at least some people
as a move to reinforce such an identity. One member of the New England
Society, Camilius Kidder, noted that "the consolidation of the Oranges
would help to avert a possible absorption by Newark, which he did not
think desirable, because the Oranges would in that event probably lose their
identity." If there was no conflict in terms of culture or class in the consolidation of the Oranges, however, several of the communities still viewed
themselves as separate and were aided in that identity by separate infrastructure systems. Resistance to the Greater Orange idea was apparently
greatest in South Orange and East Orange. As one resident of South Orange
noted, his community "had water, was about to get sewerage, neither of
these two being offered them on any better lines through consolidation,
and it feared nothing from Newark."[84] As in the case of Mount Vernon and
Pelham from Chapter 2, infrastructural development served to maintain
suburban autonomy not only from the central city, but from other suburbs,
thus reinforcing metropolitan fragmentation.

South Orange saw little to fear from Newark in 1903—not a good sign
for the Greater Newark idea. The annexation of Vailsburg proved to be the
high point of the Greater Newark movement, although hopes apparently
still remained for the plan throughout the first decade of the twentieth
century. In 1905 the board of trade claimed that "before twenty years have
passed the Greater Newark no doubt will have been accomplished, and our
city boundaries will extend and include the towns east of the Hackensack
to the top of the Orange Mountains, and may reach and include the
present city of Elizabeth; ranking Newark among the first cities in the
United States in manufactures, commerce and financial wealth." By 1908
the plan for a Greater Newark had grown even more grandiose. Newark
was envisioned by the board of trade as an expanded city that would
include the majority of Essex and Hudson Counties, as well as parts of

Bergen and Union Counties, thus creating "THE FOURTH LARGEST CITY IN THE U.S. . . . ahead of St. Louis in population, manufactures, banking and property valuations, and covering a territory about equal to that territory."[85] Yet all indications suggest that the possibilities for annexing surrounding communities had grown smaller. Another attempt to annex Irvington was rejected by the residents of that town in 1908. By 1910 the board of trade had retreated from its grandiose plans of 1908 to a Greater Newark that encompassed only "Belleville, Bloomfield, Montclair, Glen Ridge, The Oranges, South Orange, Irvington and Elizabeth."[86]

Newark was largely unsuccessful in annexing outlying territories because it had little to offer its suburbs in terms of infrastructural development. We have already seen that in its reluctance to develop an adequate water supply system, Newark ceded much of the control over water in the region to the East Jersey Water Company. In addition, by the first decade of the twentieth century, authority over sewerage in Essex County was in large part being taken over by a regional organization, the Passaic Valley Sewerage Commission. In 1899 the legislature passed a general law authorizing the creation of sewerage districts that would serve participating municipalities. In 1902 the legislature created a sewerage district that contained fifteen (later twenty-two) municipalities, including Newark, that were affected by the increasingly polluted Passaic River. The sewerage district was governed by the Passaic Valley Sewerage Commission, "composed of five members appointed from the district by the governor for terms of five years each," which was empowered to finance, construct, and manage a trunk sewer that drained into New York Bay.[87]

The Passaic Valley Sewerage Commission was analogous to the East Jersey Water Company as an organization that had no inherent interests in the expansion of the central city but could supply infrastructural development to outlying suburbs, thus reinforcing municipal independence and metropolitan fragmentation. When authority for infrastructural development was given over to regional special districts such as the Passaic Valley Sewerage Commission, central cities gave up an asset that could be used to compel annexations. It thus seems appropriate that the decline of the Greater Newark idea coincided with the establishment of the Passaic Valley Sewerage Commission, which began construction on its trunk sewer in 1912.[88]

In 1911, possibly reflecting the loss of momentum for its plan, the tone of the board of trade's call for a Greater Newark had changed noticeably, from the grandiose booster project of previous years to a more plaintive appeal:

> WHY NOT GREATER NEWARK . . . Witness the impediment placed in the way of securing the commencement of the work of ridding the Passaic Valley from the pollution of the river; town officials absolutely indifferent to the crying need of relief. The urgent necessity of a wise policy for the conserving of an adequate supply of potable water to provide for the future, compelling the authorities of Newark to include in their estimates the wants of the Oranges, Montclair and other suburbs . . . Why should the property owners of Newark pay the entire costs for an improvement such as the Clay street opening when the larger benefit will be conferred upon the towns across the river?[89]

The general question posed by the board of trade—why should Newark pay for physical improvements that would benefit the surrounding communities?—was in essence the same question the board of trade had asked twenty and thirty years earlier, but in a new context that underscored the more general problem that Newark faced in its short-lived quest for metropolitan greatness. In the nineteenth century Newark and its board of trade had concluded that it should not pay for infrastructural development in the suburbs and had thus resisted their annexation. By 1910 Newark and its board of trade had concluded similarly that the city should not have to pay for infrastructural development that benefited the suburbs, but now saw consolidation as the solution. Yet by the twentieth century the suburban municipalities had supplied themselves with service delivery systems in the face of Newark's neglect and no longer had any incentive to consolidate with a city that could only provide them with the unwanted intrusion of foreign populations and cultures. The pattern of infrastructural development in the metropolitan region, shaped by the previous decisions of city officials, residents, and other private actors, had determined the pattern of government jurisdiction and could not easily be undone.

Besides the outlying municipalities where annexation became a genuine local issue, there was another set of communities surrounding Newark, including Montclair and the Oranges, where annexation was never seriously considered, despite the calls for a Greater Newark in which they were consistently included. East Orange, for instance, was a community consistently pointed out by Newark mayor Seymour as one acceptable for annexation and was included in every Greater Newark plan devised by the board of trade. In East Orange, however, the issue of annexation was never taken seriously. There was never any referendum on the issue, and no town president or, later, mayor of East Orange ever made mention of annexation or the Greater Newark plan in any of their annual messages between 1892 and 1910.

Located immediately west of Newark, between Vailsburg and Bloomfield, East Orange was certainly in a likely geographic position to consolidate with Newark. From the standpoint of geography and topography, it in fact made more sense that East Orange should have become part of Newark than that Bloomfield should be annexed. East Orange shared contiguous roadways and trolley service with Newark, while Bloomfield had a common border of only about half a mile with the central city and shared no roadways; to get between Bloomfield and Newark, a traveler had to take Bloomfield Avenue, which passed through Belleville Township. As one Bloomfield resident mentioned in 1904, "Somewhere in a swamp, Bloomfield met Newark, but not on a contiguous highway."[90]

Despite the extensive border and transportation routes that it shared with Newark, East Orange was probably the least likely of all the municipalities in Essex County to consolidate with the central city. Local officials and residents had maintained a rigorous control of their town's identity as an affluent suburb and thus preserved a strong social separation between it and Newark. Residents had elected Republican reformers to town offices in 1890 on the platform that they would make the town a "progressive residential haven." The cost of progress was that East Orange had the second-highest tax rate in the county, which had the added benefit of keeping out undesirable elements.[91]

East Orange's progressivism was evident in infrastructural development. The town had participated with Bloomfield and Montclair in constructing an outlet sewer that discharged into the Passaic River, construction of which was completed in 1894. Even before construction of the outlet sewer, East Orange had installed a separated sewer system and was, at least according to Mayor Edward Bruen in 1900, one of the first municipalities in the country to have done so.[92] By 1892 the township sewerage system included approximately thirty-one miles of street mains that ran through approximately sixty-two miles of streets. Approximately half of the houses in the township were connected to the sewerage system. Most households that could take advantage of the sewerage system did so. As Figure 13 indicates, the number of houses with sewer connections increased along with the steady growth of the sewerage system throughout the last decade of the nineteenth century and the first decade of the twentieth.[93] Indeed, relative to population growth, sewerage construction in East Orange during the turn of the twentieth century probably outpaced sewerage construction in Newark.[94]

Among the cities and suburbs of Essex County, East Orange was also at the vanguard of water supply. It was the first of the Oranges to develop a comprehensive supply system. East Orange's water supply originated with the creation of the Orange Water Company, which was "granted a special charter" by the legislature in 1867 that gave it the right to construct a waterworks and lay pipes "through the streets of the city of Orange and adjoining townships." The company was inactive during the 1860s and 1870s until a drought in the summer of 1880 revived the "water question" throughout northern New Jersey. The company began to sell its stock, most of which was purchased by the "citizens of Orange and East Orange." Despite its initial participation, the city of Orange failed to secure a contract with the Orange Water Company, while the township of East Orange

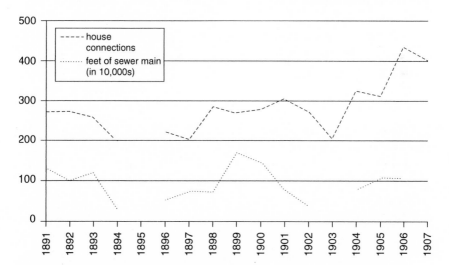

Figure 13. Sewers laid and connections made annually, East Orange, 1891–1907. *Data sources: Report of the Township Committee of the Township of East Orange, 1891–1898,* and *Annual Report of the City of East Orange, New Jersey, 1899–1907.*

entered into a contract with the company at the end of 1881 to be supplied with water for ten years, "which, with modifications, [w]as renewed for another term."[95]

By the end of the second ten-year contract with the Orange Water Company, East Orange had become a city, had experienced a significant increase in population, and was actively considering the option of a municipal water supply system. Taking his cue from what was by that time a national trend, the city's first mayor, Edward Bruen, announced to the common council in 1900 that since "the tendency throughout the country has been, and is, toward . . . municipal ownership . . . the question of the purchase of or construction of a public water supply should receive earnest consideration." Approximately one year later, in February 1901, the Orange Water Company offered to sell its waterworks to the city for $825,000. The water committee of the city council rejected the offer, as it did a subsequent offer of $800,000. While negotiations were at a standstill, East Orange residents voted by a ratio of twenty-five to one in favor of a municipal waterworks in a referendum that December. City officials then initiated proceedings to take the company's franchise and waterworks (including "the pipes and attachments thro-out") by condemnation, and the water company responded by accepting the city's standing offer of $350,000 for the distributing system. Thus the "East Orange Water Department became a reality on January 1, 1903."[96]

Unlike the case of Vailsburg but similar that of Bloomfield, the process by which East Orange officials were able to reduce the price of the water company's system from $825,000 to $350,000 suggests that the city could responsibly engage in infrastructural development without incurring exorbitant costs resulting from corrupt practices.[97] Furthermore, the overwhelming vote in favor of municipal ownership also suggests that East Orange residents trusted their local government to engage in infrastructural development. They therefore had little reason to consider annexation to Newark. Certainly East Orange officials portrayed themselves as being able to exercise fiscal responsibility in the physical development of their community. Evidence of fiscal responsibility is suggested by the early adoption of a separated sewerage system, which, as discussed in Chapter 1, was a system distinguished among other things by its "comparative cheapness." Mayor Bruen claimed further in 1900 that

> the improvements made by the municipality have cost less . . . than in most other communities; . . . we are able to construct sewers more cheaply

by day's work than by contract, a circumstance which reflects great credit upon our engineering department; our sidewalks have, in the past, cost the property-owners less money per running foot than where the individual owners have given their personal attention to doing the work themselves. Whatever statements are made to the contrary, it is confidently asserted that our macadamized roads have been resurfaced at less expense than is done by contract elsewhere; that it has been done well is evidenced by the excellent condition of the roads themselves.[98]

Even if Bruen's comments reflect the bravado of a booster mayor, the fact that more than fifty miles of the city's streets—approximately 83 percent of the total city street system—were paved by 1906 suggests a marked level of success in infrastructural development and a proven capacity for municipal autonomy.[99]

Part of the impetus for municipal ownership had been that the Orange Water Company's water supply was insufficient.[100] After purchasing the company's distributing system, East Orange had begun to purchase water from Newark on a temporary basis, and a further contract stipulating that East Orange would buy water from the city for ten years at $50 per million gallons had been at least informally agreed to. Early in 1903, however, East Orange officials reversed themselves and notified the Newark Board of Works that they would not sign a contract for a water supply from the city (at which point Newark demanded an additional $30 per million gallons for the water it was then currently supplying). Instead of entering into a ten-year contract with Newark, East Orange officials had hired an engineer, Cornelius C. Vermeule, "to make tests for artesian water at some available point, in order to find a supply that would be free from interference from outside interests." Vermeule found land in the Passaic Valley under which there was a sufficient supply of water, which the city then purchased. Municipal water became available to East Orange residents in January 1905.[101]

There were at least two reasons why the city of East Orange decided not to enter into a contract with Newark for its water supply, both of which are significant for understanding the relationship between infrastructural development and municipal autonomy. First, at least some residents and officials were aware that a dependence on Newark's water, especially during the Greater Newark movement, posed a threat to East Orange's municipal autonomy. Commenting on the water supply issue, the *Sunday Call* noted, "The East Orange people appeared to have been somewhat frightened in their negotiations by threats of annexation with Newark."[102] Second, even if East Orange had decided to purchase water by contract, Newark was not the only possible supplier nor necessarily the city's best option. Arthur Reimer, superintendent of the East Orange Water Department, noting that Newark charged a high price for water, commented further that "the East Jersey Water Company, or one of its subsidiary companies, could furnish practically the same service as Newark."[103] Thus the water company that was formed as a result of Newark's initial intransigence over the Pequannock watershed in the 1880s could compete against Newark to supply outlying areas with water in the 1900s. Furthermore, the case of East Orange suggests that because outlying communities could depend on private suppliers such as the East Jersey Water Company, Newark's ability to use water as leverage for geographic expansion was significantly reduced.

In the cases of Jersey City and New York City, central city infrastructural development helped build political machines, which stimulated resistance to annexation in the suburbs. At the same time, expertise generated by infrastructural development in the cities provided the means by which suburbs could resist annexation. Newark's suburbs may have also resisted annexation because of perceived political corruption in the central city. Newark's procurement of a water supply from the East Jersey Water Company was accompanied by charges of political corruption on the part of Mayor Joseph Haynes and political bosses Gottfried Kruegel and James Smith Jr. The water supply scandal in Newark could only have made outlying communities more resistant to annexation. As we have seen, suburban residents in Essex County feared that their communities would be subjected to Sunday beer drinking and other ethnic activities were they annexed to Newark. Since Newark's two political bosses were German and Irish, suburbanites' nativist fears were probably indistinguishable from fears of central city political machines. Thus to the extent that the water supply scandal elevated a perception of corrupt activities of ethnic politicians in Newark, central city infrastructural development probably created resistance to annexation in the suburbs of Essex County.

If infrastructure politics in Newark gave suburbanites their motivation for municipal independence, the city also provided the means for suburbs to attain that independence, though in a different fashion than did New York City and Jersey City. Through infrastructural development in New York City and Jersey City, a cadre of engineers was trained who then went into the private market to sell their expertise to surrounding suburban communities.

By contrast, it was Newark's inaction that gave a private company the opportunity to take control of the city's water supply. The private company could then sell water to surrounding communities without any demands that they be annexed to the central city. In fact, because different municipalities bid against one another to purchase water, the company probably benefited from metropolitan fragmentation.

Despite their differences, the process by which central city infrastructural development set limits to geographic expansion was similar in Newark, Jersey City, and New York City. Central city government action (or inaction, in the case of Newark) stimulated private interests that promoted independent suburban infrastructural development. Newark's relative intransigence in regard to infrastructural development simply strengthened this process. While city engineers facilitated suburban autonomy, Jersey City and New York City could at least use their municipal water supplies as an incentive for suburbanites to desire consolidation. Cities with more developed infrastructure systems had more in the way of urban services to offer surrounding communities. Because its intransigence allowed private actors to play a more substantial role in infrastructural development, Newark was the least successful of the three cities at annexing outlying land.

Despite the fact that it was laggard compared to New York City and Jersey City, Newark was still the largest municipality in Essex County, with the largest physical plant. The proactive steps that Newark took toward infrastructural development had an effect on suburban infrastructural development similar to that of the steps in New York City and Jersey City. In the case of engineering expertise, East Orange and other suburban communities used specialists from Newark, as well as engineers throughout the Northeast. When Orange began to consider a water supply system in the 1880s, the town government hired an engineer from Connecticut, William B. Rider, but when Orange officials began plans to develop a sewerage system, they hired an engineer from Newark, Carroll P. Bassett. At the same time, Orange officials also hired "F. P. Stearns, of Boston, and Samuel M. Gray, of Providence," as consulting engineers to review the plans made by Bassett. When East Orange embarked on construction of a sewerage system, township officials also hired Bassett and an out-of-state consulting engineer, the renowned Rudolph Hering. James Owen, the civil engineer who was supervising the construction of the outlet sewer in 1894, also had his offices in Newark. Both Owen and Hering were hired by South Orange to review the plans for that township's proposed sewerage system. Plans for the sewerage system had originally been drawn up by an engineer from Orange, Frederick T. Crane.[104]

The suburbs around Newark also relied on experts from New York City and the Stevens Institute of Technology in Hoboken. For instance, in East Orange's search for a water supply in 1903, the city hired the previously mentioned Vermeule, who was "one of the best known water supply engineers of the State" and "a resident of East Orange, tho practicing in New York." Vermeule, along with John J. Boyd (from Hudson County) and Nicholas Hill Jr., who had formerly been the "engineer of the Water Department of New York City," were both hired by South Orange in 1910 to find new water sources in the village. In conjunction with the question of finding new water supplies, both East Orange and Orange relied on professors from the Stevens Institute; East Orange hired Professor Thomas B. Stillman to test the quality of the water provided by the Orange Water Company, and Orange hired a Professor Denton to draw up recommendations for a new water supply for the city.[105]

With regard to street lighting, the suburban municipalities in Essex County depended in some small degree on expertise and resources from Newark. Throughout the 1890s East Orange relied on the Citizens' Gas Light Company, which was initially established primarily to serve Newark.[106] After the citizens of Orange approved the establishment of a municipal electric lighting system in 1909, "Specifications prepared by Runyon and Carey, consulting engineers, of Newark, were worked out under the general superintendence of Frederick O. Runyon, senior member of the firm." Of course, Orange and East Orange also relied on cities other than Newark for information and assistance. In Orange "Illuminating gas was introduced by John P. Kennedy, of Trenton." In 1896 East Orange Township president William C. Schmidt reported that over the previous months, he had "communicated with the Mayors of fifty cities, whose population was about equal to that of our township, upon the subject of electric street lighting," and urged the township committee to begin investigations on the subject as well.[107]

Overall, of the fourteen engineers and other experts known to have worked on infrastructure projects in Newark's suburbs in the late nineteenth and early twentieth centuries, eight either worked or lived in New Jersey. Of these eight experts, three had offices in Newark. Thus experts from Newark certainly facilitated infrastructural development in the suburbs, although they do not appear to have been any more significant in this regard than experts in the wider metropolitan region or even experts from out of state.

There is some evidence that Newark's suburbs used contractors from the central city. There is little evidence, however, that infrastructural development in the suburbs depended on contractors from Newark. The available evidence suggests that somewhere between 9 and 36 percent of the contractors who either worked or bid on infrastructure projects in East Orange had also worked on infrastructure projects in Newark.[108] More anecdotal evidence suggests that there were many suburban contractors in Essex County. George Spotiswoode appears to have been one well-connected contractor in Orange, having served on a "special committee" that originally planned that town's water supply system in 1882. Spotiswoode worked on a large land development in Orange in the 1890s, which he later came to own after the initial owners went bankrupt. There is no evidence that Spotiswoode ever had an infrastructure contract with the city of Newark, although he did bid unsuccessfully for at least one infrastructure project in East Orange. In the construction of the Orange waterworks, the contractor who "laid all the pipe," Frank C. O'Reilly, also had at least one infrastructure contract with the city of Newark, while the contractor who built a dam for the waterworks, Freel and McNamee, apparently never had an infrastructure contract with the central city.[109]

Being located near a large city that was actively engaged in infrastructural development was probably not as crucial to suburban infrastructural development by the time of the Greater Newark movement as it had been earlier in the nineteenth century. The diffusion of urban infrastructure technology throughout the nineteenth century meant that affluent suburbs built after 1890 had modern infrastructure systems "uniformly installed . . . in advance of settlement."[110] The relative ease with which Newark's suburbs were able to engage in infrastructural development in the 1890s no doubt made them less susceptible to annexation than the suburban municipalities around Jersey City in the late 1860s. Thus Jersey City could annex three entire municipalities between 1870 and 1873, while Newark was only able to annex one municipality and part of another during the first decade of the twentieth century, in large part because infrastructure systems were more readily available to suburban communities at the turn of the century than they had been in the years after the Civil War.

In short, at least three aspects of infrastructural development contributed to the failure of Greater Newark. First, urban infrastructure technology and expertise had become more readily available to smaller communities by the time Newark began to pursue an expansionist policy, making consolidation less attractive. Second, because Newark had ceded control of its water supply to a private company, it had less to offer suburban municipalities. Finally, the labor and expertise that in large part depended on infrastructural development in Newark could also be used to develop independent infrastructure systems in surrounding municipalities. Suburban infrastructural development in Essex County would probably have occurred without labor and expertise from Newark, since there were many other sources from which they could draw, but the presence of engineers and contractors in the neighboring central city no doubt made the job of infrastructural development easier in many instances and may in some cases have been a determining factor between building independent infrastructure systems or being annexed to the central city.

Repeating the diagram from Figure 5 in Chapter 1 and Figure 10 in Chapter 3, Figure 14 summarizes the evidence for the general argument provided in this and the previous two chapters. As in Figure 10, the arrows are dashed to indicate that there is not a causal link between all of the municipalities within each general category. For instance, infrastructural development in Newark and Jersey City was an important factor in the development of political machines in those two cities. However, infrastructural development in Newark and Jersey City did not necessarily have anything to do with political machines in Greenville, Hudson City, Bergen City, or Vailsburg. The outlying communities with political machines are marked with asterisks in Figure 14 (as they were in Figure 10) to indicate that suburban infrastructural development in those cases would not be expected to lead to suburban autonomy.

Infrastructural Development and Metropolitan Fragmentation: Newark's Decline

By the 1910s the suburbs around Newark were sufficiently developed to be independent of the central city. The only successful annexation after the demise of the Greater Newark movement was of an eleven-block area west of Vailsburg, known as Ivy Hill, which became part of the city in 1927. Reflecting characteristics that were typical of areas that had previously been absorbed into Newark, Ivy Hill was largely undeveloped when it was annexed,

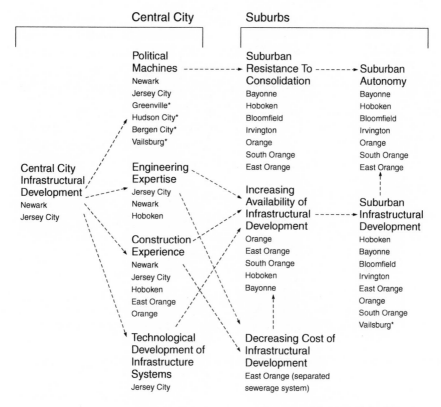

Figure 14. Relationship between central city public works in Newark and Jersey City and suburban autonomy in Essex and Hudson Counties

containing not more than twenty buildings (including the convalescent branch of the Newark City Hospital and the Ivy Hill Home for the Aged and Infirm) and less than half a mile of paved streets, sewers, and water and gas lines.[111]

This final annexation occurred during the last stage of business-inspired boosterism in Newark. The Newark Chamber of Commerce (previously the board of trade), in league with the city government, pursued aggressive development projects for the city during the 1920s, including a port deepening, "a comprehensive city plan for street improvements," a subway system, and an airport. These development projects served the interests of the city's business community, but they also reflected, in the words of

Newark historian Paul Stellhorn, "a spirit of civic pride and city building in all its facets, from new and improved transportation possibilities to libraries and cultural programs." But the city's campaign of capital development came to a halt with the onset of the Great Depression. The depression also exposed a latent cleavage between the city and its business community. Reflecting their different constituencies, the city government sought desperately to raise funds for relief projects, while the chamber of commerce opposed most local spending programs on behalf of fiscal retrenchment.[112]

The city government and the business community might have been expected to reunite under the banner of boosterism and civic pride after the depression, but the divergent interests of the city and its business community persisted, and the chamber of commerce continued to promote fiscal retrenchment into the economic resurgence during World War II. The permanent division between business and government interests in Newark was in large part a result of the proliferation of municipalities in Essex County. During the 1920s an increasing number of Newark's business elite no longer lived in the city. For instance, between 1921 and 1929 the proportion of officers and members of the board of directors of the chamber of commerce who actually lived in the city dropped from approximately 71 to 36 percent. Thus when the city and its business community came into conflict over government spending during the depression, the business elite easily transferred their allegiances to the suburban communities in which they lived. As Stellhorn has explained, "By the midthirties it had become quite apparent that the city's non-resident business community had little interest in any program which required the use of their tax dollars. More important, the members of the business elite were losing interest in Newark as the cultural and social focal point of their lives." Even after the depression, Newark was no longer seen as a source of civic pride in which investments should be made, but as a tax liability from which the business community slowly extracted itself as it moved its capital into the suburbs.[113]

Thus suburban autonomy in Essex County underwrote the eventual breakdown of a sense of community within the metropolitan region, which further enhanced the need for autonomy among the suburbs. As one Newark journalist commented in January 1939, "Talk of annexation to Newark brings only shoulder-shrugging in Irvington and Belleville. It brings sharp retorts in the Oranges. It brings derisive guffaws in Nutley and Bloomfield, exclamations of horror in Montclair and Glen Ridge . . . Greater Newark looks less certain on January 1, 1939, than it did on January 1,

1905."[114] The physical development of Newark and other central cities made the municipal autonomy of suburbs such as Irvington, Bloomfield, and East Orange possible. The physical separation of these communities then facilitated Newark's social and economic isolation during the Great Depression and arguably played no small role in the final insult—being named worst city in the nation in 1975.[115]

Conclusion: The Evolution
of Urban Politics

Among the many factors that contributed to Newark's decline from booster metropolis to worst city in the nation was the city's relatively small geographic size, which made it easier for residents and businesses to leave for surrounding municipalities. Newark's "minuscule 24-square mile size," says Kenneth Jackson, "is the dominant cause of many of its contemporary problems." Yet even New York City lost residents and businesses to the suburbs in the twentieth century. The General Foods Corporation moved its corporate headquarters from Manhattan to White Plains in 1954, marking the start of a mass exodus of business from New York City to surrounding communities in Westchester County, New Jersey, and Connecticut. Even when businesses remained in the city, thousands of their workers abandoned New York to live in the suburbs. The movement of the city's middle class into the independent, outlying suburbs is one of the more prominent explanations of New York's fiscal problems in the 1970s.[1]

Metropolitan fragmentation created a problem for suburbs as well as central cities. In 1961, Robert Wood pointed out that fragmentation in the New York metropolitan region created a situation where "the communities under the heaviest density pressures to spend have a tendency to be poorly equipped to meet those needs." With territory divided "among hundreds of jurisdictions . . . the political economy goes forward in ways localized, limited, and largely negative in character." Twenty years later Michael Danielson and Jameson Doig, while disagreeing in significant ways with Wood's description of the regional political economy, agreed that political fragmentation was one of the key variables that created "a significant mismatch of resources and needs in the region's suburbs."[2]

David Rusk and others have argued that one solution for metropolitan fragmentation is continued consolidations that maintain cities' "elasticity."[3]

194

But the infinite expansion of central cities is clearly not a feasible solution to the problems of metropolitan fragmentation. Even if New York City had continued to expand its borders after 1898, it would eventually have come up against state borders dividing New York, New Jersey, and Connecticut. New Jersey communities that New York City could never annex served as suburbs to the central city throughout the nineteenth century. Barring radical changes in the American political system that redistribute power and authority from states to metropolitan regions, state borders present permanent barriers to consolidation in many metropolitan districts. In any case, even within states, residents of metropolitan regions have shown a marked disinclination to approve city-county consolidations and other forms of regional government.[4]

The argument that I have made in this book is that metropolitan fragmentation was a process inherent in urban growth in the United States. Many outlying communities within metropolitan regions confronted population growth not by joining forces with the central city, but by installing infrastructure systems that enabled them to provide their own services and remain independent municipalities. Political corruption associated with the physical development of the central city often generated the motivation for suburban autonomy. Suburban infrastructure systems reinforced municipal boundaries and in at least some instances contributed to a sense of place identity that was distinct from the central city. Thus my argument would in fact predict that urbanization made consolidation an increasingly unlikely solution to the problems of metropolitan fragmentation.

Other authors regard the proliferation of independent municipalities within metropolitan regions as a virtue. For instance, Geoffrey Brennan and James Buchanan have argued that consolidated local governments will be less efficient because they will operate as monopolies and seek to maximize tax revenues for their own benefit. If municipalities must compete against one another for residents and businesses, they will be forced to provide services more efficiently. Similarly, according to Charles Tiebout's well-known argument, if municipalities must compete against one another for residents, they will be compelled to match the services they provide to the preferences of residents and businesses. Metropolitan fragmentation should thus lead to more satisfied "consumer-voters."[5]

Although rarely discussed in this manner, the free-market or "public choice" defense of government decentralization can be seen as part of Jane Jacobs's evolutionary explanation of urban growth. Jacobs argues that the economic diversity and differentiation of cities make them engines of innovation. In large part, innovation—what Jacobs calls "new work"—arises from existing divisions of labor. Thus "the greater the sheer numbers and varieties of divisions of labor already achieved in an economy, the greater the economy's inherent capacity for adding still more kinds of goods and services." Of course, only some innovations succeed. As Jacobs notes, between "old work" and "new work" is a good deal of trial and error.[6] The mechanism that distinguishes useful innovations from nonuseful innovations (a question Jacobs never directly addresses) is the marketplace. Those innovations that succeed in creating new work are those that produce saleable goods in a competitive market. Similarly, advocates of local government decentralization argue that competition among municipalities distinguishes those government activities that are useful from those that are not useful and will be eliminated.

The argument made here extends the argument for local government decentralization. In a sense, municipal governments competed in the production of infrastructure—sewerage, water supply, street lighting, and street pavements. Expertise developed around each of these public commodities, and this expertise was largely responsible for innovations in public works—new illuminants such as naphtha, new water-pumping systems, new street pavements, and new sewerage systems. The test of these new forms of infrastructure was the willingness of municipalities to purchase them.

But central city infrastructural development was also an inherently political process. Much of the motivation for building infrastructure systems was rooted in the potential political rewards that they generated—padded contracts, patronage jobs, insider real estate deals, and new political alliances. Civil engineers were not the only experts who emerged from the process of infrastructural development. Politicians "invented" new ways to extract illicit profits from the multimillion-dollar infrastructure projects over which they had control, the Tweed Ring being a well-known case in point.

Some degree of illicit profit making was probably a necessary component of infrastructural development. Seymour Mandelbaum and James Buchanan and Gordon Tullock have argued, in different ways, that monetary side payments can facilitate desired outcomes in institutional contexts where decision making is highly fragmented, as it is in a city or a legislative body.[7] Certainly in massive projects such as the construction of a comprehensive water supply or sewerage system, which in their implementation had to pass through numerous veto points, cash became the currency of consensus.

Central city infrastructural development was also promoted by the mutually beneficial relationship between politicians and engineers. In the marketplace of municipalities, however, politicians and engineers fared quite differently. Suburban communities eagerly sought engineers who could assist them in the construction of infrastructure systems. By contrast, suburbs were not eager to place themselves in the hands of self-serving politicians who would supply their friends and political allies with padded contracts and other benefits of infrastructural development at taxpayer expense. Because outlying municipalities could purchase selectively from the innovations wrought by infrastructural development, taking the engineers but leaving the political machines, only some of the characteristics of central city infrastructural development survived the struggle for municipal existence. In fact, as I have argued throughout this book, outlying municipalities used engineers from the city as a way to keep out political machines. Engineers who made suburban infrastructural development possible also facilitated suburban autonomy from the central city.

Engineers were not the only agents of technology diffusion from cities to suburbs. As we have seen in Chapter 5, the East Jersey Water Company in large part owed its existence to the demand for adequate drinking water in Newark. The East Jersey Water Company also came to provide drinking water to several of the municipalities surrounding Newark. With a third party supplying water, suburban municipalities had less incentive to consolidate with the central city. Similarly, the New York and New Jersey Globe Gas-light Company first supplied naphtha for streetlights in New York and then took on street lighting in suburban communities such as Pelham. The Citizens' Gas Light Company followed a similar pattern, first supplying gas to Newark and then only later to East Orange and other surrounding municipalities. The combination of local engineers with gas and water companies indicates that infrastructural development in the city provided a substantial resource for infrastructural development in the suburbs.

The case studies have suggested at least two important qualifications to this general argument. First, the New York metropolitan region demonstrates clearly that no simple distinction can be made between a "central city" and "outlying municipalities" or "suburbs." New York was obviously the primary city in the region, but there were numerous others municipalities, such as Brooklyn or Yonkers, that could lay claim to being major cities in their own right. Other municipalities such as Hoboken, Greenville, East Orange, and Bloomfield were more or less suburbs of their most proximate major city, such as Newark or Jersey City, but also suburbs of New York City.

Because the metropolitan region was so entangled in crosscutting city-suburb relations, the general diffusion of infrastructure technology from central city to suburb was not always clear. For instance, engineers from a smaller city, Jersey City, assisted both Brooklyn and Newark in the development of their respective water supply systems. As the home of the Stevens Institute of Technology, Hoboken appears to have been the source of expertise related to infrastructural development to a degree disproportionate to its size. Despite these qualifications, however, the general process was for large central cities both within and outside the metropolitan region to serve as the primary source of expertise for infrastructural development in the suburbs.

A second qualification to the general argument is that some outlying municipalities not only imported engineers but also embraced politicians from the central cities. While more outlying municipalities appear to have resisted their annexation to the central city because they feared political corruption and higher taxes (as in Bayonne, Hoboken, Yonkers, Mount Vernon, and Flushing), the available evidence also suggests that Long Island City, Greenville, and possibly Vailsburg and Brooklyn had even more corrupt politicians than the central city, and residents in these municipalities desired consolidation as an anticorruption measure. The case of Greenville indicates that there was a type of corruption possibly unique to the suburbs, namely, factional splits that assumed greater importance in smaller communities than in big cities. Such a factional split may have also been the cause of the apparent dissatisfaction with the Bayonne city government among the residents of Salterville.

The case studies have also shown that the residents of outlying municipalities considered more than questions of economy and efficiency when they voted either for or against consolidation. Most residents probably had a good deal less than perfect information concerning the costs and benefits of consolidation. In the case of Jersey City, the effects of consolidation could not be known until after the consolidation referendum, when residents knew which municipalities had voted to join the central city. Because residents had imperfect knowledge, they probably relied on general characterizations of central cities as being corrupt—infested with *"ringology* or *ringgold"*[8]—and therefore inefficient. Moreover, the case studies have shown that many residents subscribed to characterizations of their own municipalities as "suburban" in nature and therefore fundamentally incompatible with the central city. In the cases of Pelham and Bayonne, infrastructural development was carried out for the explicit purpose of defining a suburban place identity, thus differentiating these two municipalities from their larger neighbors.

Ironically, if infrastructural development at first served to distinguish suburbs from cities, the fact that municipalities also used public works to compete against one another for labor and capital ultimately began to blur the distinction between cities and suburbs, as the case of the Greater Mount Vernon movement indicates. Several decades later, shopping malls would begin to do the same thing. Much as outlying communities adapted water, sewerage, and street pavements for their suburban needs in the late nineteenth century, they later adapted the downtown commercial shopping district to the suburban environment in the form of the shopping mall. As urban-planning historian Margaret Crawford has explained the suburban shopping mall, "Architects manipulated space and light to achieve the density and bustle of a city downtown—to create essentially a fantasy urbanism devoid of the city's negative aspects: weather, traffic and poor people." In contrast to Crawford's claim that shopping malls create a "fantasy urbanism," my argument holds that the evolutionary process by which outlying municipalities take aspects of the city environment and adapt them to their needs is the very essence of urbanization. Indeed, as Crawford notes, cities have responded to the suburban shopping mall with their own versions of shopping malls that seek to capitalize on the unique aspects of the central city as a point of history and culture—Boston's Faneuil Hall, Baltimore's Inner Harbor, and New York's South Street Sea Port.[9]

While the case of infrastructural development in the nineteenth and early twentieth centuries involved the diffusion of infrastructure technology from larger to smaller cities and suburbs, the case of mall building suggests a more recursive diffusion of development technology, from cities to suburbs and back again from suburbs to cities. As suburban municipalities have established their autonomy and independence through developmental policies, from infrastructure systems to shopping malls, they have become increasingly equal competitors with central cities and have also further blurred the distinctions between the urban and the suburban.

If cities pursue developmental polices because they have to compete with other cities for labor and capital, we would expect to find that cities and suburbs face more pressure to pursue new developmental policies as they become increasingly indistinguishable from one another and thus more equal competitors. Development proceeds independently within each municipality, yet at the same time is shaped by development in surrounding municipalities. As development proceeds, it reinforces the competition between those municipalities and at the same time reformulates the object of that competition, for example, from sewerage systems to shopping malls. Although the object of competition changes, it is always part of a developmental policy.

The mutually reinforcing processes of intercity competition and the pursuit of developmental policies create a further process of standardization and commodification that extends from individuals to institutions. City engineers commodified their expertise in the form of consulting practices, and the physical infrastructure of the city was standardized and commodified into prefabricated systems such as the Holly pump that could be sold as service delivery packages in the suburbs. Consulting engineers and prefabricated infrastructure systems reinforced suburban autonomy by making infrastructural development possible for smaller and smaller communities. In turn, the proliferation of municipalities created a larger market for contracted services. Armed with the ability to provide their own services, independent municipalities themselves became commodities, packages of public services from which residents within a metropolitan region could choose. In Bayonne, for instance, infrastructural development was carried out for the explicit purpose of making the city a bedroom community for New Yorkers.

In the pursuit of new developmental policies, the old developmental policies become less visible as they become more ubiquitous—the "hidden function" of local government.[10] The growing standardization, proliferation, and thus decreasing awareness of public works has both practical and ideological consequences. On the practical side, as modern infrastructure systems became increasingly an accepted element of the urban and suburban landscape, they were easily ignored and thus subject to neglect. As a former city manager of Oklahoma City explained, "It is easier for politicians to extend the street, water, and sewerage systems into newly developing areas than it is to maintain an aging, deteriorating system . . . So long as the maintenance problems are invisible, so long as water comes out of the tap and disappears down the hole in the sink, it is hard to convince people that their sanitary systems need major repairs or upgrading."[11] Similarly, Martin Melosi has written that "it takes a major disruption . . . to demonstrate graphically the importance of the streets and alleys, bridges, power and communication networks, water and sewer lines, and waste-disposal facilities to urban survival."[12] Certainly it was the specter of such a "major disruption" that aroused various authors in the 1980s to write about an impending "infrastructure crisis."[13]

The growing ubiquity of urban and suburban infrastructure systems also involved an ideological shift. By the 1890s infrastructure systems were being installed in new residential developments prior to settlement. Mary Corbin Sies has argued that these new suburbs were characterized by a "suburban ideal" that embraced technology "as a potential social cure-all."[14] With infrastructure systems preinstalled, residents' uncritical acceptance of technology would not have been disturbed by any political conflict or corruption experienced in the process of infrastructural development, as happened in many of the communities that have been examined in this study. When the provision of infrastructure was privatized as part of the overall suburban package, there was no longer any public role for politicians to corrupt. New political issues have of course arisen, including privatization and increased concerns over pollution, but these political issues do not question the fundamental necessity of urban infrastructure systems, and they often see further technological advances, such as new filtration and incineration systems, as the solution. The turn-of-the-century "suburban ideal" is embedded in the modern politics of infrastructure.

John Stuart Mill argued in the mid-nineteenth century that the unthinking acceptance of democracy eroded its very meaning and significance. It was those individuals who had fought and argued for democratic government who best understood its meaning. Later generations who simply received democratic government without question would ultimately undermine its spirit because they had never understood democracy in the first place.[15] Similarly, those residents in cities and suburbs who participated in the process of infrastructural development a century ago were in a privileged position to understand the meaning of urban life, much of which is still relevant to contemporary society. Our thoughtless acceptance of urban infrastructure and other features of the urban environment contributes to our ignorance, which has led—and will lead in the future—to new urban crises. These new crises will provide us with the opportunity to reformulate and reinvigorate the meaning of urban life and will take us beyond the suburban ideal.

Notes

Introduction: Urbanism, Infrastructure, Politics

1. A sizable body of literature exists on the contemporary relationship between infrastructural development and economic growth. For good literature reviews, see David Alan Aschauer, "Why Is Infrastructure Important?" in Alicia Munnell, ed., *Is There a Shortfall in Public Capital Investment?* (Boston: Federal Reserve Bank of Boston, 1990), pp. 21–68, and Christine Kessides, "A Review of Infrastructure's Impact on Economic Development," in David F. Batten and Charlie Karlsson, eds., *Infrastructure and the Complexity of Economic Development* (New York: Springer, 1996), pp. 213–230.

2. Louis Wirth, "Urbanism as a Way of Life," *American Journal of Sociology* 44 (July 1938): 10n10.

3. William Mulholland, quoted in Gerard T. Koeppel, *Water for Gotham: A History* (Princeton, NJ: Princeton University Press, 2000), p. 6. For a good overview of infrastructural development in American cities, see Joel A. Tarr, "Building the Urban Infrastructure in the Nineteenth Century: An Introduction," in *Infrastructure and Urban Growth in the Nineteenth Century* (Chicago: Public Works Historical Society, 1985). On the relationship between water supply and city population, see the description of population loss in Philadelphia as a result of the 1793 yellow fever epidemic in Nelson M. Blake, *Water for the Cities: A History of the Urban Water Supply Problem in the United States* (Syracuse, NY: Syracuse University Press, 1956), p. 6; on street lighting, see Mark Bouman, "Luxury and Control: The Urbanity of Street Lighting in Nineteenth-Century Cities," *Journal of Urban History* 14 (November 1987): 7–37. For good historical overviews of infrastructural development, see Ellis L. Armstrong, ed., *History of Public Works in the United States, 1776–1976* (Chicago: American Public Works Association, 1976), and Martin V. Melosi, *The Sanitary City: Urban Infrastructure in America from Colonial Times to the Present* (Baltimore: Johns Hopkins University Press, 2000).

4. Kenneth T. Jackson, *Crabgrass Frontier: The Suburbanization of the United States* (New York: Oxford University Press, 1985), p. 146; Sam B. Warner Jr., *Steetcar*

Suburbs: The Process of Growth in Boston, 1870–1900 (Cambridge, MA: Harvard University Press and MIT Press, 1962), pp. 41, 113.

5. Thomas J. Sugrue, *The Origins of the Urban Crisis: Race and Inequality in Postwar Detroit* (Princeton, NJ: Princeton University Press, 1996), pp. 245–246.

6. Paul E. Peterson, *City Limits* (Chicago: University of Chicago Press, 1981), chs. 2–3.

7. Proponents of polycentricity make up the "public choice" school of urban political economy, the origins of which are usually traced to Charles M. Tiebout's landmark article, "A Pure Theory of Local Expenditures," *Journal of Political Economy* 64 (October 1956): 416–424. For a good literature review, see Alan Altshuler and David Luberoff, *Mega-projects: The Changing Politics of Urban Public Investment* (Washington, DC: Brookings Institution Press; Cambridge, MA: Lincoln Institute of Land Policy, 2003), pp. 53–62, esp. p. 57n30. See also Geoffrey Brennan and James Buchanan, *The Power to Tax: Analytical Foundations of a Fiscal Constitution* (New York: Cambridge University Press, 1980), and Alex Anas, "The Costs and Benefits of Fragmented Metropolitan Governance and the New Regionalist Policies," *Planning and Markets* 2 (September 1999), *www-pam.usc.edu*.

8. For an excellent summary, bibliography, and critique of this literature, see Elinor Ostrom, "The Social Stratification–Government Inequality Thesis Explored," *Urban Affairs Quarterly* 19 (September 1983): 91–112. Later works that fall within the tradition of the social stratification–government inequality literature include David Rusk, *Cities without Suburbs*, 2nd ed. (Washington, DC: Woodrow Wilson Center Press, 1995); David Rusk, *Inside Game/Outside Game: Winning Strategies for Saving Urban America* (Washington, DC: Brookings Institution Press, 2001); Myron Orfield, *Metropolitics: A Regional Agenda for Community and Stability*, rev. ed. (Washington, DC: Brookings Institution Press; Cambridge, MA: Lincoln Institute of Land Policy, 1997); and Orfield, *American Metropolitics: The New Suburban Reality* (Washington, DC: Brookings Institution Press, 2002).

9. See Henry C. Binford, *The First Suburbs: Residential Communities on the Boston Periphery, 1815–1860* (Chicago: University of Chicago Press, 1985), chs. 5 and 9; Ann Durkin Keating, *Building Chicago: Suburban Developers and the Creation of a Divided Metropolis* (Columbus: Ohio State University Press, 1988), pp. 8–9, chs. 5–6; Michael N. Danielson and Jameson W. Doig, *New York: The Politics of Urban Regional Development* (Berkeley: University of California Press, 1982), p. 76; and Marc A. Weiss, *The Rise of the Community Builders: The American Real Estate Industry and Urban Land Planning* (New York: Columbia University Press, 1987).

10. See Steven P. Erie, *Rainbow's End: Irish-Americans and the Dilemmas of Urban Machine Politics, 1840–1985* (Berkeley: University of California Press, 1988), pp. 80–81.

11. Jackson, *Crabgrass Frontier*, p. 115; Warner, *Streetcar Suburbs*, p. 31. On the relationship between transportation and suburbanization in the New York metropolitan region, see Danielson and Doig, *New York*, pp. 58–64.

12. Peterson, *City Limits*, p. 4. See also Paul Kantor, *The Dependent City Revisited: The Political Economy of Urban Development and Social Policy* (Boulder, CO: Westview Press, 1995).

13. See also Nancy Burns and Gerald Gamm, "Creatures of the State: State Politics and Local Government, 1871–1921," *Urban Affairs Review* 33 (September 1997): 59–96.

Chapter 1. Private Benefits, Public Goods

1. The classic formulations of public goods and the dilemma of supplying them efficiently are Paul A. Samuelson, "The Pure Theory of Public Expenditures," *Review of Economics and Statistics* 36 (November 1954): 387–389, and Richard A. Musgrave, *The Theory of Public Finance* (New York: McGraw-Hill, 1959). For specific illustrations of urban infrastructure systems as various types of public goods, see Vivienne Bennett, *The Politics of Water: Urban Protest, Gender, and Power in Monterrey, Mexico* (Pittsburgh: University of Pittsburgh Press, 1995), pp. 23–24; Christine Meisner Rosen, *The Limits of Power: Great Fires and the Process of City Growth in America* (New York: Cambridge University Press, 1986), p. 47; and E. S. Savas, *Privatization and Public-Private Partnerships* (New York: Chatham House, 2000), chs. 3 and 9.

2. Mancur Olson, *The Logic of Collective Action: Public Goods and the Theory of Groups* (Cambridge, MA: Harvard University Press, 1971), pp. 60–66.

3. See, for instance, Richard Child Hill, "Separate and Unequal: Government Inequality in the Metropolis," *American Political Science Review* 68 (December 1974): 1557–1568. For an example that relates specifically to infrastructure, see Sarah S. Elkind, *Bay Cities and Water Politics: The Battle for Resources in Boston and Oakland* (Lawrence: University Press of Kansas, 1998).

4. See John H. Gray, "The Difficulties of Control as Illustrated in the History of Gas Companies," in *Corporations and Public Welfare: Addresses at the Annual Meeting of the American Academy of Political and Social Science, Philadelphia, April Nineteenth and Twentieth, MDCCCC* (New York: McClure, Phillips and Co., 1900), and Mark H. Rose, *Cities of Light and Heat: Domesticating Gas and Electricity in Urban America* (University Park: Pennsylvania State University Press, 1995), p. 6.

5. Nelson M. Blake, *Water for the Cities: A History of the Urban Water Supply Problem in the United States* (Syracuse, NY: Syracuse University Press, 1956), pp. 77, 267; Rosen, *Limits of Power*, pp. 48–49. See also Carl V. Harris, *Political Power in Birmingham, 1871–1921* (Knoxville: University of Tennessee Press, 1977), ch. 11; Maureen Ogle, "Water Supply, Waste Disposal, and the Culture of Privatism in the Mid-Nineteenth-Century American City," *Journal of Urban History* 25 (March 1999): 321–347; and Richard Alan Levitan, "Corruption, Reform, and Institutional Change: Public Choice in Nineteenth Century Urban America" (Ph.D. diss., University of Pennsylvania, 1999), ch. 3.

6. Blake, *Water for the Cities*, pp. 88–89; Kate Foss-Mollan, *Hard Water: Politics and Water Supply in Milwaukee, 1870–1995* (West Lafayette, IN: Purdue University Press, 2001), ch. 4.

7. Joel A. Tarr, "Building the Urban Infrastructure in the Nineteenth Century: An Introduction," in *Infrastructure and Urban Growth in the Nineteenth Century*

(Chicago: Public Works Historical Society, 1985), p. 64; Stuart Galishoff, *Newark, the Nation's Unhealthiest City, 1832–1895* (New Brunswick, NJ: Rutgers University Press, 1988), p. 41. The narrative reports in the 1880 census volumes on the *Social Statistics of Cities* suggest that there was a good deal of variation between cities in how they charged residents for sewers. For instance, in Detroit the city government paid for all main sewers, manholes, and catch basins, but "laterals usually built in the alleys and back streets are paid for by the abutting property. Assessments are laid on the basis of the area of abutting lots." In Hoboken "assessment upon abutters is made solely in proportion to the benefit rendered, and of this each assessor is the judge." In Cincinnati and Milwaukee residents were charged assessments for sewers based on the footage of their property abutting the street in which it was laid. In Savannah the city paid for all sewerage construction but charged individual property owners $14 for "connections," "supervision," and "permits." George E. Waring Jr., *Report on the Social Statistics of Cities*, published as part of the Tenth Census (1886; reprint, New York: Arno Press, 1970), pt. 1, p. 694; pt. 2, pp. 177, 368, 610, 668.

8. James W. Howard, "The Paving Problem," *Paving and Municipal Engineering* 1 (November 1890): 93–95; Tarr, "Building the Urban Infrastructure in the Nineteenth Century," pp. 64–65. On utilities as natural monopolies, see Harris, *Political Power in Birmingham*, pp. 263–268.

9. Matthew A. Crenson, "Urban Bureaucracy in Urban Politics: Notes toward a Developmental Theory," in J. David Greenstone, ed., *Public Values and Private Power in American Politics* (Chicago: University of Chicago Press, 1982), pp. 209–225.

10. Olson, *Logic of Collective Action*, p. 11.

11. Crenson, "Urban Bureaucracy in Urban Politics," p. 226.

12. On "nesting," see Elinor Ostrom, *Governing the Commons: The Evolution of Institutions for Collective Action* (New York: Cambridge University Press, 1990), p. 50, and George Tsebelis, *Nested Games: Rational Choice in Comparative Politics* (Berkeley: University of California Press, 1990), p. 94.

13. On the private contracting method in street cleaning, see Seymour J. Mandelbaum, *Boss Tweed's New York* (New York: John Wiley and Sons, 1965), p. 13, and Levitan, "Corruption, Reform, and Institutional Change," ch. 2. On the police, see James F. Richardson, *The New York Police: From Colonial Times to 1901* (New York: Oxford University Press, 1970), pp. 29–50.

14. See Robert W. Bailey, "Uses and Misuses of Privatization," in Steve H. Hanke, ed., *Prospects for Privatization* (New York: Academy of Political Science, 1987), pp. 138–152, and Paul Starr, "The Limits of Privatization," ibid., pp. 124–137, esp. p. 130.

15. Gustavus Myers, *The History of Tammany Hall*, 2nd ed. (1917; reprint, New York: Dover Publications, 1971), pp. 310–311.

16. Zane L. Miller, *Boss Cox's Cincinnati: Urban Politics in the Progressive Era* (New York: Oxford University Press, 1968), pp. 82, 101–102, 104–105; Lincoln Steffens, *The Shame of the Cities* (1904; reprint, New York: Sagamore Press, 1957), pp. 83–84.

17. Paul E. Peterson, *City Limits* (Chicago: University of Chicago Press, 1981), p. 148. See also Alan Altshuler and David Luberoff, *Mega-projects: The Changing Politics of Urban Public Investment* (Washington, DC: Brookings Institution Press; Cambridge, MA: Lincoln Institute of Land Policy, 2003), p. 47.

18. Rosen, *Limits of Power*, p. 58.

19. Galishoff, *Newark, the Nation's Unhealthiest City*, p. 111; Clay McShane, "Transforming the Use of Urban Space: A Look at the Revolution in Street Pavements, 1880–1924," *Journal of Urban History* 5 (May 1979): 283.

20. The 1850s inaugurated an era of unprecedented municipal defaults in the United States, approximately 20 percent of which were the result of bonds issued to pay for infrastructural development. Eric H. Monkkenen, "The Politics of Municipal Indebtedness and Default, 1850–1936," in Terrence J. McDonald and Sally K. Ward, eds., *The Politics of Urban Fiscal Policy* (Beverly Hills, CA: Sage Publications, 1984), p. 130. For a specific case where residents resisted infrastructural development out of concerns for municipal debt and higher taxes, see Terrence J. McDonald, *The Parameters of Urban Fiscal Policy: Socioeconomic Change and Political Culture in San Francisco, 1860–1906* (Berkeley: University of California Press, 1986), pp. 137–138.

21. Stanley K. Schultz and Clay McShane, "To Engineer the Metropolis: Sewers, Sanitation, and City Planning in Late-Nineteenth-Century America," *Journal of American History* 65 (September 1978): 397–402; Jon C. Teaford, *The Unheralded Triumph: City Government in America, 1870–1900* (Baltimore: Johns Hopkins University Press, 1984), pp. 133–141.

22. Alan I. Marcus, "Professional Revolution and Reform in the Progressive Era: Cincinnati Physicians and the City Elections of 1897 and 1900," *Journal of Urban History* 5 (February 1979): 191; McShane, "Transforming the Use of Urban Space," p. 298; Joel A. Tarr, "The Separate vs. Combined Sewer Problem: A Case Study in Urban Technology Design Choice," *Journal of Urban History* 5 (May 1979): 320; Martin V. Melosi, *The Sanitary City: Urban Infrastructure in America from Colonial Times to the Present* (Baltimore: Johns Hopkins University Press, 2000), pp. 155–160. For an earlier perspective on the relationship between engineers and other professionals, specifically in regard to the New York metropolitan region, see "Water Sources: Investigation Should Go On at Once," *Brooklyn Daily Eagle*, July 10, 1894, p. 10.

23. John R. Logan and Harvey L. Molotch, *Urban Fortunes: The Political Economy of Place* (Berkeley: University of California Press, 1987), pp. 1–2. Crenson also notes that real estate interests are exceptional as an organized interest on the demand side of municipal policy ("Urban Bureaucracy in Urban Politics," p. 215).

24. Teaford, *Unheralded Triumph*, pp. 199–207.

25. Charles C. Euchner, "The Politics of Urban Expansion: Baltimore and the Sewerage Question, 1859–1905," *Maryland Historical Magazine* 86 (Fall 1991): 276, 279.

26. Teaford, *Unheralded Triumph*, p. 201; Rosen, *Limits of Power*, p. 58.

27. Euchner, "Politics of Urban Expansion," p. 275; Rosen, *Limits of Power*, pp. 251–252, 264–270, 315–321.

28. As Amy Bridges notes, the political issues that arose around public works in large part led to the development of an "urban party system" that focused on local rather than national issues. See Amy Bridges, *A City in the Republic: Antebellum New York and the Origins of Machine Politics* (New York: Cambridge University Press, 1984), esp. pp. 33–38.

29. Tsebelis, *Nested Games*, ch. 3. A good description of the Prisoner's Dilemma and similar games is given in Donald P. Green and Ian Shapiro, *Pathologies of Rational Choice Theory: A Critique of Applications in Political Science* (New Haven, CT: Yale University Press, 1994), pp. 74–88.

30. Alan Lessoff, *The Nation and Its City: Politics, "Corruption," and Progress in Washington, D.C., 1861–1902* (Baltimore: Johns Hopkins University Press, 1994), ch. 3.

31. Ibid., p. 91.

32. Schultz and McShane, "To Engineer the Metropolis," pp. 396–400, 407–411.

33. While the game between engineers and politicians was "assurance," the game between reformers and politicians could be characterized as either prisoner's dilemma or "deadlock," depending on whether it was actually in the best interests of reformers and politicians to attempt to usurp the power of the other. See Tsebelis, *Nested Games*, ch. 3. The literature on progressive reformers and their goals is extensive and varied. Of particular interest for the discussion here is Kenneth Finegold, *Experts and Politicians: Reform Challenges to Machine Politics in New York, Cleveland, and Chicago* (Princeton, NJ: Princeton University Press, 1995).

34. Kenneth T. Jackson, *Crabgrass Frontier: The Suburbanization of the United States* (New York: Oxford University Press, 1985), pp. 144–146; Sam B. Warner Jr., *Streetcar Suburbs: The Process of Growth in Boston, 1870–1900* (Cambridge, MA: Harvard University Press and MIT Press, 1962), pp. 41–42, 112–113; Ann Durkin Keating, *Building Chicago: Suburban Developers and the Creation of a Divided Metropolis* (Columbus: Ohio State University Press, 1988), p. 105.

35. Jackson, *Crabgrass Frontier*, pp. 144–146; Jon C. Teaford, *City and Suburb: The Political Fragmentation of Metropolitan America, 1850–1970* (Baltimore: Johns Hopkins University Press, 1979), pp. 141–145.

36. Henry C. Binford, *The First Suburbs: Residential Communities on the Boston Periphery, 1815–1860* (Chicago: University of Chicago Press, 1985), pp. 223–225; Warner, *Streetcar Suburbs*, p. 163; Elkind, *Bay Cities and Water Politics*, pp. 72–73.

37. Vincent Ostrom, *Water and Politics: A Study of Water Policies and Administration in the Development of Los Angeles* (Los Angeles: Haynes Foundation, 1953), pp. 11–20, 148–159; quotes on pp. 156–157.

38. Harris, *Political Power in Birmingham*, p. 106; Graham R. Taylor, *Satellite Cities: A Study of Industrial Suburbs* (1915; reprint, New York: Arno Press and the New York Times, 1970), p. 243.

39. U.S. Bureau of the Census, *General Statistics of Cities, 1915* (Washington, DC: Government Printing Office, 1916), pp. 156–158. On metropolitan districts, see Elkind, *Bay Cities and Water Politics*, esp. chs. 3–4; Schultz and McShane, "To

Engineer the Metropolis," pp. 398–399; and Nancy Burns, *The Formation of American Local Governments: Private Values in Public Institutions* (New York: Oxford University Press, 1994), esp. pp. 25–32.

40. Jackson, *Crabgrass Frontier*, pp. 150–153; Teaford, *City and Suburb*, pp. 5–9; Burns, *Formation of American Local Governments*, pp. 4–6, 16–21.

41. "The Waring System of Sewerage," *Paving and Municipal Engineering* 1 (June 1890): 4; "Future of the Water-Works Business," *Paving and Municipal Engineering* 1 (July 1890): 26–27; "The Improved Welsbach Incandescent Gas Light," *Paving and Municipal Engineering* 4 (March 1893): 175–177.

42. Letty Anderson, "Fire and Disease: The Development of Water Supply Systems in New England, 1870–1900," in Joel A. Tarr and Gabriel Dupuy, eds., *Technology and the Rise of the Networked City in Europe and America* (Philadelphia: Temple University Press, 1988), pp. 150–152.

43. Ibid., pp. 140, 148–149.

44. The *Descriptive Index of Current Engineering Literature, 1884–1891*, vol. 1 (Chicago: Association of Engineering Societies, 1892), reported 406 articles on water supply systems under 29 separate subject headings, 224 articles on sewerage systems under 10 subject headings, 85 articles on street paving under 3 headings, and 61 articles on street lighting under 9 headings in approximately 100 American and European engineering journals between 1884 and 1891. (Transcripts from congressional hearings and annual reports, also included in the index, were excluded in this count.) The journal *Paving and Municipal Engineering* (not included in the index) listed articles in its index on infrastructure systems in New York, New Jersey, Nebraska, Tennessee, Minnesota, Texas, Massachusetts, Washington, Illinois, Missouri, Pennsylvania, Iowa, Ohio, Alabama, Georgia, Michigan, and Delaware, as well as France, Holland, England, China, and Japan, between June 1891 and May 1892 alone.

45. Harold L. Platt, *City Building in the New South: The Growth of Public Services in Houston, Texas, 1830–1910* (Philadelphia: Temple University Press, 1983), pp. 64–65; see also Schultz and McShane, "To Engineer the Metropolis," pp. 393–396, 399–405.

46. Raymond H. Merritt, *Engineering in American Society, 1850–1875* (Lexington: University Press of Kentucky, 1969), p. 159; Platt, *City Building in the New South*, p. 33. See also Melosi, *Sanitary City*, pp. 95–99, 163–164.

47. Platt, *City Building in the New South*, pp. 34, 66.

48. Anderson, "Fire and Disease," p. 148.

49. Merritt, *Engineering in American Society*, p. 6. See also Frank Knight, "Original Responsibility of City Civil Engineers," *Paving and Municipal Engineering* 4 (March 1893): 139–142.

50. Steffens, *Shame of the Cities*, p. 7.

51. See chapter 3 in this volume.

52. Richardson Dilworth, "From Sewers to Suburbs: Transforming the Policy-Making Context of American Cities," *Urban Affairs Review* 38 (May 2003): 726–739.

53. Charles M. Tiebout, "A Pure Theory of Local Expenditures," *Journal of Political Economy* 64 (October 1956): 416–424.

54. Cf. Vincent Ostrom, Charles M. Tiebout, and Robert Warren, "The Organization of Government in Metropolitan Areas: A Theoretical Inquiry," *American Political Science Review* 55 (December 1961): 831–842.

Chapter 2. Independent Yonkers, Expansionist New York

1. Quoted in Arthur Everett Peterson and George William Edwards, *New York as an Eighteenth Century Municipality*, vol. 1 (1917; reprint, Port Washington, NY: Ira J. Friedman, 1967), pp. 5–6. See also Edwin G. Burrows and Mike Wallace, *Gotham: A History of New York City to 1898* (New York: Oxford University Press, 1999), pp. 72–73, 77–79.

2. Burrows and Wallace, *Gotham*, p. 43. See also Peterson and Edwards, *New York as an Eighteenth Century Municipality*, vol. 1, pp. 75–76; vol. 2, pp. 166–167.

3. On the Colles waterworks, see Carl Bridenbaugh, *Cities in Revolt: Urban Life in America, 1743–1776* (New York: Alfred A. Knopf, 1938), pp. 106, 296; Nelson M. Blake, *Water for the Cities: A History of the Urban Water Supply Problem in the United States* (Syracuse, NY: Syracuse University Press, 1956), pp. 15–17; Peterson and Edwards, *New York as an Eighteenth Century Municipality*, vol. 2, pp. 139–141. Eugene P. Moehring notes that Colles's system "would have serviced Broadway and adjacent streets" (*Public Works and the Patterns of Urban Real Estate Growth in Manhattan, 1835–1894* [New York: Arno Press, 1981], p. 25), but he is probably only referring to water mains. As Gerard T. Koeppel notes, "Colles proposed a network of . . . six-inch bore mains buried four feet beneath the town's seven major streets, and three-inch pipe beneath the rest." Gerard T. Koeppel, *Water for Gotham: A History* (Princeton, NJ: Princeton University Press, 2000), p. 42.

4. Edward K. Spann, "The Greatest Grid: The New York Plan of 1811," in Daniel Schaffer, ed., *Two Centuries of American Planning* (Baltimore: Johns Hopkins University Press, 1988), pp. 14–25.

5. Burrows and Wallace, *Gotham*, p. 421. See also Elizabeth Blackmar, *Manhattan for Rent, 1785–1850* (Ithaca, NY: Cornell University Press, 1989), pp. 97, 159–161.

6. Erastus C. Benedict, *New York and the City Travel: Omnibus and Railroad. What Shall Be Done* (New York: n.p., 1851). Mentioned in Spann, "Greatest Grid," pp. 26–27. The definition of developmental policies comes from Paul E. Peterson, *City Limits* (Chicago: University of Chicago Press, 1981), p. 41.

7. Spann, "Greatest Grid," p. 21.

8. Sidney I. Pomerantz, *New York: An American City, 1783–1803*, 2nd ed. (Port Washington, NY: Ira J. Friedman, 1965), pp. 187–192; Blake, *Water for the Cities*, ch. 3; Beatrice G. Reubens, "Burr, Hamilton, and the Manhattan Company, Part I: Gaining the Charter," *Political Science Quarterly* 72 (December 1957): 578–607.

9. This debate centers on whether or not New York State legislators were aware that the Manhattan Company charter was to be used primarily to create a bank.

. For instance, Burrows and Wallace claim that in regard to Burr's clandestine efforts to create a bank, "no one was really fooled" (*Gotham*, p. 361), but Gustavus Myers has claimed that "the legislators . . . were much surprised later to hear that it contained a carefully worded clause vesting the Manhattan Company with banking powers." Gustavus Myers, *The History of Tammany Hall*, 2nd ed. (1917; reprint, New York: Dover Publications, 1971), p. 14. See also Pomerantz, *New York*, pp. 190–191; Reubens, "Burr, Hamilton, and the Manhattan Company," pp. 589–591; and Koeppel, *Water for Gotham*, ch. 5. Reubens extends her argument in "Burr, Hamilton and the Manhattan Company, Part II: Launching a Bank," *Political Science Quarterly* 73 (March 1958): 100–125; see especially pp. 100–106.

10. Blake, *Water for the Cities*, pp. 56–62, 101–102, 123; Pomerantz, *New York*, p. 200.

11. Jon C. Teaford, *The Municipal Revolution in America: Origins of Modern Urban Government, 1650–1825* (Chicago: University of Chicago Press, 1975). See also Gerald Frug, *City Making: Building Cities without Building Walls* (Princeton, NJ: Princeton University Press, 1999), chs. 1–2, and Judith Spraul-Schmidt, "Reconstituting City Government: Midcentury State Constitution Making, Defining the Municipal Corporation, and the Public Welfare," in Robert B. Fairbanks and Patricia Mooney-Melvin, eds., *Making Sense of the City: Local Government, Civic Culture, and Community Life in Urban America* (Columbus: Ohio State University Press, 2001).

12. Blake, *Water for the Cities*, pp. 101–103.

13. The quote is from Burrows and Wallace, *Gotham*, p. 439. On the origins of gas street lighting in New York City, see Louis Bader, "Gas Illumination in New York City, 1823–1863" (Ph.D. diss., New York University, 1970), and Frederick L. Collins, *Consolidated Gas Company of New York: A History* (New York: Consolidated Gas Company of New York, 1934), chs. 1–5. See also Myers, *History of Tammany Hall*, p. 78, and "An Act to Incorporate the Gas Light Company of the City of New York," *Laws of the State of New York*, 46th Session, March 26, 1823, pp. 99–101.

14. Blake, *Water for the Cities*, chs. 7–8 (for the cost of the Croton Aqueduct, see pp. 170–171); Koeppel, *Water for Gotham*, chs. 8–11; Burrows and Wallace, *Gotham*, ch. 35; Charles H. Weidner, *Water for a City: A History of New York City's Problem from the Beginning to the Delaware River System* (New Brunswick, NJ: Rutgers University Press, 1974), chs. 4–6.

15. In 1907, 117 American cities with populations of more than 30,000 had public water supply systems. The average year that those systems had either been built or acquired was 1871. U.S. Bureau of the Census, *Statistics of Cities Having a Population of over 30,000: 1907* (Washington, DC: Government Printing Office, 1910), pp. 131–133, 372–377.

16. Frank Parsons, *The City for the People, or, The Municipalization of the City Government and of Local Franchises*, rev. ed. (Philadelphia: C. F. Taylor, 1901). Parsons claims that when "The Philadelphia Councils attempted to take possession of the [gas] works" in 1841, "it was found that they had merely succeeded in creating

a trust which under the rulings of the courts made the managing board trustees for the bond holders and the absolute masters of the situation till all the bonds had matured and were paid. So that the first real public gas works were established in Richmond in 1852" (p. 205). Other than Philadelphia and Richmond, Parsons does not indicate which cities had municipal gas works. Among cities with populations of more than 30,000, only five had municipal gasworks by 1907. U.S. Census Bureau, *Statistics of Cities Having a Population of over 30,000, 1907*, p. 386.

17. Bader, "Gas Illumination in New York City," p. 287.

18. Collins, *Consolidated Gas Company of New York*, pp. 102–108, ch. 12; quote on p. 92. See also Bader, "Gas Illumination in New York City," pp. 192–194, 301.

19. *Minutes of the Common Council of the City of New York, 1784–1831*, vol. 19, *May 3, 1830, to May 9, 1831* (New York: City of New York, 1917), p. 320.

20. Collins, *Consolidated Gas Company of New York*, chs. 13–15; Bader, "Gas Illumination in New York City," p. 301. See also New York City Streets Department, Bureau of Lamps and Gas, *Fourth Quarterly Report*, 1866, p. 73; and New York City Department of Public Works, *Report for the Quarter Ending December 31, 1876*, p. 30.

21. Harold De Wolf Fuller, *Myndert Van Schaik, 1782–1865* (New York: Alumni Federation of New York University, 1926). Reprinted online at *www.marblecemetery.org*. For more on Van Schaik, see Blake, *Water for the Cities*, pp. 133–143, and Koeppel, *Water for Gotham*, pp. 145–167. On the cholera epidemic that preceded authorization of the Croton Aqueduct, see Charles E. Rosenberg, *Cholera Years: The United States in 1832, 1849, and 1866* (Chicago: University of Chicago Press, 1962).

22. See Roy Rosenzweig and Elizabeth Blackmar, *The Park and the People: A History of Central Park* (Ithaca, NY: Cornell University Press, 1992), pp. 24–25. On the crisis in public safety in the 1830s, see Paul A. Gilje, *The Road to Mobocracy: Popular Disorder in New York City, 1763–1834* (Chapel Hill: University of North Carolina Press, 1987), chs. 9–10.

23. "Since the water pipes of the Manhattan Company extended only to such parts of the city as had promised to be profitable, all the district north of Pearl Street on the east side and Grand street on the west side were totally unsupplied" (Blake, *Water for the Cities*, p. 123). Joanne Abel Goldman, speaking of the Croton system, notes, "In stark contrast to the city's other efforts to provide public services, the pattern of water supply did not mirror the distribution of wealth. Water was first introduced into the poorer, densely populated southern wards of the city." Joanne Abel Goldman, *Building New York's Sewers: Developing Mechanisms of Urban Management* (West Lafayette, IN: Purdue University Press, 1997), p. 53.

24. Moehring, *Public Works*, pp. 28–37. Moehring notes that "as the Industrial Revolution gained momentum and factories invaded cities everywhere, a consensus arose among New York's political and economic leaders that the massive aqueduct had to be built" (p. 37). Industrial demand for water apparently had little

to do with the need for steam power, however. See Burrows and Wallace, *Gotham*, p. 663. The overlapping membership between city government and local fire insurance companies fits with a positive and statistically significant relationship that I have found between the number of fire insurance companies and the miles of water main in cities with populations of more than 30,000 in 1905. Richardson Dilworth, "Paving Bodies Politic: Government Fragmentation and Infrastructural Development in the American Metropolis" (Ph.D. diss., Johns Hopkins University, 2001), ch. 3.

25. Rosenzweig and Blackmar, *Park and the People*, p. 48; Amy Bridges, *A City in the Republic: Antebellum New York and the Origins of Machine Politics* (New York: Cambridge University Press, 1984), p. 132.

26. Moehring, *Public Works*, pp. 41–42. See also Goldman, *Building New York's Sewers*, pp. 77–79.

27. The historian quoted is Eugene Moehring, "Space, Economic Growth, and the Public Works Revolution in New York," in *Infrastructure and Urban Growth in the Nineteenth Century* (Chicago: Public Works Historical Society, 1985), p. 42; Rosenzweig and Blackmar, *Park and the People*, pp. 37, 40–41, 45. See also Myers, *History of Tammany Hall*, p. 181n4; Burrows and Wallace, *Gotham*, pp. 790–791.

28. Rosenzweig and Blackmar, *Park and the People*, pp. 24, 42, 50–54, 57.

29. George Mazaraki, "The Public Career of Andrew Haswell Green" (Ph.D. diss., New York University, 1966), p. 27; Burrows and Wallace, *Gotham*, p. 832; Rosenzweig and Blackmar, *Park and the People*, pp. 54–58.

30. Burrows and Wallace, *Gotham*, pp. 836–837.

31. Mazaraki, "Public Career of Andrew Haswell Green," pp. 38–39. The 1857 charter was not wholly political. Mazaraki notes, for instance, that making the Central Park Commission a state-appointed body "seems to have been motivated as much by the desire to develop the Park as to deny the Wood Democrats the patronage connected with the work" (p. 26).

32. Bridges, *City in the Republic*, p. 117; Myers, *History of Tammany Hall*, pp. 186–187; Mazaraki, "Public Career of Andrew Haswell Green," pp. 41–42.

33. "The Street Department," *New York Times*, October 25, 1860, p. 4.

34. Mazaraki, "Public Career of Andrew Haswell Green," pp. 61–69, 90–112. For more on Green, see John Foord, *The Life and Public Services of Andrew Haswell Green* (New York: Doubleday, Page and Company, 1913), and Barry J. Kaplan, "Andrew H. Green and the Creation of a Planning Rationale: The Formation of Greater New York City, 1865–1890," *Urbanism Past and Present* 8 (1979): 32–41.

35. Green's 1868 report to the Central Park Commission is reprinted in Foord, *Life and Public Services of Andrew Haswell Green*, pp. 279–310; the quote is on p. 289.

36. Mazaraki, "Public Career of Andrew Haswell Green," p. 112.

37. Ibid., p. 96; Goldman, *Building New York's Sewers*, pp. 129–135. See also Kaplan, "Andrew H. Green and the Creation of a Planning Rationale," p. 34.

38. Alexander B. Callow Jr., *The Tweed Ring* (New York: Oxford University Press, 1966), pp. 224–228.

39. Burrows and Wallace, *Gotham*, pp. 1008–1012, 1027–1028; Callow, *Tweed Ring*, chs. 17–18 (the quote about Hall is on p. 286). The best account of the fall of the Tweed Ring is provided by Leo Hershkowitz, *Tweed's New York: Another Look* (Garden City, NY: Anchor Press, 1977), chs. 19–30.

40. Burrows and Wallace, *Gotham*, pp. 1027–1028, 1010; Mazaraki, "Public Career of Andrew Haswell Green," pp. 195–211; Seymour J. Mandelbaum, *Boss Tweed's New York* (New York: John Wiley and Sons, 1965), chs. 9–11.

41. The traditional explanation, given, for instance, by Callow, is that infrastructure projects were used simply as the basis for padded contracts through which members of the "ring" and their associates could make money. A slight variation on this theme has been offered by Mandelbaum, who has argued that the infrastructure projects and the padded contracts were both a necessary price paid by Tweed and his associates to bring some semblance of political order to the fragmented city. A more radical departure from the traditional explanation has been offered by Leo Hershkowitz, who contends that infrastructural development stemmed from Tweed's genuine concern for the health and welfare of the city, and that Tweed was personally a very minor player in the "ring." Callow, *Tweed Ring*, ch. 11; Mandelbaum, *Boss Tweed's New York*, chs. 6–7; Hershkowitz, *Tweed's New York*, pp. xiii–xx.

42. Moehring, *Public Works*, p. 313; this difference is statistically significant at $p \leq .10$.

43. Mandelbaum, *Boss Tweed's New York*, p. 70; Moehring, *Public Works*, p. 315.

44. Goldman, *Building New York's Sewers*, pp. 152, 169–170.

45. Richard Stone, "The Annexation of the Bronx, 1874," *Bronx County Historical Society Journal* 6 (January 1969): 1–24.

46. "Equalization of Assessments," *Yonkers Examiner*, January 7, 1858; Stone, "Annexation of the Bronx," pp. 1, 5, 16; Edward K. Spann, *The New Metropolis: New York City, 1840–1857* (New York: Columbia University Press, 1981), p. 191. Population figures for Yonkers come from Charles Elmer Allison, *The History of Yonkers, Westchester County, New York* (1896; reprint, Harrison, NY: Harbor Hill Books, 1984), p. 265, and "Yonkers in the U.S.A.," *Yonkers Historical Bulletin* 2 (April 1954): 5.

47. Arnold L. Steigman, "Mayor-Council Government: Yonkers, New York, 1908–1939—A Study of 'Failure and Abandonment,'" 3 vols., vol. 1 (Ph.D. diss., New York University, 1967), pp. 14–16, 19–21; Arnold L. Steigman, "The Emergence of Executive Power in the Government of Yonkers: A Political-Administrative History Documenting the Period 1853–1908" (M.P.A. thesis, Baruch College, City University of New York, 1954), pp. 20–22.

48. "Yonkers by a New Yorker," article from the *Missouri Republican*, reprinted in the *Yonkers Examiner*, May 14, 1857.

49. "Westchester: Interesting Historical Reminiscences," *Yonkers Gazette*, November 13, 1869.

50. Spann, *New Metropolis*, p. 202.

51. Ibid. Spann is of course mistaken when he claims that Morrisania was annexed to New York City as part of the Greater New York consolidation in 1898.

52. See the classic arguments made by Zane L. Miller, *Boss Cox's Cincinnati: Urban Politics in the Progressive Era* (New York: Oxford University Press, 1968), and Sam B. Warner Jr., *Streetcar Suburbs: The Process of Growth in Boston, 1870–1900* (Cambridge, MA: Harvard University Press and MIT Press, 1962).

53. "Synopsis of the City Charter" and "The Proposed City Charter," *Statesman*, February 3, 1870; "The City Charter," *Yonkers Gazette*, January 22, 1870.

54. Discussion of incorporation received heavy coverage in the *Yonkers Gazette* from January 22 to February 26, 1870, and in the *Statesman* from January 13 to February 17, 1870. The quote noting that there was no use pressing the matter appeared in the *Gazette* on March 19, 1870. The *Statesman* noted on April 4, 1870, that in the recent town and county elections, more Republicans had been elected to office.

55. "Westchester County," *New York Times*, December 11, 1870, reprinted in Denis Tilden Lynch, *The Wild Seventies* (New York: D. Appleton-Century Co., 1941), pp. 90–91. At least some town residents were aware of the possibility of being annexed at this time. See, for instance, in the *Gazette*, a reprint from the *New York World* in the "Local News and Gossip" section, April 11, 1869, and a front-page article on the history of Westchester County that noted, "It is quite safe to predict that in a few years the lower end of Westchester county will be absorbed by the city" ("Westchester," *Yonkers Gazette*, November 13, 1869). In 1954 the *Yonkers Historical Bulletin* claimed that the incorporation of the city of Yonkers was a move "reportedly to prevent absorption by New York City" ("Yonkers and the U.S.A." p. 5). Stone makes a similar claim in "Annexation of the Bronx," p. 5.

56. "The Proposed Annexation of Westchester Towns," *New York Times*, December 28, 1870; "The Coming City," *Yonkers Gazette*, August 20, 1870. There had been an annexation bill presented in the previous legislative session, although, as the *Statesman* noted, "No action . . . was taken. The plan was not ripe" ("Are We Going to New York?" January 5, 1871, p. 4). Richard Stone ("Annexation of the Bronx," p. 3), who claims that "the first actual attempt in the Legislature at annexation came in 1869," appears to be referring to the 1871 bill, although he mentions only Morrisania, West Farms, and Mount Vernon as areas that were proposed to be annexed. Considering that Mount Vernon was only a village in the town of Eastchester at this time, such a proposed annexation would have made little sense.

57. Annexation received heavy coverage in the *Gazette* from December 10, 1870, to February 18, 1871, and in the *Statesman* from December 29, 1870 to February 16, 1871.

58. *Statesman*, January 5, 1871 ("Are We Going to New York?"), and January 26, 1872.

59. "Opposed to Annexation," *Yonkers Gazette*, December 17, 1870; *New York Daily Times* article reprinted in the *Gazette*, January 14, 1871; "Local News and Gossip—Westchester County," *Yonkers Gazette*, January 28, 1871. Stone claims that Morrisania was interested in being annexed to New York as early as 1864, but on the basis of questionable evidence ("Annexation of the Bronx," p. 2).

60. "Annexation Dead!" and "Now for a City Charter," *Yonkers Gazette*, February 11, 1871. The quote is from "The City of Yonkers," *Yonkers Gazette*, December 9, 1871. See also "Imperial New York," *Yonkers Gazette*, January 13, 1872. At least one version of the annexation bill may have included only Morrisania and West Farms, see "Annexation," *Yonkers Gazette*, December 2, 1871.

61. *Yonkers Gazette*, December 9, 1871 ("The City of Yonkers"), and March 9, 1872 ("City and County of Yonkers"); "The City of Yonkers," *Statesman*, March 21, 1872. For more on the incorporation, see the *Gazette*, March 9, April 13 and 27, May 11, and June 8 and 29, 1872; and the *Statesman*, March 21, May 30, and June 6, 1872. The southern border for the city was established as "the north line of Mt. St. Vincent" ("The City Charter," *Yonkers Gazette*, May 25, 1872). Apparently there was no referendum on the city charter within the village of Yonkers or the surrounding area that was to be included in the city, although there does appear to have been majority support among village residents. Steigman has claimed, for instance, that in regard to the city charter, "the whole village was in agreement . . . the villagers presented a united front on this matter and rallied behind their token leader, the village president, until victory was assured." Steigman also claims that residents in the southern section of the town were "given a choice as to whether they wished to join in the consolidation or remain outside of it" and did in fact register their disapproval of being included within the jurisdiction of the proposed city. "Emergence of Executive Power," pp. 26, 62–64.

62. "The Annexation of Kingsbridge," *Yonkers Gazette*, January 18, 1873. Spaulding's comment was also treated critically by the *Statesman* on January 23 ("Town of Kingsbridge") and January 30 ("Kingsbridge and Yonkers"), 1872. Spaulding owned a plot of land between the Hudson River and Kings Bridge Road in the Riverdale section of the town of Yonkers. See Frederick W. Beers, *Atlas of New York and Vicinity from Actual Surveys* (New York: Beers, Ellis and Soule, 1868), plates 20, 21.

63. Articles and other commentary on the annexation of Kingsbridge, Morrisania, and West Farms appeared in the *Gazette* on January 18, February 8 and 22, March 1, April 19, May 3 and 10, September 13, and November 1 and 8, 1873, and in the *Statesman* on January 1 and 16, February 6, April 24, and May 8, 1873.

64. Joel Schwartz, "The Evolution of the Suburbs," in Philip Dolce, ed., *Suburbia: The American Dream and Dilemma* (Garden City, NY: Anchor Press/Doubleday, 1976), p. 8 (paraphrased by Martin V. Melosi in "Environmental Crisis in the City: The Relationship between Industrialization and Urban Pollution," in Martin V. Melosi, ed., *Pollution and Reform in American Cities, 1870–1930* [Austin: University of Texas Press, 1980], pp. 16–17); Stone, "Annexation of the Bronx," p. 14; *Yonkers Gazette*, August 20, 1870 ("The Coming City"), and May 10, 1873 ("Annexation"); *Statesman*, April 24 ("Annexation to New York") and May 8 ("The City" and "Our Water Supply"), 1873.

65. "Annexation! Town Meeting," *Yonkers Gazette*, January 21, 1871.

66. "Minor Topics," *New York Times*, January 6, 1873.

67. David C. Hammack, *Power and Society: Greater New York at the Turn of the Century* (New York: Russell Sage Foundation, 1982), p. 187. For discussion of the costs and benefits of annexation, see *Yonkers Gazette*, February 19 and December 10 and 24, 1870, and January 7, 14, 21, and 28 and February 4, 1871; and *Statesman*, February 3 and 17, 1870, and January 5, 1871.

68. "Department of Public Parks and Yonkers," *Statesman*, December 12, 1872; Stone, "Annexation of the Bronx," pp. 1–2.

69. "Metropolitan Annexation and Incorporation," *New York Times*, July 20, 1869.

70. Paul Pierson, "Increasing Returns, Path Dependence, and the Study of Politics," *American Political Science Review* 94 (June 2000): 251–267.

71. The establishment of the road district was in part an effort to take road building out of the hands of a "Boulevard Ring" that controlled the town highway commission and had incurred an exorbitant amount of debt. Indeed, the final city charter "abolished" both "the power of commissioner of highways" and "the boulevard bills." Steigman, "Emergence of Executive Power," pp. 42–46; "The City Charter," *Yonkers Gazette*, May 25, 1872. On the Boulevard Ring, see also the letter to the editor from "Fair Play" in the *Yonkers Gazette*, February 2, 1870.

72. J. Thomas Scharf, *History of Westchester County, New York, Including Morrisania, King's Bridge, and West Farms, Which Have Recently Been Annexed to New York City*, vol. 2 (Philadelphia: L. E. Preston and Company, 1886), p. 25. On infrastructural development in Yonkers in the late 1850s, see the minutes of the board of trustees published in the *Yonkers Examiner*, 1857–1858.

73. For discussion of the waterworks, see *Yonkers Gazette*, October 9 and 23 and December 25, 1869; February 5, 1870; December 16, 23, and 30, 1871; and January 13, 1872; *Statesman*, September 2, 23, and 30, 1869; January 27 and February 3, 1870; December 21 and 28, 1871; and January 11, 1872. See also Allison, *The History of Yonkers, Westchester County, New York*, pp. 240–246; Scharf, *History of Westchester County*, vol. 2, p. 37; and Harry B. Evans, "The Early History of the Yonkers Water System," *Yonkers Historical Society Newsletter* 4 (Summer 1995): 1–2. At a taxpayers' meeting in December 1871, on the subject of supplying Yonkers with water, the president of the board of trustees, Robert P. Getty, noted that "the project of supplying this village with water is something which has been agitated for seventeen or eighteen years" (*Yonkers Gazette*, December 21, 1871). Unfortunately, there is no record that I have found of the previous agitations that Getty was referring to.

74. "The Water Bill," *Statesman*, January 16, 1873; common council minutes and letter to the editor from "Economist," *Yonkers Gazette*, March 8, 1873. There is no direct evidence to show that the residents of Yonkers wanted to incorporate as a city in order to facilitate the development of a water supply system. However, incorporation was generally desired in order for an area to better supply residents with services. The development of a water supply system would thus certainly be a likely reason for the residents of Yonkers to want to incorporate as a city. Only one letter to the editor from "L" in the *Gazette* made the connection

between incorporation and the water supply explicit: "I have two suggestions to make: First—To incorporate the city of Yonkers. Second—To incorporate the Yonkers Water Works Company, and then issue city . . . water loan bonds for building of the same. I shall be a liberal subscriber if the thing is put in this shape" (*Yonkers Gazette*, January 22, 1870).

75. As Steigman notes of Yonkers's government, "Most of the political figures were large property holders and business or professional men . . . these people had the greatest stake in community welfare as their own prosperity was linked to its, and so they were active in community affairs primarily to promote its growth and development." Steigman notes that there was apparently a second referendum on the Yonkers waterworks in November 1872 that "showed an affirmative vote." However, he provides no documentation of this referendum ("Emergence of Executive Power," pp. 26, 203–204). In my own examination of the *Yonkers Gazette* and *Statesman* for this period, I found nothing to suggest that there had been a second referendum.

76. Letty Anderson, "Fire and Disease: The Development of Water Supply Systems in New England, 1870–1900," in Joel A. Tarr and Gabriel Dupuy, eds., *Technology and the Rise of the Networked City in Europe and America* (Philadelphia: Temple University Press, 1988), pp. 141–142. Rosenberg discusses the 1873 epidemic in the conclusion of *Cholera Years*, pp. 226–234.

77. "The Water Question—A Comprehensive Scheme for a Good Supply," *Yonkers Gazette*, December 14, 1872.

78. Burrows and Wallace, *Gotham*, pp. 1228–1229.

79. "Our Water Supply," *Statesman*, May 8, 1873. See also *Statesman*, June 27 ("A Slow Commission") and July 4 ("The Water Commissioners"), 1873.

80. *Yonkers Gazette*, August 9 ("Our Water Supply") and 30 ("Our Water Supply—Prompt Action of the Commissioners"), 1873. See also *Statesman*, August 1 and 29, 1873.

81. "Systematic Sewerage," *Statesman*, December 2, 1869, p. 4; Minutes of the Board of Trustees, *Yonkers Gazette*, July 24, 1869; Minutes of the Board of Trustees, *Yonkers Gazette*, September 11, 1869.

82. "The Water Question—Surface or Subterranean Supply?" *Yonkers Gazette*, December 7, 1872, and *Statesman*, December 12, 1872. See also the letter to the editor from "Practical Engineer" in the *Gazette*, January 11, 1873.

83. *Yonkers Gazette*, August 30, 1873 ("Our Water Supply"); September 27, 1873 ("The Introduction of Water"); and December 21, 1871 ("Water: Taxpayers' Meeting").

84. "The Water Question," *Yonkers Gazette*, November 23 and December 7, 1872; "Report on Water Supply for the Village of Yonkers," *Statesman*, February 3, 1870; *Boyd's Westchester County Directory, 1887–88* (New York: W. Andrew Boyd, 1887), p. 264.

85. *Boyd's Westchester County Directory, 1887–88*, p. 258. The names of these contractors appear frequently in the announcements on bids for various projects, published in the *Gazette* as part of the board of trustees and common council

minutes. These contractors also ran advertisements in the *Statesman* in the late 1860s and early 1870s, indicating that they were located in Yonkers.
86. Burrows and Wallace, *Gotham*, p. 969.

Chapter 3. Greater New York and Later Annexation Schemes

1. David C. Hammack, *Power and Society: Greater New York at the Turn of the Century* (New York: Russell Sage Foundation, 1982), p. 192; Richard Stone, "The Annexation of the Bronx, 1874," *Bronx County Historical Society Journal* 6 (January 1969): 18; J. Thomas Scharf, *History of Westchester County, New York, Including Morrisania, King's Bridge, and West Farms, Which Have Recently Been Annexed to New York City*, vol. 1 (Philadelphia: L. E. Preston and Company, 1886), p. 761. New York City began to provide water from the Bronx and Bryam Rivers to the annexed territories in 1885. Nelson M. Blake, *Water for the Cities: A History of the Urban Water Supply Problem in the United States* (Syracuse, NY: Syracuse University Press, 1956), p. 277.
2. Charles H. Weidner, *Water for a City: A History of New York City's Problem from the Beginning to the Delaware River System* (New Brunswick, NJ: Rutgers University Press, 1974), pp. 70–77.
3. Hammack, *Power and Society*, pp. 192–196.
4. Ibid.; "New-York's Place in Danger," *New York Times*, November 4, 1894, p. 2. This article notes that "The Greater New-York will . . . include two cities and fifteen towns." Of these locales, Jamaica Bay is listed under both Kings and Queens Counties, with different square mileage and population figures for each listing. Albert E. Henschel, *Municipal Consolidation: Historical Sketch of the Greater New York* (n.p., 1895), p. 13 (New York Public Library). For indications of earlier movements toward consolidation, see Jeffrey A. Kroessler, "Building Queens: The Urbanization of New York's Largest Borough" (Ph.D. diss., City University of New York, 1991), pp. 232–233.
5. Hammack, *Power and Society*, p. 204. On resistance to the Consolidation Inquiry Commission, see p. 196; on the meaning of the referendum vote, see also "The Question of Annexation," *Mount Vernon Daily Argus*, September 26, 1894, p. 2 (article reprinted from the *New York Sun*), and also the *Brooklyn Daily Eagle*, October 30, 1894, reprinted in Harold Coffin Syrett, *The City of Brooklyn, 1865–1898: A Political History* (1944; reprint, New York: AMS Press, 1968), p. 255.
6. Henschel, *Municipal Consolidation*, p. 15. On the geographic distribution of support for consolidation as expressed in the referendum, the *Brooklyn Daily Eagle* commented, "By a majority what is meant? . . . Conceivably if every man in Brooklyn voted against consolidation and every man in New York voted for it, it would be carried by two to one. There are twice as many voters in New York as in Brooklyn" ("Consolidation or Not?" September 2, 1894, p. 6).
7. Hammack, *Power and Society*, p. 206n88; Hammack incorrectly identifies Mount Vernon as a town. See also Henschel, *Municipal Consolidation*, pp. 15–16.

8. Alfred M. Franko, *Your Mount Vernon Board of Water Supply: An Historical Account of a Community's Struggle for a Pure Water Supply with a Description of the Present System* (Mount Vernon, NY: Mount Vernon Board of Water Supply, 1959), p. 15.

9. Mount Vernon was divided into five wards, each of which was broken down into one to three districts, making a total of ten districts. Every district voted against consolidation by majorities ranging from 59 to 82 percent except for the Second District of the Second Ward, which voted for consolidation by a majority of 65 percent. Why the residents of this district voted for consolidation is unclear. The residents of the First District of the Second Ward voted against consolidation by a majority of 68 percent. The Second Ward comprised the heart of Mount Vernon's downtown district and bordered New York City. Possibly there was a more unequal distribution of wealth in this ward, which could account for the disparate vote, or possibly those residents who lived immediately across the border from New York City voted in favor of consolidation. If we exclude the vote of the residents of the Second District of the Second Ward, the majority voting against consolidation in Mount Vernon jumps to 66 percent. For the election returns in 1892, see Franko, *Your Mount Vernon Board of Water Supply*, p. 15, and for 1894, see the *Mount Vernon Daily Argus*, November 7, 1894, p. 1; for the wards in Mount Vernon, see Joseph R. Bien, *Atlas of Westchester County, New York* (New York: Julius Bien and Company, 1893), plates 4, 9–12.

10. Bien, *Atlas of Westchester County*, plates 4, 9–12.

11. Franko, *Your Mount Vernon Board of Water Supply*, pp. 8–14; "Consolidation— The New York and Mount Vernon Water Company Merged," *Mount Vernon Daily Argus*, June 28, 1892, p. 2. The reasons behind this consolidation are largely lost to history, but Franko speculates that the cause was "corporate high jinks . . . and sleight of hand shuffling of directorships" (p. 14). Accounts of the New York City Suburban Water Company are contradictory. By Franko's account, the New York and Mount Vernon Water Company was "suddenly superseded" by the New York City Suburban Water Company in 1891 (p. 14). However, the *Daily Argus* reported in 1894 that "the New York City Suburban Water Company was incorporated in June, 1892 . . . to consolidate the Mount Vernon Water Company and the New York and Mount Vernon Water Company, two established concerns" ("Our Water Company in Receiver's Hands," October 9, 1894, p. 1).

12. Franko, *Your Mount Vernon Board of Water Supply*, p. 12. According to Franko, the water company "had 1,700 subscribers (8,500 users)" in 1890 (p. 13). Franko makes mention only of "a neighboring water company." That it was the New Rochelle Water Company that was taking water upstream from Mount Vernon's intake is suggested in "Mr. Wood in Behalf of Annexation," *Mount Vernon Daily Argus*, November 5, 1894, p. 3.

13. Franko, *Your Mount Vernon Board of Water Supply*, pp. 15–16.

14. *Mount Vernon Daily Argus*, June 16, 1892 ("City Government Inaugurated"), and November 17, 1894 ("Extra: Our Sewerage System Outlet Assailed"). Jared Sandford, the village president, served as the city's interim mayor until June 1892. "Honorable Jared Sandford," *Mount Vernon Centennial Journal, 1892–1992* (Mount Vernon, NY: Mount Vernon City Centennial Committee,

1992). Mount Vernon's Republican newspaper, the *Mount Vernon Record*, claimed that under Democratic rule, only one street in Mount Vernon had been macadamized by 1892 ("An Admirable Statement," May 14, 1897, p. 1). In 1892, however, the *Daily Argus* reported that "with the creation of macadamized streets comes the demand for bicycles. Our local dealers report a good trade" ("Local News," May 2, 1892). On street assessments, see the *Daily Argus*, June 15, 1892, p. 2; on street lighting, see "The Gas Question and Its History," *Daily Argus*, September 20, 1894.

15. The water company was put into receivership in either September or October 1894. *Mount Vernon Daily Argus*, October 27 ("A Successful Annexation Meeting"), November 17 ("Extra: Our Sewerage System Outlet Assailed"), and November 5 ("Mr. Wood in Behalf of Annexation," p. 3), 1894; Franko, *Your Mount Vernon Board of Water Supply*, p. 17. Franko claims that the company's financial problems were due to its investments in the waterworks. For coverage of the water company being put into receivership, see the *Daily Argus*, October 9, 11, and 26 and November 1, 1894.

16. "Extra: Our Sewerage System Outlet Assailed," *Mount Vernon Daily Argus*, November 17, 1894.

17. By the early twentieth century Wood had changed his mind and "vigorously opposed a municipally owned water system and had made several trips to Albany to urge defeat of the Fiske and Brush sponsored bills permitting Mount Vernon to purchase the Inter-Urban" (Franko, *Your Mount Vernon Board of Water Supply*, p. 21).

18. "Injunction against the Water Company," *Mount Vernon Daily Argus*, October 11, 1894, p. 1.

19. Ibid. See also "The Gas Contract," *Mount Vernon Daily Argus*, October 13, 1894, p. 2.

20. The area annexed to New York City in 1874 was actually used by both annexationists and antiannexationists in Mount Vernon to argue their different points. For the antiannexationist argument, see "Annexation: A Drive through the Annexed District," *Mount Vernon Daily Argus*, September 26, 1894, p. 1; Judge Isaac N. Mills, though an antiannexationist, presented the annexationist argument concerning lower Westchester County, "Against Annexation!" *Mount Vernon Daily Argus*, October 6, 1894, p. 1.

21. "Against Annexation!" *Mount Vernon Daily Argus*, October 6, 1894, p. 1.

22. Blake, *Water for the Cities*, pp. 77, 267.

23. "City Government Inaugurated," *Mount Vernon Daily Argus*, June 16, 1892, p. 1.

24. *Manual of American Water-works, 1890–91* (New York: Engineering News Publishing Company, 1892), p. xxxii.

25. Mount Vernon in fact acquired a municipal water supply in 1922, when its population had more than doubled from what it was in the nineteenth century (Franko, *Your Mount Vernon Board of Water Supply*, pp. 30–34).

26. "More Consolidation Arguments," *Brooklyn Daily Eagle*, November 3, 1894; Edwin G. Burrows and Mike Wallace, *Gotham: A History of New York City to 1898* (New York: Oxford University Press, 1999), pp. 1192–1193.

27. Kroessler, "Building Queens," p. 240.

28. Advertisement for the Flushing and North Side Railroad in F. W. Beers, *Atlas of Long Island, New York* (New York: Beers, Comstock and Cline, 1873), pp. 18–19.

29. The Flushing Village Association was "organized in 1886 and incorporated in 1900." Henry D. Waller, *History of the Town of Flushing* (1899; reprint, Flushing, NY: J. H. Ridenour, 1975), p. 218; August Kupka, *History of Flushing, N.Y.: Its Development from a Colonial Village to a Community in Greater New York* (Flushing, NY: Flushing Historical Society, 1949), pt. 2; *History of Queens County* (New York: W. W. Munsell and Co., 1882), p. 109. The number of gas streetlights in the village increased from 18 to 101 between 1860 and 1880. Electric streetlights were introduced in 1896.

30. Waller, *History of the Town of Flushing*, p. 212.

31. The name "Long Island City" had been around for about two decades prior to the actual city. See "Origin of 'Long Island City,'" *Long Island City Star*, May 14, 1870, in Vincent F. Seyfried, *Index to First Volume, Long Island City Star and Transcript of News Articles, 1864–1871* (n.p., n.d.), p. 58.

32. *History of Queens County*, p. 257.

33. Kroessler, "Building Queens," pp. 249, 268.

34. Vincent F. Seyfried, *300 Years of Long Island City, 1630–1930* (n.p., 1984), pp. 31, 75–95.

35. "Incorporation Meeting," *Long Island City Star*, January 8, 1869, quoted in Seyfried, *300 Years of Long Island City*, p. 100; Seyfried, *300 Years of Long Island City*, p. 101; *Long Island City Star*, January 8, 1869; "Public Ad," *Long Island City Star*, April 1, 1870; "The Day of Jubilee!" *Long Island City Star*, May 6, 1870. In *300 Years of Long Island City* (pp. 75, 93–102), Seyfried contends that Astoria residents opposed the city charter because their village "already had good streets, good municipal services, an efficient and responsive village government and a low tax rate" (p. 100). Yet Astoria residents may have actually expected a lower tax rate once they were independent of Newtown. See "Astoria," *Long Island City Star*, February 26, 1869, in Seyfried, *Index to First Volume*, p. 25. The *New York Times* reported cryptically of Long Island City that "the great opposition to the incorporation of the new city arises from a number of Brooklyn politicians, who look upon the 'handful of helpless' villages as rightfully belonging to them" ("Long Island City—Its Growth and Prospects," May 8, 1870, p. 6).

36. Seyfried, *300 Years of Long Island City*, pp. 103–107.

37. The waterworks were put into operation in 1875, and by 1877 fifteen miles of water main had been laid. Ibid., p. 109; see also "John Quinn," *Long Island City Weekly Star*, December 30, 1894, in Vincent F. Seyfried, *Long Island City Star, Transcript of News Articles, 1894* (n.p., n.d.), p. 374.

38. *History of Queens County*, p. 283; *Long Island City Weekly Star*, March 13, 1891 ("The City Debt"), and August 18, 1893 ("Our Water Supply"), in Seyfried, *Long Island City Star, Transcript of News Articles, 1891*, pp. 23–25, and *1893*, pp. 304–305. The Steinway waterworks became the most extensive water

supply system in Queens County and remained so well into the twentieth century (Vincent F. Seyfried, personal communication, February 2000).

39. Seyfried, *300 Years of Long Island City*, pp. 120–125.

40. Ibid., pp. 124–125; *Long Island City Star*, December 25, 1891 ("Electric Contract"), and February 17, 1893 ("Long Island City Water Supply"); see also December 14, 1894 ("City Fathers Decide in Favor of Electric Lights"), in Seyfried, *Long Island City Star, Transcript of News Articles, 1891*, p. 146; *1893*, pp. 228–229; *1894*, p. 377.

41. Seyfried, *300 Years of Long Island City*, pp. 114, 124–125, 133; "The City Debt," *Long Island City Weekly Star*, March 13, 1891, in Seyfried, *Long Island City Star, Transcript of News Articles, 1891*, pp. 24–25.

42. *The City of Brooklyn* (New York: J. H. and C. M. Goodsell, 1871), pp. 10, 14–17. After Chicago increased its population by annexing outlying territory in 1889, Brooklyn dropped to being the fourth-largest city in the country. U.S. Census Office, *Abstract of the Eleventh Census*, 2nd ed. (Washington, DC: Government Printing Office, 1896), pp. 34–37.

43. According to Kroessler, "In both Kings and Queens, the most urbanized sections and the areas closest to Manhattan voted in favor of consolidation, while the sparsely settled towns on the periphery generally opposed the idea" ("Building Queens," p. 245). While this is true for Queens County, the ten wards farthest away from New York in Brooklyn provided the bulk of support for consolidation. Hammack, *Power and Society*, p. 208; "New-York's Place in Danger," *New York Times*, November 4, 1894, p. 2; "A Movement against Consolidation under Way," *Brooklyn Daily Eagle*, November 12, 1894, p. 10. On the consolidation vote in the outlying towns, see also the *Brooklyn Daily Eagle*, November 13 ("Loyal Citizens' League") and November 14 ("Consolidation Arguments"), 1894. The town of Flatlands was annexed in December 1895, thus making the city of Brooklyn coterminous with Kings County ("Consolidation or Not?" *Brooklyn Daily Eagle*, September 2, 1894, p. 6). There had also been an attempt to annex Flatlands, New Lots, Flatbush, Gravesend, and New Utrecht to Brooklyn in 1873. See Marc Linder and Lawrence S. Zacharias, *Of Cabbages and Kings County: Agriculture and the Formation of Modern Brooklyn* (Iowa City: University of Iowa Press, 1999), ch. 7.

44. "Although it is difficult to ascertain the extent of the daily migration, it would not be an exaggeration to assume that by ten o'clock on any week day Brooklyn had lost one-tenth of its citizens to the larger metropolis." Syrett, *City of Brooklyn*, p. 11. An earlier account contends that "Brooklyn held the anomalous position of out-numbering, at night, its day population by tens of thousands." Henry R. Stiles, *A History of the City of Brooklyn*, vol. 2 (Brooklyn, NY: Published by subscription, 1867–1870), pp. 420–421.

45. Syrett, *City of Brooklyn*, pp. 19–20.

46. "Greater New York Is Brooklyn," *Brooklyn Daily Eagle*, March 29, 1894, p. 6.

47. Syrett, *City of Brooklyn*, p. 12.

48. Stiles, *History of the City of Brooklyn*, vol. 2, pp. 420–421.

49. *Souvenir of Brooklyn: Descriptive, Historical, and Statistical Review* (Brooklyn, NY: Anderson and Gillette, 1890), p. 7; "Loyal Citizens' League," *Brooklyn Daily*

Eagle, November 13, 1894, p. 7. On industry in Brooklyn, see also Syrett, *City of Brooklyn*, pp. 13–18, 140, and Stiles, *History of the City of Brooklyn*, vol. 3, p. 586.

50. Stiles, *History of the City of Brooklyn*, vol. 2, pp. 208, 211, 262, 279, 283 (quotes on pp. 419 and 422).

51. "The Brooklyn Water Works," *New York Herald*, June 9, 1857.

52. Stiles, *History of the City of Brooklyn*, vol. 3, pp. 596–597. The account in the *Herald* lists the ponds used by the Brooklyn waterworks, although different ponds are named in *History of Queens County*, p. 151, and in William P. Sander, "The Early Uses of Water Power on Long Island," *Nassau County Historical Journal* 15 (1952): 62–73; see also William E. McCauley, "A History of the Use and Control of the Ground Waters of Long Island," *Nassau County Historical Journal* 21 (Spring 1960): 1–12. Joel A. Tarr has claimed that Brooklyn, Chicago, and Jersey City were the major American cities to have built comprehensive sewerage systems; see Joel A. Tarr, "Sewerage and the Development of the Networked City in the United States, 1850–1930," in Joel A. Tarr and Gabriel Dupuy, eds., *Technology and the Rise of the Networked City in Europe and America* (Philadelphia: Temple University Press, 1988), p. 164.

53. Stiles, *History of the City of Brooklyn*, vol. 2, p. 430; vol. 3, p. 589n2. Even before its incorporation as a city, the residents of Brooklyn were discussing the possibility of forming a water company to supply residents with water from "springs on the East River shore" (vol. 2, p. 236).

54. At least one member of Brooklyn's common council, John A. Dayton, had a vested interest in the Long Island Water Company. As chairman of the council's water committee, Dayton was largely responsible for the 1854 water supply plan, which would have required the city to purchase the property of the Long Island Water Company. Ibid., vol. 3, p. 589n2.

55. Ibid.; Joanne Abel Goldman, *Building New York's Sewers: Developing Mechanisms of Urban Management* (West Lafayette, IN: Purdue University Press, 1997), p. 111.

56. *City of Brooklyn*, p. 26; "Senator Reynolds on Consolidation," *Brooklyn Daily Eagle*, September 28, 1894, p. 9. In regard to Brooklyn's tax base, Reynolds noted that "Brooklyn is a city of homes and will undoubtedly remain so, consequently its real estate valuations will increase very slowly. If such is the fact, it will be impossible to lower the tax rate to any appreciable extent."

57. *Brooklyn Daily Eagle*, March 6, 1894 ("Met with Slight Favor: Young Republicans Not Wildly Desirous for Consolidation," p. 10); see also March 17, 1894 ("The Greater New York," p. 5), and September 2, 1894 ("Consolidation or Not?" p. 6).

58. "Senator Reynolds on Consolidation," *Brooklyn Daily Eagle*, September 28, 1894, p. 9; Syrett, *City of Brooklyn*, pp. 25, 30–31, 46. While Syrett is highly critical of the special commissions, he does credit them with having done some good work in the city on pp. 140–141.

59. Syrett, *City of Brooklyn*, pp. 50, 89, 91–94; see also pp. 64, 118.

60. "Senator Reynolds on Consolidation," *Brooklyn Daily Eagle*, September 28, 1894, p. 9; see also Hammack, *Power and Society*, pp. 198–199; *Brooklyn Daily Eagle*, September 28 ("General John B. Woodward's Views," p. 7) and

October 30 ("Twelve Reasons That Are Twelve Frauds," p. 6), 1894; Syrett, *City of Brooklyn*, pp. 230, 254–255 (emphasis in original).

61. Burrows and Wallace, *Gotham*, p. 1228. Cf. Eugene P. Moehring, "Space, Economic Growth, and the Public Works Revolution in New York," in *Infrastructure and Urban Growth in the Nineteenth Century* (Chicago: Public Works Historical Society, 1985), pp. 45–51.

62. Hammack, *Power and Society*, p. 206; George W. Bromley and Walter S. Bromley, *Atlas of the City of Brooklyn, New York* (Philadelphia: G. W. Bromley and Co., 1893), plates 9–13, 37–43; Syrett, *City of Brooklyn*, p. 191; see also "A Water Famine Is Possible," *Brooklyn Daily Eagle*, August 21, 1894, p. 10.

63. "Near the Danger Line," *Brooklyn Daily Eagle*, May 22, 1894; see also "Radical Notions," *Brooklyn Daily Eagle*, June 24, 1894, p. 15.

64. *Brooklyn Daily Eagle*, March 17 ("We Are Short of Water"), March 18 ("As to Increased Water Supply"), June 24 ("Radical Notions"), June 27 ("The Park Water Supply"), June 28 ("Are We Drinking Impure Water?"), and June 29 ("The Increase in Water Consumption"), 1894.

65. *Brooklyn Daily Eagle*, May 18 ("Two Millions Needed," p. 5), May 28 ("Water Extension Plan," p. 12), July 2 ("Our Scant Supply of Water," p. 12), July 16 ("Aldermen Holding Out," p. 10), July 17 ("Aldermen and Increased Water Supply," p. 4, and "The Aldermen Dodged," p. 5), and July 19 ("The Cat out of the Bag," p. 1), 1894.

66. *Brooklyn Daily Eagle*, July 9 ("Jahn Refused to Sign," p. 12), July 10 ("Halting Aldermen," p. 6, and "Lots of Wind, No Water," p. 7), and July 17 ("Aldermen and Increased Water Supply," p. 4), 1894; Syrett, *City of Brooklyn*, pp. 194–197.

67. Syrett, *City of Brooklyn*, pp. 197–224.

68. *Brooklyn Daily Eagle*, October 31, 1894, quoted in Syrett, *City of Brooklyn*, p. 256; "Greater New York," *Brooklyn Daily Eagle*, January 23, 1894, p. 9.

69. *Brooklyn Daily Eagle*, June 26 ("The Water Supply," p. 6), July 7 ("Let the Aldermen Take the Large View of the Water Question," p. 4), July 23 ("Adopted the Water Plan," p. 10), and July 24 ("Signed by the Mayor," p. 1), 1894; see also May 18 ("As to Increased Water Supply," p. 4), June 8 (letter to the editor from J. H. Griffith, p. 8), and June 15 (letter to the editor from "Independent," p. 12), 1894. Despite these and other articles in the *Eagle*, Kroessler makes the highly contestable claim that "the water question scarcely entered into the debate over consolidation, dominated as it was by issues of taxation, corruption, home rule, and party politics" ("Building Queens," p. 264).

70. *Brooklyn Daily Eagle*, July 7 ("Money for More Water," p. 5) and March 17 ("The Greater New York," p. 5), 1894; Blake, *Water for the Cities*, p. 277. On the cost of the New Croton Aqueduct, see Weidner, *Water for a City*, pp. 68–69.

71. "Senator Reynolds on Consolidation," *Brooklyn Daily Eagle*, September 28, 1894, p. 9.

72. Hammack, *Power and Society*, pp. 214–216, 223.

73. Ibid., pp. 221–222; Barry J. Kaplan, "Metropolitics, Administrative Reform, and Political Theory: The Greater New York City Charter of 1897," *Journal of*

Urban History 9 (February 1983): 186. Wurster, Schieren's fire commissioner, was elected mayor of Brooklyn in 1896. Mayor Schieren declined to run again after his election in 1894 (Syrett, *City of Brooklyn*, p. 231).

74. "Profiting by Consolidation," *Newtown Register*, July 15, 1897, in Vincent F. Seyfried, *Newtown Register, Transcript of News Articles, 1897*, p. 119.

75. On infrastructural development and the 1897 charter, see Hammack, *Power and Society*, pp. 225–229, and Kaplan, "Metropolitics, Administrative Reform, and Political Theory," pp. 167, 177, 181.

76. For a discussion of "Dillon's Law," see Gerald E. Frug, *City Making: Building Communities without Building Walls* (Princeton, NJ: Princeton University Press, 1999), pp. 45–51.

77. "Board of Trade," *Mount Vernon Record*, March 26 and April 9, 1897.

78. "The Honorable Jared Sandford," *Mount Vernon Centennial Journal, 1892–1992* (Mount Vernon, NY: Mount Vernon City Centennial Committee, 1992); "Annexationists in Conference," *Mount Vernon Daily Argus*, December 29, 1897; "Annexation," *Mount Vernon Record*, January 28 and February 11 and 18, 1898.

79. *Mount Vernon Daily Argus*, January 6 ("Bill to Annex Yonkers") and February 3 (letter to the editor from George T. Lovell), 1898; "Board of Trade," *Mount Vernon Record*, November 19, 1897, p. 1; Gustavus Myers, *The History of Tammany Hall*, 2nd ed. (1917; reprint, New York: Dover Publications, 1971), p. 284. Myers notes that Van Wyck "was in no sense the organization's candidate, but represented merely Mr. Croker's choice and dictation" (p. 282). The *Mount Vernon Record* gave conflicting reports as to the opinions of Tammany Hall regarding the annexation of Mount Vernon to New York, reporting in January 1898 that "it is rumored that King Croker is opposed to annexation. He believes that New York has quite enough to attend to now without bothering with Mount Vernon" ("Annexation," January 21, 1898). In February, however, the *Record* reported that "the Tammany Democracy favor annexation" ("Annexation," February 18, 1898).

80. "An Admirable Statement," *Mount Vernon Record*, May 14, 1898.

81. Letter to the editor from George T. Lovell, *Mount Vernon Daily Argus*, January 14, 1898.

82. "Board of Trade," *Mount Vernon Record*, January 14, 1898.

83. Franko, *Your Mount Vernon Board of Water Supply*, pp. 19–20; "The Water Supply Question Again," *Mount Vernon Daily Argus*, July 7, 1896; "Extra: Mount Vernon's Ample Water Supply," *Mount Vernon Daily Argus*, December 10, 1897; *Mount Vernon Record*, March 19 ("Aldermen in Session") and August 27 ("The Water Question"), 1897. For a critical response to the purchase of the Mamaroneck Water Company, see "The Water Company," *Mount Vernon Record*, September 3, 1897, p. 4; on a possible competing water company in Mount Vernon, see the *Mount Vernon Record*, June 11 ("Interesting Meeting") and June 18 (letter to the editor from "Citizen," p. 6), 1897.

84. *Mount Vernon Record*, March 26 ("Hutchinson Valley Sewer") and April 2 ("Sewage Questions"), 1897; "Common Council," *Mount Vernon Daily Argus*, February 2, 1898.

85. *Mount Vernon Record*, April 2 ("Consistency on the Sewer Question"), April 9 ("The Great Question" and "Mass Meeting to Oppose the Sewer"), and April 16 ("Some Sewer Facts"), 1897.

86. *Mount Vernon Record*, April 16 ("The Bill Passed"), April 23 ("The Sewer Bill" and "The Sewer Hearing"), April 30 ("The Bill Not Approved" and "The Hearing before the Common Council"), and September 3 ("The Sewer"), 1897.

87. *Mount Vernon Record*, February 19 ("The Sewer Problem" and "Those Sewer Bills"), March 12 ("The Sewers"), April 9 ("Joseph S. Wood, Esq., Hon. Isaac N. Mills"), and April 23 ("The Sewer Hearing"), 1897.

88. The estimated cost of the sewer outlet proposed by Wood ranged between $125,000 and $297,000, in contrast to the final estimated cost to Mount Vernon of $445,000 for the sewerage plan proposed in the sewer bill. *Mount Vernon Record*, April 16 ("Unfair and Untrue" and "Some Sewer Facts"), July 2 ("The Sewer Question Again"), September 3 ("The Sewer"), September 10 ("The Sewer Question"), and December 17 ("Common Council"), 1897; "A Feasible Sewer Outlet Proposed," *Mount Vernon Daily Argus*, December 17, 1897. On Louis Haffen (whom the *Record* incorrectly refers to as "Commissioner Heffen" in "The Sewer Question Again"), see Gary Hermalyn, "The Bronx at the Turn of the Century," *Bronx County Historical Journal* 26 (Fall 1989): 98.

89. "Mount Vernon: Vale, 1897; Hail 1898," *Mount Vernon Daily Argus*, January 3, 1898. For a similar statement in the *Mount Vernon Record*, see "Greater Mount Vernon," January 14, 1898.

90. *Mount Vernon Daily Argus*, June 1 ("A Busy Man Is H. P. McTague"), June 6 ("A Contractor with a Proud Record"), and June 16 ("Sketches of Our City Offi-cers"), 1892; *Mount Vernon Record*, April 16 ("Some Sewer Facts"), May 7 ("De-partment of Public Works"), July 16 ("At Last" and "What Shall Be Done about It?"), and July 30 ("Danger Ahead" and "Another Good Officer Gone"), 1897.

91. *Turner's Mount Vernon City Directory, Embracing the Residents of Pelham, for the Years 1897–98* (Port Chester, NY: Turner and Co. Publishers, 1897), p. 268.

92. *Mount Vernon Record*, April 16 ("Mr. Fairchild's Letter" and "Some Sewer Facts") and April 23 ("Unfair and Untrue"), 1897.

93. *Mount Vernon Record*, August 20 ("For Mt. Vernon") and November 12 ("Favor Factories"), 1897. See also "Factories, Yes or No," *Mount Vernon Daily Argus*, February 12, 1898.

94. "The Board of Trade," *Mount Vernon Record*, July 8 and 15, 1898.

95. "Town of Pelham: Annexation," *Pelham Record* (supplement to the *Mount Vernon Record*), August 26, 1898. See also "Eulogized Our City," *Mount Vernon Record*, February 12, 1897. On the consolidation of Mount Vernon and Yonkers, see "A Question of Annexation," *Yonkers Gazette*, February 9, 1889. Another report includes Bronxville in Greater Mount Vernon; see "Greater Mount Vernon," *Mount Vernon Record*, January 14, 1898.

96. See, for instance, the advertisements in the *Pelham Record* on May 21 and 28, 1897. For information on infrastructural development in all three villages in Pelham, see the *Pelham Record*, July 9 ("Work on the Sewers") and August 6

("Improvements Wanted"), 1897; April 29 ("Worth Considering"), 1898; and Lockwood Barr, *Ancient Town of Pelham, Westchester County, State of New York* (Richmond, VA: Dietz Press, 1947), pp. 113, 128, 130, 139–141. On the negative reaction of Mount Vernon to the construction of sewers in Pelham Manor, see "Another Outrage," *Mount Vernon Record*, July 16, 1897.

97. "The Oneness of Pelham," *Pelham Record*, October 1, 1897.

98. Barr, *Ancient Town of Pelham*, pp. 139–140; "Village Fathers," *Pelham Record*, August 13, 1897. The 1897–98 edition of *Turner's Mount Vernon City Directory*, which included Pelham, listed only five civil engineers for both Mount Vernon and Pelham, all of whom were located in Mount Vernon (see note 91). Fairchild is identified as the president of the Pelham Heights Company in advertisements that ran weekly in the *Pelham Record;* see, for instance, February 25, 1898.

99. At the monthly meeting of the North Pelham Village Board of Trustees, "Mr. Hoey, representing the Naphtha Light Co., of New York, was . . . present, and was ready to renew the contract of lighting by the present system for another year, if the Board desired" ("Village Fathers," *Pelham Record*, August 13, 1897). However, at the trustees' meeting the following month, "The Eastchester Gas Company, Pelham Gas Light Company, and the N.Y. and N.J. Globe Gas Co., each had representatives present to submit bids" ("Street Lighting," *Pelham Record*, September 10, 1897). In saying that the New York and New Jersey Globe Gas-light Company supplied North Pelham with naphtha in 1897, I am assuming that this was the company that the *Pelham Record* meant when it made reference to the "Naphtha Light Company." The New York and New Jersey Globe Gas-light Company had been supplying New York City with naphtha since the late 1870s; see New York City Department of Public Works, *Report for the Quarter Ending December 31, 1882.*

100. Clinton Hood, *722 Miles: The Building of the Subways and How They Transformed New York* (Baltimore: Johns Hopkins University Press, 1993), pp. 48–55.

101. *Pelham Record*, July 8 ("Bids Opened") and July 15 ("Village Fathers" and "Highway Improvements"), 1898; "Common Council," *Mount Vernon Record*, August 19, 1898.

102. *Mount Vernon Daily Argus*, June 1 ("A Busy Man Is H. P. McTague") and June 6 ("A Contractor with a Proud Record"), 1892; *Mount Vernon Record*, May 7 ("Department of Public Works"), July 16 ("What Shall Be Done about It?"), and July 30 ("Danger Ahead"), 1897.

103. Victor Mays, *Pathway to a Village: A History of Bronxville* (Bronxville, NY: Nebko Press, 1961), pp. 107–113, 120; Anita Inman Comstock, "1898: Bronxville's First Year," in *Bronxville: Views and Vignettes, 1898–1973* (Bronxville, NY: Bronxville Diamond Jubilee Committee, 1974), pp. 26–27; "Village Trustees Report to the Taxpayers of Bronxville," reprinted in Jean S. Bartlett, "The Bronxville Four," in *Bronxville: Views and Vignettes.*

104. Edward J. Smits, "The Creation of Nassau County," *Long Island Historical Journal* 1 (Spring 1989): 170–182; Kroessler, "Building Queens," pp. 252–265; M. H. Smith, *History of Garden City*, rev. ed. (Garden City, NY: Garden City Historical

Society, 1980), pp. 20–29, 61–69. See also Roger A. Wines, "A. T. Stewart and Garden City," *Nassau County Historical Journal* 19 (Winter 1958): 1–15.

105. Cf. Mary Corbin Sies, "The City Transformed: Nature, Technology, and the Suburban Ideal, 1877–1917," *Journal of Urban History* 14 (November 1987): 83–84.

106. Hammack, *Power and Society*, pp. 209–210.

107. The Barber Asphalt Company was founded in 1878; *Long Island City Weekly Star*, March 27, 1894, in Seyfried, *Long Island City Star, Transcript of News Articles, 1894*, pp. 340–341.

Chapter 4. Expansionist Jersey City and Its Discontents

1. "Consolidation—What Our Neighbors Think of It," *Evening Journal*, September 30, 1869 (excerpted from the *New York Evening Post*). The *Jersey Journal* was commonly known as the *Evening Journal* and is listed as such at the Jersey City Public Library. I will refer to it as the *Evening Journal* hereafter.

2. On the final vote and the actual consolidation, see Alexander McLean, *History of Jersey City, N.J.: A Record of Its Early Settlement and Corporate Progress* (Jersey City: Press of the Jersey City Printing Company, 1895), p. 79; and William H. Shaw, *History of Essex and Hudson Counties, New Jersey*, vol. 2 (Philadelphia: Everts and Peck, 1884), p. 1142.

3. Jane Jacobs, *The Economy of Cities* (New York: Vintage Books, 1970), p. 142. The three largest stockholders in the Jersey Company, Richard Varick, Jacob Radcliff, and Anthony Dey, were all prominent New York Federalists, and Alexander Hamilton himself drafted the company's charter. Radcliff served on the New York Supreme Court and as mayor of New York City from 1810 to 1811 and 1815 to 1818; Varick served as mayor of New York from 1789 to 1801; and Dey "was one of the most successful lawyers and largest owners of real estate in his day." J. Owen Grundy, *The History of Jersey City, 1609–1976* (Jersey City: W. E. Knight, 1976), p. 29 (Grundy rounds the number of lots in Jersey City to 1,000); William H. Richardson, *The Federalist Fathers and the Founding of Jersey City* (Jersey City: Historical Society of Hudson County, NJ, 1927), p. 6. Hermann Platt notes that Hamilton "saw the Jersey Company as a companion to the Society for the Establishment of Useful Manufactures, his earlier venture in Paterson." See Hermann Platt, "The Jersey City Water Rights Controversy, 1845–1850," *New Jersey History* 94 (Winter 1976): 141–142. See also McLean, *History of Jersey City*, pp. 21–24.

4. Quotes from McLean, *History of Jersey City*, pp. 27–28, 32–33. See also Daniel Van Winkle, *History of the Municipalities of Hudson County, New Jersey, 1630–1923* (New York: Lewis Historical Publishing Company, 1924), pp. 80–81; Richardson, *Federalist Fathers*, p. 35.

5. McLean, *History of Jersey City*, p. 34.

6. Ibid., pp. 36–39.

7. The conflict between New Jersey and New York over control of the Hudson River continued after 1834, but in Jersey City the initial treaty "lifted a cloud

which had prevented shore improvements for thirty years." McLean, *History of Jersey City*, p. 36. On the railroad and the Morris Canal, see Van Winkle, *History of the Municipalities of Hudson County*, p. 104.

8. On the Associates' lasting power in Jersey City after the 1838 charter, see Platt, "Jersey City Water Rights Controversy," pp. 142–154; on the relationship between the Associates and the New Jersey Rail Road and Transportation Company, see Van Winkle, *History of the Municipalities of Hudson County*, pp. 104–107 (quote on pp. 104–105).

9. As one author explains in regard to the 1838 charter, "The efforts made by the Associates to attract men of means and enterprise were moderately successful, but the more that men of this class established homes and business in the city, the more the influence of the Associates declined" (McLean, *History of Jersey City*, p. 39).

10. The quote is from McLean, *History of Jersey City*, p. 24. The 1829 population figure for Jersey City was given by the Reverend E. D. Barry and reported in the "History and Statistical Memoranda of Jersey City" section of the *Directory of Jersey City, Harsimus, and Pavonia, for 1849–50* (Jersey City: John H. Vorhees, 1849). The 1834 population figure for Jersey City comes from Van Winkle, *History of the Municipalities of Hudson County*, p. 99. The claim that Newark experienced a slower rate of growth during this period is based on the fact that Newark's population increased by approximately 60 percent between 1830 and 1840. Assuming a constant rate of growth in these years, the population would have increased by only 30 percent between 1830 and 1835, which I assumed to be roughly comparable to the period 1829–34.

11. "Improvements of the City," *Jersey City Gazette and Bergen Advertiser*, March 30, 1836 (reprinted as "Jersey City Improvements," *Newark Daily Advertiser*, April 1, 1836); McLean, *History of Jersey City*, p. 37. See also Van Winkle, *History of the Municipalities of Hudson County*, pp. 95–99. On the rising price of real estate in Jersey City, see "Real Estate," *Jersey City Gazette and Bergen Advertiser*, June 3, 1835.

12. "An Act to Incorporate Jersey City," *Acts of the Sixty-second General Assembly of the State of New Jersey* (Trenton: James Adams, 1838), secs. 12, 18 (pp. 115–116, 119–120).

13. Van Winkle, *History of the Municipalities of Hudson County*, p. 100. Quotes from McLean, *History of Jersey City*, p. 40. The area of land filled in between 1841 and 1855 was determined by comparing two maps: L. F. Douglass, *Topographical Map of Jersey City, Hoboken, and the Adjacent County* (1841; reprint, New York: Benjamin S. Demarest, 1876), and William H. Wood, *Map of Jersey City, Hoboken, and Hudson Cities* (Jersey City: R. B. Kashow, 1855).

14. U.S. Census Office, *Preliminary Report on the Eighth Census* (Washington, DC: Government Printing Office, 1862), p. 243.

15. McLean, *History of Jersey City*, p. 39.

16. On the original corporators of the Jersey City Gas Light Company, see *Directory of Jersey City, Harsimus, and Pavonia, for 1849–50*, pp. 40, 19, 12, 5, 47, and McLean, *History of Jersey City*, p. 40. For more on Bacot, see Adrian C. Leiby

and Nancy Wichman, *The Hackensack Water Company, 1869–1969* (River Edge, NJ: Bergen County Historical Society, 1969), pp. 36–38. The "overlord class" quote comes from Edlow W. Harrison, *The Public Water Supplies of Hudson Co., N.J., Particularly with Reference to the Jersey City Supply*, Historical Society of Hudson County, Paper no. 8 (November 18, 1909), p. 7. The "men in whom everyone has confidence" quote is from McLean, *History of Jersey City*, p. 56.

17. On Ward, see McLean, *History of Jersey City*, p. 56, and Van Winkle, *History of the Municipalities of Hudson County*, pp. 110–111.

18. McLean, *History of Jersey City*, pp. 56–58; "An Act for the Appointment of Commissioners in Relation to Supplying the Townships of Hoboken, Van Vorst, and the City of Jersey City with Pure and Wholesome Water," *Acts of the Seventy-fifth Legislature of the State of New Jersey, and Seventh Session under the New Constitution* (Trenton: Phillips and Boswell, 1851), pp. 389–390.

19. For the election results, see "Official" and "The New Charter Accepted," *Sentinel and Advertiser*, March 28, 1851.

20. "Our Window View," *Sentinel and Advertiser*, March 20, 1851.

21. Quote from *Daily Telegraph*, March 19, 1851; *Sentinel and Advertiser*, March 19 ("Jersey City Charter"), March 20 ("Election"), March 21 ("A Bull, That Was a Bull" and "Carping Critics"), and March 24 ("The Charter"), 1851. On the advantages that Van Vorst residents would expect to get from consolidation, see the *Sentinel and Advertiser*, March 10 (letter to the editor from "Jersey"), March 11 ("To Correspondents," "Van Vorst Square," and letter to the editor from "Harsimus"), and March 18 ("City Charter" and "Van Vorst Square"), 1851. See also Van Winkle, *History of the Municipalities of Hudson County*, p. 114 (who gives somewhat different figures for the consolidation referendum), and Platt, "Jersey City Water Rights Controversy," p. 151.

22. On the development of the Jersey City water supply, see McLean, *History of Jersey City*, pp. 56–58; Van Winkle, *History of the Municipalities of Hudson County*, pp. 110–111; Harrison, *Public Water Supplies of Hudson Co.*; "An Act to Authorize the Construction of Works for Supplying Jersey City and Places Adjacent with Pure and Wholesome Water," *Acts of the Seventy-sixth Legislature of the State of New Jersey* (Somerville, NJ: Donaldson and Brokaw, 1852), ch. 174, March 25, 1852. The only mention of the water bill that I could find in the local press was the following: "Among the acts passed by the Legislature, is the important one appointing Commissioners to supply Jersey City with water. The bill passed the Assembly by an unanimous vote. Thanks to the good management of our representatives." *Sentinel and Advertiser*, March 25, 1852. On the sewerage system, see the minutes of the Jersey City Common Council, May 24, June 21, August 2 and 16, September 6, 13, and 21, and October 4, 1853. By November sewers were being laid in accordance with the sewerage plan. Ironically, although sewers were laid in accordance with the plan, the plan itself was apparently never fully implemented because a navigable canal that was essential to the plan was never built. See "Chief Engineer's Report for 1877," in Board of Public Works of Jersey City, *Reports of the Chief Engineer, 1871–1887* (n.p., n.d.), pp. 15–16.

23. *Reports of the Jersey City Water Commissioners, 1851–1860* (n.p., n.d.); *1861–1870* (n.p., n.d.).

24. Van Winkle, *History of the Municipalities of Hudson County*, pp. 95–96.

25. The "ambitious little city" quote comes from Van Winkle, *History of the Municipalities of Hudson County*, p. 95. William E. Sackett, *Modern Battles of Trenton, Being a History of New Jersey's Politics and Legislation from the Year 1868 to the Year 1894*, vol. 1 (Trenton, NJ: John L. Murphy, 1895), pp. 98, 109, 227. Gilchrist later also served as the state attorney general. See also McLean, *History of Jersey City*, p. 79, and the following articles from the *Evening Journal:* "Consolidation. Arguments for and against the Measure," September 27, 1869; "Consolidation—No. 4," March 2, 1869; and "Consolidation—What Our Neighbors Think of It," September 30, 1869 (excerpted from the *New York Evening Post*).

26. Douglas V. Shaw, "The Making of an Immigrant City: Ethnic and Cultural Conflict in Jersey City, New Jersey, 1850–1877" (Ph.D. diss., University of Rochester, 1972), pp. 147–150.

27. Ibid.

28. Letter to the editor from "F," *Evening Journal*, October 5, 1869. Several meetings were held to discuss consolidation in the various cities. They were reported in the *Evening Journal* on September 28 and October 10 ("Consolidation"), 1869.

29. The claim about "giving away" the waterworks is in "Consolidation," *Evening Journal*, September 28, 1869. See also the *Evening Journal*, September 29 ("Consolidation") and October 5 ("The Consolidation Bill" and "Last Words on Consolidation"), 1869.

30. "More Light at Last," *Evening Journal*, October 6, 1869. See also James C. G. Conniff and Richard Conniff, *The Energy People: A History of PSE&G* (Newark: Public Service Electric and Gas Co., 1978), p. 26.

31. "Gas," *Evening Journal*, March 19, 1869. The four gas companies in Hudson County in 1869 were the People's Gas Light Company of the City of Hudson (chartered in 1868; its name was changed to the People's Gas Light Company of Jersey City in 1870), the Hoboken and Weehawken Gas Light Company (1863), the Hudson County Gas Light Company (1863), and the Bergen Point Gas Light Company (1864). In addition, the Consumers Gas Company of Jersey City was granted a charter in 1876. *Corporations of New Jersey, List of Certificates to December 31, 1911* (Trenton, NJ: Macrellish and Quigley, State Printers, 1914), pp. 74, 153, 302, 312, 552. On the possibility of municipal ownership of the gasworks, see the common council minutes reprinted in the *American Standard*, March 18, 1870, and the *Evening Journal*, March 16, 1870.

32. "Consolidation—Objections Considered," *Evening Journal*, September 30, 1869.

33. "First Annual Message of His Honor Mayor O'Neill," *Evening Journal*, May 3, 1870; McLean, *History of Jersey City*, p. 80.

34. "Council Proceedings," *Hoboken Standard*, May 8, 1869.

35. William H. Shaw, *History of Essex and Hudson Counties*, vol. 2, p. 1207.

36. John Stevens, broadside, reprint of the 1804 original, Hoboken Public Library Archives; *History of Hoboken* (Hoboken: Hoboken Board of Trade, 1907), p. 13;

"Some Interesting History of Hoboken and Environments," *Hudson Observer*, December 30, 1921. For more on the founding of Hoboken, see also William Shaw, *History of Essex and Hudson Counties*, vol. 2, pp. 1208–1211. McLean (*History of Jersey City*, p. 22) has contended that Stevens was "stimulated" to sell lots at Hoboken by a feeling of "competition" with the Associates of the Jersey Company.

37. *The Evening News and Hoboken: The Record of the Progress of the Hoboken Evening News together with the History of the City of Hoboken, from Its Settlement to the Present Time* (Hoboken: Evening News, 1893), pp. 76–78. On Stevens's ferries, see William Shaw, *History of Essex and Hudson Counties*, vol. 2, p. 1210, and George Long Moller, *The Hoboken of Yesterday* (Hoboken: Poggi Press, 1964), pp. 35–38.

38. *Message of Hon. Cornelius V. Clickener, First Mayor of the City of Hoboken, under Its New Charter, Presented to the City Council, May 7th, 1855* (Hoboken: Wm. L. S. Harrison, 1855), pp. 3–4. See also Van Winkle, *History of the Municipalities of Hudson County*, p. 288.

39. *Evening News and Hoboken*, p. 78; Moller, *Hoboken of Yesterday*, p. 38. According to one source, Stevens's sons John, Robert, and Edwin bought out their father's other heirs and became the corporation's sole owners. In 1856 John Stevens died and left his portion of the company to Edwin, who subsequently bought out his brother Robert (*History of Hoboken*, p. 19). However, the minutes of the HLIC directors' meetings indicate that other people besides the Stevenses were large stockholders in the company through the 1840s (Stevens family collection, manuscript group 409, New Jersey Historical Society, Newark).

40. HLIC, "Charter, By-laws, etc.," 1840, Box 45, File 1, p. 11, Stevens family collection, New Jersey Historical Society.

41. "An Act to Incorporate the Hoboken Land and Improvement Company," passed February 21, 1838, *Acts of the Sixty-second General Assembly of the State of New Jersey, at a Session Begun at Trenton on the Twenty-fourth Day of October, Eighteen Hundred and Thirty-seven. Being the First Sitting* (Trenton: James Adams, 1838), pp. 92–95, quotes on pp. 92 and 94.

42. *History of Hoboken*, pp. 19–20. HLIC officers were involved in most important Hoboken institutions. For instance, HLIC president W. W. Shippen served on the board of directors of the Hoboken City Bank, while Edwin Stevens served on the board of directors and was also a manager, of the Hoboken Bank for Savings. Both banks were incorporated in 1857. In 1884 William H. Macy, who had come to Hoboken in 1854 to work for the HLIC and was on the board of directors by the 1880s, was elected a tax commissioner to the city's Third Ward. Macy had also been a large property holder in the city since the 1860s. William Shaw, *History of Essex and Hudson Counties*, vol. 2, pp. 1218–1222; *Evening News and Hoboken*, p. 81.

43. See the directors' meeting minutes of the HLIC on November 14, 1840; April 14 and July 1 and 6, 1841; and May 14, 1842 (microfilm reel no. 32, Stevens family collection, New Jersey Historical Society). A record of the petition to repeal the HLIC charter can be found in the *Journal of the Legislative Council*, 65 sess., 2 sit. (1841), p. 245, located at the New Jersey State Library in Trenton.

The notice of the petition to repeal the HLIC charter found in the *Journal of the Legislative Council* gives no indication why residents wanted the charter repealed. Interestingly, the New Jersey State Archives has a copy of the *Journal of the Legislative Council* that makes no reference to the petition. See also John W. Cadman Jr., *The Corporation in New Jersey: Business and Politics, 1791–1875* (Cambridge, MA: Harvard University Press, 1949), p. 385n110. The list of subsidiary companies owned by the HLIC comes from the pamphlet from the *Stevens Family Papers Exhibit* at the New Jersey Historical Society, 1970. A copy of this pamphlet is located in the Hoboken Public Library Archives.

44. *New York Atlas*, October 26, 1856, reprinted in an unnamed Hudson County newspaper, November 1, 1856. Mayors file, Hoboken Public Library Archives.

45. Ibid., p. 1.

46. Contemporary accounts claim that one-third of the taxes collected by the city came from the HLIC. *Evening News and Hoboken*, p. 78, taken verbatim from William Shaw, *History of Essex and Hudson Counties*, vol. 2, p. 1218.

47. *Message of Hon. Cornelius V. Clickener*, p. 12.

48. "An Act to Authorize the Construction of Works for Supplying Jersey City and Places Adjacent with Pure and Wholesome Water," approved March 25, 1852, *Acts of the Seventy-sixth Legislature*, pp. 419–430, quotes on pp. 419–420, 428. Emphasis added.

49. "Act to Incorporate the Hoboken Land and Improvement Company," sec. 4; "Act for the Appointment of Commissioners in Relation to Supplying the Townships of Hoboken, Van Vorst, and the City of Jersey City with Pure and Wholesome Water," sec. 1.

50. HLIC, "Charter, By-laws, etc.," 1840, Box 45, File 1, p. 11, Stevens family collection, New Jersey Historical Society.

51. "A Supplement to the Act Entitled, 'An Act to Incorporate the Hoboken Land and Improvement Company,' Passed the Twenty-first Day of February, Anno Domini Eighteen Hundred and Thirty-eight," approved March 17, 1855, *Acts of the Seventy-ninth Legislature of the State of New Jersey, and Eleventh under the New Constitution* (Trenton: Phillips and Boswell, 1855), p. 327; "An Act to Incorporate the City of Hoboken," approved March 28, 1855, Title IV, sec. 40, ibid., p. 463.

52. In conjunction with purchasing water from Jersey City, Hoboken established its own board of water commissioners and registrars, which was "elected by the people and the commissioners served without salary . . . All the mains [in Hoboken] became the property of the city." "An Act to Amend an Act Entitled 'An Act to Incorporate the City of Hoboken,' Approved March Twenty-Eight, Eighteen Hundred and Fifty-five," approved March 14, 1856, *Acts of the Eightieth Legislature of the State of New Jersey, and Twelfth under the New Constitution* (New Brunswick: A. R. Speer, 1856), pp. 285–286; "An Act to Authorize the Water Commissioners of the City of Hoboken to Contract for and Introduce Water into Said City, and to Provide for the Payment Thereof," approved March 20, 1857, *Acts of the Eighty-first Legislature of the State of New Jersey, and Thirteenth under the New Constitution* (New Brunswick: A. R. Speer, 1857),

pp. 500–504; William Shaw, *History of Essex and Hudson Counties,* vol. 2, pp. 1207, 1210, 1217; Van Winkle, *History of the Municipalities of Hudson County,* pp. 289, 293.

53. Hoboken got its own gas company in 1863. The founders of the Hoboken Gas Company are unknown, but at least by 1884 HLIC president W. W. Shippen was the gas company's president. William H. Shaw, *History of Essex and Hudson Counties,* vol. 2, pp. 1218–1219.

54. Report, March 26, 1861, in *Reports of the Jersey City Water Commissioners, 1861–1870.* The 1855 Hoboken city charter had actually prohibited Hoboken residents from being charged for water at rates higher than the rates charged in either Jersey City or New York (see note 51).

55. "Hoboken," *Evening Journal,* October 2, 1869, p. 4.

56. "Anti-consolidation Meeting held in Hoboken," *Evening Journal,* October 2, 1869.

57. William Shaw, *History of Essex and Hudson Counties,* vol. 2, pp. 1217–1219.

58. "Hoboken and Consolidation," *Evening Journal,* October 7, 1869. The tract of land was later returned to Hoboken in 1874. See John P. Snyder, *The Story of New Jersey's Civil Boundaries, 1606–1968* (Trenton: New Jersey Bureau of Geology and Topography, 1969), pp. 146, 148, 151. William Shaw gives the date for Weehawken's "reannexation" as 1876 (*History of Essex and Hudson Counties,* vol. 2, p. 1210).

59. William Shaw, *History of Essex and Hudson Counties,* vol. 2, p. 1210; Van Winkle, *History of the Municipalities of Hudson County,* p. 289. The U.S. Census Bureau did not start counting the population of Hoboken until 1880, when it counted 30,999 people living in the city. Constant population growth from 1860 to 1880 would have given Hoboken a population of 20,329 in 1870.

60. "Council Proceedings," *Hoboken Standard,* May 8, 1869; William Shaw, *History of Essex and Hudson Counties,* vol. 2, p. 1207.

61. Around the same time as the consolidation referendum, the Hoboken common council began to let contracts for the filling, grading, curbing, guttering, flagging, and draining of several streets in the "uptown" section of the city. Hoboken mayor Edward Stanton described these street projects in his first annual message to the common council in 1891: "The fruits of official stupidity and extravagance . . . are maturing in the shape of a large block of bonded indebtedness which was incurred about twenty years ago, when the measure which has been popularly but somewhat inaccurately described as the 'uptown street improvements' was consummated." *First Annual Message of the Hon. Edward R. Stanton, Mayor of the City of Hoboken, May 4, 1891* (n.p., n.d.), pp. 4–5. Even in the early 1870s the uptown street improvements provoked a reaction against the city government and appear to have been the impetus behind the formation of the Hoboken Tax-payers' and Citizens' Association. The association's primary complaint was that the street improvements were exorbitantly expensive, and thus the property owners who were ostensibly benefited by the projects were assessed at exorbitant rates. The street projects had

become exorbitantly expensive because they were used as a source of graft for politicians, contractors, and local engineers. *By-laws of the Hoboken Tax-payers' and Citizens' Association, together with a Statement of Facts and Principles, with Which Every Tax-payer Should Be Familiar* (n.p., 1873), pp. 8–16.

62. "Hoboken and Consolidation," *Evening Journal,* October 7, 1869.

63. *By-laws of the Hoboken Tax-payers' and Citizens' Association,* pp. 15–16. Emphasis in original.

64. James Madison, "The Federalist No. 10," in Robert Scigliano, ed., *The Federalist* (New York: Random House, 2000), p. 60.

65. *Message of Hon. Cornelius V. Clickener,* pp. 11–13.

66. For instance, after his long tenure as a member of the Hoboken Board of Water Commissioners, HLIC president W. W. Shippen served as a member of the board of directors of the Hackensack Water Company Reorganized. Leiby and Wichman, *Hackensack Water Company,* pp. 49–62. See also William Shaw, *History of Essex and Hudson Counties,* vol. 2, p. 1219; Harrison, *Public Water Supplies of Hudson Co.; Evening News and Hoboken,* p. 19.

67. *Evening News and Hoboken,* pp. 34–35.

68. On engineers in Hoboken, see ibid., pp. 24–33.

69. For the residences of these contractors, see *Gopsill's Jersey City and Hoboken Directory, for the Year Ending April 30, 1871* (Jersey City: John H. Lyon, 1871), pt. 1, pp. 87, 124, 169; pt. 2, p. 359. The directory lists four John McDermotts, three of whom are listed as "laborer" and one of whom is listed as "mason." One John McDermott listed as "laborer" lived in Bergen City, while the other three lived in Jersey City. James Coughlin and Michael Callahan worked as partners in the firm of Coughlin and Callahan. For more on these contractors, see *By-laws of the Hoboken Tax-payers' and Citizens' Association,* pp. 10–11.

70. Walter F. Robinson, "The Historical Heritage of Modern Bayonne," in *Bayonne Centennial Historical Revue* (Progress Printing Company, n.d.), p. 26 (Robinson's work is actually unpaginated. I have numbered the pages myself, using the first page of the text as page 1). On the population of Bayonne, see Carmela A. Karnoutsos, "The Founding of the City of Bayonne, 1859–1869," in Carmela A. Karnoutsos, ed., *From Township to City: Papers about the Founding of Bayonne* (n.p., 1996), pp. 3–5. Karnoutsos writes that "after the Civil War, Bayonne's population grew rapidly from approximately 1,700 residents in 1865 to 3,834 in 1869" (p. 5). See also Van Winkle, who estimated that at the time of incorporation, the city of Bayonne's population "probably exceeded 2,500" (*History of the Municipalities of Hudson County,* p. 242). For general histories of Bayonne, see also Gladys Mellor Sinclair, *Bayonne Old and New: The City of Diversified Industry* (New York: Maranatha Publishers, 1940), and Royden Page Whitcomb, *First History of Bayonne, New Jersey* (Bayonne: published by the author, 1904).

71. Robinson, "Historical Heritage of Modern Bayonne," p. 17; "Local Items," *Bayonne Herald,* August 28, 1869. See also Richard G. Shahpazian, "Henry Meigs: Bayonne's Unsung Hero," in Carmela A. Karnoutsos, ed., *From Township to City: Papers about the Founding of Bayonne* (n.p., 1996), pp. 13–38.

72. All state legislation relative to street openings in Bayonne was conveniently reprinted in one volume, *The Revised Charter of the City of Bayonne, Approved March 22, 1872* (Bayonne: Bayonne Herald Print, 1872). For the original act creating the street commission, see pp. 67–70. The commissioners named in the 1857 act—A. D. Mellick, Jacob A. Van Horn, Jacob M. Vreeland, Hartman Vreeland, and Egbert Waters—were all prominent residents of the peninsula. On the commissioners, see Van Winkle, *History of the Municipalities of Hudson County*, p. 236–240; Karnoutsos, "Founding of the City of Bayonne," p. 3; and Robinson, "Historical Heritage of Modern Bayonne," pp. 14–15.

73. Robinson, "Historical Heritage of Modern Bayonne," p. 8. For a description of the lower villages, which were evidently wealthier and more populated than Salterville, see Van Winkle, *History of the Municipalities of Hudson County*, pp. 239–240 (Van Winkle refers incorrectly to "Satterville"). Two supplements to the 1857 act passed in 1863 and 1864 repealed the requirements of the 1857 act and "all proceedings of the Commissioners held pursuant to the act" for various areas between Forty-fifth and Fifty-second Streets in Salterville. *Revised Charter of the City of Bayonne*, pp. 71–74.

74. In place of the commission, an 1864 act stipulated that any ten "freeholders, and residents in the said Township of Bayonne," desirous of opening a street could apply to the Hudson County court, and the court would "nominate and appoint three intelligent, judicious and disinterested freeholders of the said Township of Bayonne" as "Commissioners to view the said street, avenue or square, and determine whether the same shall be opened or not." No street could be opened if "five-eighths of the owners of property in value on the line of such streets, avenues or squares shall object thereto in writing." *Revised Charter of the City of Bayonne*, pp. 76–77.

75. "Bayonne As It Was," *Bayonne Herald*, September 18, 1869.

76. Real estate circular, quoted in "Bergen Point," *Bayonne Herald*, October 2, 1869; Robinson, "Historical Heritage of Modern Bayonne," p. 24; Van Winkle, *History of the Municipalities of Hudson County*, p. 238. The railroad required significant changes to the Ryan Map (*Revised Charter of the City of Bayonne*, pp. 99–103).

77. Shahpazian, "Henry Meigs," p. 19; Robinson, "Historical Heritage of Modern Bayonne," pp. 13, 25; "Local Items," *Bayonne Herald*, September 25, 1869.

78. "Bayonne As It Was," *Bayonne Herald*, September 18, 1869.

79. Karnoutsos, "Founding of the City of Bayonne," p. 4; *Revised Charter of the City of Bayonne*, pp. 104–106.

80. Van Winkle, *History of the Municipalities of Hudson County*, p. 242. The city charter proposal faced some initial resistance, once again by the Salters and their allies, who charged that the establishment of a city was a continuation of the unfair process of infrastructural development that they had seen under the township government and the map and grade commission. Shahpazian, "Henry Meigs," pp. 19–20.

81. "Influence of the Latourette House," *Bayonne Herald*, September 11, 1869; *Bayonne Herald*, August 21 ("What the Press Say of Us") and August 28

("Bayonne: What New Yorkers Think of it"), 1869; see also Van Winkle, *History of the Municipalities of Hudson County*, p. 240; Shahpazian, "Henry Meigs," pp. 16–17, 30.

82. Shahpazian, "Henry Meigs," p. 22; "Wait until Next Year," *Bayonne Herald*, August 21, 1869. See also "The Common Council at Work," *Bayonne Herald*, July 24, 1869.

83. "Pavement on Avenue S," *Bayonne Herald*, September 4, 1869.

84. *Bayonne Herald*, April 30, 1870 ("The Mayor's Message"), and July 24, 1869 ("The Common Council at Work" and "Councilmanic Proceedings").

85. The initial stock offering was apparently unsuccessful, because the *Herald* asked two months later, "What has become of the Bayonne Gas Company? Our streets are as dark as the deepest pit at night, and even a cat could lose its way." *Bayonne Herald*, September 11, 1869 ("Local Items"). Another sale of stock was offered in April 1870, and the streets of the city were finally lit in February 1872. The map and grade commissioner (of those appointed in 1868) who opposed the city charter was John Combes. Shahpazian, "Henry Meigs," pp. 19–20, 27; *Bayonne Herald*, July 24, 1869 ("Local Items"), and April 30, 1870 ("The Bergen Point Gas Light Company"). The Erastus Randall who was a map and grade commissioner and founder of the Bergen Point Gas-Light Company in 1869 may be the same Erastus Randall who was a founder of the Jersey City Gas Light Company in 1849. The evidence suggests that Randall had lived in Jersey City (see note 16 of this chapter) and later moved to Bayonne, as he is listed in the 1879—1880 *General Directory and Manual of the City of Bayonne, Hudson County, New Jersey* (Bayonne: Bayonne Printing Company, 1879), p. 40, but not listed in *Gopsill's Jersey City and Hoboken Directory for the Year Ending April 30, 1880* (Washington, DC: William H. Boyd, 1879), p. 317.

86. *Bayonne Herald*, July 24 ("Duties of Street Commissioner") and October 9 ("A Defence of Our Council"), 1869. The relationship between the map and grade commission and the city government is unclear. Van Winkle notes cryptically that the "map and grade commission placed the power and authority of that body with the Mayor and Common Council. The revision was made necessary by reason of frequent quarrels between the commission and the Common Council." According to Van Winkle, the 1872 charter revision "was formulated for the purpose of ending the authority of the map and grade commissioners" (*History of the Municipalities of Hudson County*, p. 242). In a humorous parody of a Bayonne Common Council meeting, the *Evening Journal* commented that "the Common Council practically resolved itself into the Map and Grade Commissioners" (reprinted in "Councilmanic Proceedings," *Bayonne Herald*, September 18, 1869).

87. *Bayonne Herald*, December 4, 1869 ("How to Make the City Grow"), and April 30, 1870 ("The Mayor's Message"). Salterville is referred to as the Third Ward in the mayor's message. See also September 25 ("Local Items") and August 21 ("Wait until Next Year"), 1869.

88. "Local Items," *Bayonne Herald*, November 6, 1869.

89. "Disadvantages of Consolidation," *Bayonne Herald*, October 30, 1869. The date is misprinted on the newspaper as November 9, but is corrected by hand on the microfilm at the Bayonne Public Library. Shahpazian notes that Salterville residents "believed Jersey City was better equipped to deliver services, such as water, gas, and lighting." "Henry Meigs," p. 23.

90. "Consolidation," *Bayonne Herald*, October 2, 1869.

91. "Disadvantages of Consolidation," *Bayonne Herald*, October 30, 1869. There were apparently other later consolidation schemes in Hudson County. See, for instance, "The Proposed Consolidation of Hoboken and the Northern Townships," *Evening Journal*, January 4, 1872.

92. "Disadvantages of Consolidation," *Bayonne Herald*, October 30, 1869. On Bayonne's water supply, see Robinson, "Historical Heritage of Modern Hoboken," pp. 58–59.

93. On James Ryan and the Fouquet Map, see Robinson, "Historical Heritage of Modern Bayonne," pp. 14–15, and Karnoutsos, "Founding of the City of Bayonne," pp. 2–3. On James Ryan, see also "Tuesday Evening. Meeting of the Council," *Bayonne Herald*, July 24 and August 7, 1869. On Emmet Smith, who besides being a city surveyor and engineer was a very active member of the Bayonne community, see Sinclair, *Bayonne Old and New*, p. 43.

94. The contractors are identified in the minutes of the common council, *Bayonne Herald*, September 4 and 25, 1869. The earliest directory for Bayonne is for 1879–80, *General Directory and Manual of the City of Bayonne*. No Hutchinsons or Rokes are listed in this directory. Four John Van Buskircks are listed—one as a "bookeeper," one as a "builder," and two with unlisted occupations (p. 49). In *Gopsill's Jersey City and Hoboken Directory* for 1870–71, one John Van Buskirck is listed as a "boatman" (pt. 3, p. 576).

95. Quoted in Shahpazian, "Henry Meigs," p. 23.

96. Quoted in the *Evening Journal*, March 8, 1870 ("The Consolidation Charter"), see also March 9 ("The Caucus Charter") and March 17 ("Consolidation Troubles"), 1870. The nativist but Democratic *American Standard* hardly mentioned the 1870 charter during the time that it filled the columns of the *Evening Journal*.

97. Sackett, *Modern Battles of Trenton*, vol. 1, pp. 87–88.

98. Quoted in the *Jersey City Times*, February 3, 1871 ("How the Old Thing Works"); see also February 3 ("Several Timely Topics") and February 7 ("The Bumstead Charter"), 1871. The board of public works and the other boards created in 1871 were not the only institutions of city government that were held in contempt during this period. As Douglas Shaw notes, "That the 1870 aldermen had been 'bummers' was an accepted truth by 1872 and rarely challenged" ("Making of an Immigrant City," p. 256; for more on the 1871 charter, see p. 210).

99. *Evening Journal*, March 4 ("Bergen") and September 13 ("Bergen City"), 1870; "The New Board of Works," *Jersey City Times*, January 28, 1871.

100. See the 1871 and 1872 reports in Board of Public Works of Jersey City, *Reports of the Chief Engineer, 1871–1887*.

101. Douglas Shaw, "Making of an Immigrant City," p. 240; McLean, *History of Jersey City*, p. 84. Even before the 1871 charter had passed the state legislature, the grand jury was investigating "an alleged fraudulent transaction . . . whereby the Board of Aldermen voted to purchase a certain property at an exorbitant price, in the consummation of which sale Alderman Bumsted, who voted in the affirmative, was pecuniarily interested" (*Jersey City Times*, January 28, 1871).

102. Van Winkle, *History of the Municipalities of Hudson County*, pp. 128–129.

103. "The Greenvillians Vote 'No Charter,'" *Evening Journal*, October 2, 1869.

104. "Greenville," *Bayonne Herald*, October 16, 1869.

105. Van Winkle, *History of the Municipalities of Hudson County*, p. 129.

106. After the overhaul of the street commission in 1868, "the Legislature . . . ma[de] it obligatory on the part of the township committee to issue bonds not exceeding in amount $5,000, on the requisition of the street commission" (Van Winkle, *History of the Municipalities of Hudson County*, pp. 128–129). The legislature did away with the $5,000 limit in 1870 and gave the street commissioners the authority to "borrow such sums of money as they may deem necessary, in anticipation of the collection of assessments for street improvements." The township committee was then required to pay for the bonds through general taxes. "An Act Relating to the Street Commissioners of Greenville, Hudson County, New Jersey," approved March 2, 1870, *Acts of the Ninety-fourth Legislature of the State of New Jersey and Twenty-sixth under the New Constitution* (Newark: E. N. Fuller, 1870), pp. 389–391.

107. The tax rate was reported as being three times what it had been in the previous year. Minutes of the Greenville Street Commissioners, *Bayonne Herald and Greenville Register*, November 9, 1872; "Greenville," *Bayonne Herald and Greenville Register*, November 23, 1872.

108. *Bayonne Herald and Greenville Register*, November 23 ("Arrest of Greenville Street Commissioners" and "Greenville") and November 30 ("Greenville"), 1872.

109. *Bayonne Herald and Greenville Register*, December 7 ("Greenville Tax War Ended" and "Greenville") and December 14 ("Greenville"), 1872.

110. Van Winkle states that "it was finally determined that the only possibility of escape from the existing unsatisfactory conditions was through a union with Jersey City." *History of the Municipalities of Hudson County*, p. 129.

111. "Greenville," *Bayonne Herald and Greenville Register*, December 7 and 14, 1872.

112. See the letter to the editor from "Citizen," *Bayonne Herald and Greenville Register*, December 14, 1872.

113. Douglas Shaw, "Making of an Immigrant City," p. 250; Board of Public Works of Jersey City. 1872 report, pp. 39–41, *Reports of the Chief Engineer, 1871–1887*.

114. Data on all public works in Jersey City come from Board of Public Works of Jersey City, *Reports of the Chief Engineer, 1871–1887*. On infrastructural development in Greenville, see Spielmann and Brush, *Sanitary and Topographical Map of Hudson County, N.J.* (Hoboken, NJ: Spielmann and Brush, 1880), plates 5–8. George E. Waring Jr. also noted that Greenville had no sewers in his *Report on the Social Statistics of Cities*, published as part of the Tenth Census

.   (1886; reprint, New York: Arno Press, 1970), pt. 1, pp. 695–705. On the annexation of Greenville, see the *Jersey City Times*, January 29 ("Greenville Annexation") and February 10 ("The New District"), 1873.

115. Douglas Shaw notes of the 1877 Jersey City charter, which made the boards of public works, police, and fire protection elective, that "with so many elected bodies, responsibility, instead of being concentrated, was so diffused as to render the government ineffective . . . native-born Republicans were often able to elect three members to a board, deadlocking proceedings for months at a time." "Making of an Immigrant City," p. 259. Information on the chief engineer comes from Board of Public Works of Jersey City, *Reports of the Chief Engineer, 1871–1887.*

116. On the chief engineers after 1887, see the annual *Manual of the Board of Street and Water Commissioners, of Jersey City* (published annually from 1887 to 1907 by Noland Brothers, with locations in both New York and Jersey City). After 1907, the *Manual* stops listing the chief engineer, but Van Keuren is listed as such in the *Jersey City-Hoboken Directory* into the 1920s. On the change from the board of public works to the board of street and water commissioners, see *Manual of the Board of Public Works and Board of Street and Water Commissioners,* · 1889–1890, title page, and "An Act Concerning the Government of Cities in This State," sec. 7, *Acts of the One Hundred and Thirteenth Legislature of the State of New Jersey,* April 6, 1889 (Trenton, NJ: MacCrellish and Quigley, 1889), pp. 187–205. The number of commissioners was increased to five in 1891. On infrastructural development in Jersey City up to 1905, see U.S. Bureau of the Census, *Statistics of Cities Having a Population of over 30,000, 1905* (Washington, DC: Government Printing Office, 1907), pp. 342–354.

117. Samuel H. Popper, "Newark, N.J., 1870—1910: Chapters in the Evolution of an American Metropolis" (Ph.D. diss., New York University, 1952), p. 115.

118. Walter G. Muirhead, "Jersey City of Today," in Walter G. Muirhead, ed., *Jersey City of Today: Its History, People, Trades, Commerce, Institutions, and Industry* (Jersey City: Frank Stevens, 1910), pp. 18–22; Jersey City Department of Streets and Public Improvements and Bureau of Water Supply, "Jersey City's Water Supply," reprinted from *Aquafax,* February and March 1925, in Free Public Library of Jersey City, ed., *The Water Supply of Jersey City* (n.p., n.d.).

Chapter 5. The Rise and Fall of Greater Newark

1. "Mayor's Annual Message to the Common Council," *Newark Annual Reports,* 1904, p. 17.

2. John P. Snyder, "The Bounds of Newark: Tract, Township, and City," *New Jersey History* 86 (Summer 1968): 101–104.

3. John T. Cunningham, *Newark* (Newark: New Jersey Historical Society, 1966), pp. 25, 67, 99. Unlike New York City, where the municipal corporation owned all of the common land such as the streets and public squares, the Newark town records indicate that areas reserved for public use, including "Large

Extensive Roads," were the property of all the "Inhabitants of the Town." See *Records of the Town of Newark* (1864; reprint, Newark: New Jersey Historical Society, 1966), p. 185. On the preeminence of Perth Amboy as a trading port, see Carl Bridenbaugh, *Cities in the Wilderness: The First Century of Urban Life in America, 1652–1742* (1938; reprint, New York: Alfred A. Knopf, 1955), p. 181, and Robert G. Albion, "New Jersey and the Port of New York," *Proceedings of the New Jersey Historical Society* 58 (April 1940): 84–93.

4. Snyder, "Bounds of Newark," pp. 93–101.

5. Susan E. Hirsch, *Roots of the American Working Class: The Industrialization of Crafts in Newark, 1800–1860* (Philadelphia: University of Pennsylvania Press, 1978), p. 3; Raymond M. Ralph, "From Village to Industrial City: The Urbanization of Newark, New Jersey, 1830–1860" (Ph.D. diss., New York University, 1978), pp. 15, 18–19, 24. See also Cunningham, *Newark*, pp. 84–85, 106–109.

6. Hirsch, *Roots of the American Working Class*, p. xix.

7. See Ralph, "From Village to Industrial City," p. 40, and Hirsch, *Roots of the American Working Class*, pp. 17–18.

8. Hirsch, *Roots of the American Working Class*, pp. 16–17, 47, 50. By 1820 the town's population had reached 6,507, and by 1830 it had increased to 10,953, making Newark more than twice the size of any other town in the state (Cunningham, *Newark*, pp. 99–100).

9. *Records of the Town of Newark*, pp. 266–271; "Newark a City," *Newark Daily Advertiser*, March 19, 1836. See also the state legislature minutes printed in this paper on January 29, 1836; Ralph, "From Village to Industrial City," pp. 35–36. On the resistance of property owners, see the *Newark Daily Advertiser*, March 15 ("The Corporation") and March 17 ("Election Tomorrow"), 1836.

10. *Records of the Town of Newark*, April 1, 1831, pp. 261–262; "Newark Corporation," *Newark Daily Advertiser*, January 29, 1836. The city charter was printed in full in the *Newark Daily Advertiser*, March 5, 1836.

11. For the announcements by the street commissioner, see the classified advertisements in the *Newark Daily Advertiser*, August 15 and 19, 1835. Ralph, "From Village to Industrial City," pp. 35, 229–230; "Newark Corporation," *Newark Daily Advertiser*, January 29, 1836; Cunningham, *Newark*, p. 110; Frank J. Urquhart, *A History of the City of Newark*, vol. 1 (New York: Lewis Historical Publishing Co., 1913), pp. 569–570; Stuart Galishoff, *Newark, the Nation's Unhealthiest City, 1832–1895* (New Brunswick, NJ: Rutgers University Press, 1988), pp. 39–41.

12. Bridenbaugh, *Cities in the Wilderness*, p. 143.

13. There is no record of when sewers were first laid in the streets of Jersey City, although one author seems to indicate that the first sewers appeared on Paulus Hook in 1842 or a bit later. Alexander McLean, *History of Jersey City, N.J.: A Record of Its Early Settlement and Corporate Progress* (Jersey City: Press of the Jersey City Printing Company, 1895), p. 47.

14. See the reports on feet of sewers (both main and lateral) laid every year in *Reports of the Jersey City Water Commissioners, 1851–1860* (n.p., n.d.); *1861–1870*

(n.p., n.d.). Ralph notes that "by 1870 Newark had only 12.5 miles of sewers" ("From Village to Industrial City," p. 231).

15. Samuel H. Popper, "Newark, N.J., 1870–1910: Chapters in the Evolution of an American Metropolis" (Ph.D. diss., New York University, 1952), pp. 305–306.

16. As Elizabeth Blackmar notes of eighteenth-century New York City, "the underlying aim of the corporation's street policies was to promote commerce in the very literal sense of facilitating the unimpeded circulation of commodities." *Manhattan for Rent, 1785–1850* (Ithaca, NY: Cornell University Press, 1989), pp. 152, 159.

17. McLean, *History of Jersey City*, p. 39.

18. See Hirsch, *Roots of the American Working Class*, pp. 17–18.

19. Streetlights may have been required earlier in Jersey City because of a higher level of crime. As Hermann Platt notes, "Paulus Hook had a bad reputation; it was considered a rowdy place, with much dog fighting, bull baiting, and drunken brawls by ferrymen." "The Jersey City Water Rights Controversy, 1845–1850," *New Jersey History* 94 (Winter 1976): 142.

20. On oil streetlights in Newark, see Cunningham, *Newark*, p. 110, and the letter to the editor from "New York," *Newark Daily Advertiser*, January 8, 1836. On the relationship between street crime and population, Bridenbaugh notes that "in proportion to the number of inhabitants crime was probably no more prevalent in the towns than throughout the countryside, but it requires no hypothesis of the urban origins of wrong-doing to demonstrate that in areas of greater concentration of population and of wealth offenses against society are certainly more evident, and their punishment more vitally necessary" (*Cities in the Wilderness*, p. 68).

21. William H. Shaw, *History of Essex and Hudson Counties, New Jersey*, vol. 1 (Philadelphia: Everts and Peck, 1884), p. 638. See also James C. G. Conniff and Richard Conniff, *The Energy People: A History of PSE&G* (Newark: Public Service Electric and Gas Co., 1978), pp. 24–25. There is some confusion in the literature as to when the Newark Gas Light Company was actually granted a corporate charter. Shaw gives the date as 1847 (p. 638), while Popper gives the date as 1837 ("Newark, N.J.," p. 316), and Conniff and Conniff claim that the date of incorporation was 1845 (p. 23), which is also given as the date of incorporation in *Corporations of New Jersey, List of Certificates to December 31, 1911* (Trenton, NJ: Macrellish and Quigley, State Printers, 1914), p. 469.

22. Ralph, "From Village to Industrial City," p. 266. The original officers of the Newark Gas Light Company who served on the common council were Samuel Meeker, who served on the common council in 1842; James Keene, who served from 1840 to 1841 and from 1843 to 1845; Isaac Baldwin, who served in 1836; Reuben D. Baldwin, who served in 1842 and again from 1845 to 1848; and Beach Vanderpool, who served on the common council in 1845 and as mayor in 1846. For a complete list of the first officers of the Newark Gas Light Company, see Shaw, *History of Essex and Hudson Counties*, vol. 1, p. 638. A convenient list of the members of the common council is provided in

"Catalogue of the City Government from 1836 to 1873," *Newark Annual Reports*, 1873, pp. 252–271.

23. John W. Cadman Jr., *The Corporation in New Jersey: Business and Politics, 1791–1875* (Cambridge, MA: Harvard University Press, 1949), p. 226; Shaw, *History of Essex and Hudson Counties*, vol. 1, pp. 638–640. Conniff and Conniff note that the two gas companies "divided the city at the Morris Canal bridge" and also claim, in contrast to Shaw, that the Citizens' Gas Light Company was incorporated in 1873 (*Energy People*, p. 25). Since notices for subscriptions to the stock of the new gas company were mentioned in the "Local Matters" section of the *Newark Daily Advertiser* on April 7, 1868, it would seem that the Conniff and Conniff date is incorrect.

24. Data on the specific number of streetlights in Newark come from Shaw, *History of Essex and Hudson Counties*, vol. 1, pp. 638–639, and "Mayor's Annual Message to the Common Council," *Newark Annual Reports*, 1872, pp. 17, 28. In 1884 New York City also had 128 electric streetlights in addition to its gas streetlights, although that number does not significantly decrease the average number of people per street lamp in that year. The Newark and Citizens' Gas Light Companies consolidated in 1895 to form the Newark Gas Company. *Corporations of New Jersey*, p. 469. For street lighting in New York, see the New York City Department of Public Works, reports for the quarters ending December 31, 1882, and December 31, 1883, located in the New York City municipal archives.

25. Galishoff, *Newark*, pp. 43–44; the quote is from Urquhart, *History of the City of Newark*, vol. 1, p. 595. The Newark Aqueduct Company charter was the second granted to a water company in the state of New Jersey (the first was to the Morris Aqueduct Company). Nationally, the Newark Aqueduct Company was one of twenty-nine private water companies given a corporate charter in the United States between 1791 and 1800 (Nelson M. Blake, *Water for the Cities: A History of the Urban Water Supply Problem in the United States* [Syracuse, NY: Syracuse University Press, 1956], pp. 64, 68). A notice for subscriptions to the Newark Aqueduct Company appeared in the *Centinel of Freedom*, February 4, 1800. The directors of the Newark Aqueduct Company are listed in Shaw, *History of Essex and Hudson Counties*, vol. 1, p. 17. The directors are listed as town officials in the index to *Records of the Town of Newark*.

26. Galishoff, *Newark*, p. 3.

27. Ibid., pp. 44–45; Ralph, "From Village to Industrial City," pp. 222–225. See also Popper, "Newark, N.J.," p. 268.

28. Hirsch, *Roots of the American Working Class*, p. 116. See also Ralph, "From Village to Industrial City," p. 220.

29. Galishoff, *Newark*, pp. 45–46; Hirsch, *Roots of the American Working Class*, p. 129. The quote is from Ralph, "From Village to Industrial City," p. 226.

30. Popper, "Newark, N.J.," p. 79. Mayor William Fiedler indicated the influence of the board of trade on infrastructural development when he announced to the common council in 1880 that "we owe it to all our businessmen, but

especially to our manufacturers, to provide properly paved streets." "Mayor's Annual Message to the Common Council," *Newark Annual Reports,* 1880, p. 31.

31. Newark Board of Trade, *Annual Report,* 1874, p. 11; quoted as well in Popper, "Newark, N.J.," pp. 77–78.

32. Newark Board of Trade, *Annual Report,* 1874, p. 13; Galishoff, *Newark,* pp. 169–170. Of the Croes and Howell report, the Newark Aqueduct Board had only this to say: "Messrs. Croes & Howell finished their work of investigation as to sources of water supply other than the Passaic River at Belleville in February, and made a very full and exhaustive report thereon, which has been published in book form for the use of members of the Board, of the Common Council and citizens. It is a most interesting and valuable document" (*Newark Annual Reports,* 1879, p. 502).

33. "Mayor's Annual Message to the Common Council," *Newark Annual Reports,* 1881, p. 38.

34. Galishoff, *Newark,* p. 171; *Newark Annual Reports,* 1885, p. 198.

35. "Mayor's Annual Message to the Common Council," *Newark Annual Reports,* 1885, p. 37. When Haynes made this address to the common council, he came out explicitly in favor of the Pequannock watershed. This calls into question Galishoff's claim that Haynes's support for the Pequannock was a result of a trip that he took to the watershed with his friend Julius Pratt in 1886 (*Newark,* p. 181). Haynes's speech to the board of trade is recorded in Newark Board of Trade, *Annual Report,* 1886, pp. 38–39. On Haynes's important role in securing the Pequannock as a watershed, see Cunningham, *Newark,* pp. 223–224; Galishoff, *Newark,* p. 181; and Richard Shafer, "Haynes' 'Folly' Turns into a Profit of $94 Million," Newark *Star-Ledger,* July 16, 1961. On an alternative proposal for a waterworks, see Newark Board of Trade, *Annual Report,* 1887, p. 9.

36. Popper, "Newark, N.J.," pp. 75–76, 93, 252, 262. See also Ralph, "From Village to Industrial City," p. 64, and Hirsch, *Roots of the American Working Class,* pp. 126–127.

37. On Newark's first intercepting sewer, see "Report of the City Surveyor and Engineer and Superintendent of Newark's Improved Sewerage for the Year 1884," *Newark Annual Reports,* 1884, p. 439, and "Mayor's Message to the Common Council," *Newark Annual Reports,* 1887, p. 31. On electric street lighting in Newark, see "Mayor's Annual Message to the Common Council," *Newark Annual Reports,* 1886; Cunningham, *Newark,* pp. 179–180; Shaw, *History of Essex and Hudson Counties,* vol. 1, pp. 640–645.

38. Newark Board of Trade, *Annual Report,* 1895, p. 93.

39. Galishoff, *Newark,* p. 187; "Work on the Water Supply" and "The Water Contract in Force," *Newark Sunday Call,* September 29, 1889, pp. 1, 4. See also Popper, "Newark, N.J.," pp. 278–281.

40. "The New Haynes," *Newark Sunday Call,* September 29, 1889, p. 4. The *Newark Sunday Call* voiced similar comments on October 6 ("The Old and New Haynes" and "Haynes or Richards?") and October 13 ("Mayor Haynes"), 1889. On criti-

cism of Haynes in regard to the board of works in 1891, see "The Haynes Nomination," *Newark Sunday Call*, September 27, 1891, and "Tuesday's Results," *Newark Sunday Call*, October 18, 1891.

41. Popper, "Newark, N.J.," pp. 282, 455–457; William E. Sackett, *Modern Battles of Trenton, Being a History of New Jersey's Politics and Legislation from the Year 1868 to the Year 1894*, vol. 1 (Trenton, NJ: John L. Murphy, 1895), pp. 363–366; "The Haynes Nomination," *Newark Sunday Call*, September 27, 1981, p. 4. See also "Without Any Parallel—Nothing like the Board of Works in Other Cities" and "Our 'Executive' Board," *Newark Sunday Call*, September 27, 1891, pp. 1, 4; "Tuesday's Results," *Newark Sunday Call*, October 18, 1891, p. 4. Popper notes of the board of works that it assumed "full control of the streets, sidewalks, fountains, lamps, sewers, wharves, bridges, public buildings, the removal of ashes and garbage, and the new water system. All of those were heretofore exclusively under the control of the Common Council" ("Newark, N.J.," p. 281). In fact, as previously discussed, the water supply had not been under the control of the common council, but of the Newark Aqueduct Board. See "Mayor's Annual Message to the Common Council," *Newark Annual Reports*, 1881, p. 36.

42. "Mayor's Message to the Common Council," *Newark Annual Reports*, 1890, pp. 68–73, and 1894, pp. 22–23. On the "intercepting sewer scandal," see the *Newark Sunday Call*, October 11, 1891, p. 4.

43. As Popper notes, "Improvements in municipally sponsored services resulted in the appearance of specialized departments to cope with the complexities connected with the administration of such services. The heads of those departments became a coterie of municipal bureaucrats, who regularly pleaded for the expansion of their respective departments before the municipal legislature" ("Newark, N.J.," pp. 455–456); elsewhere, Popper is more charitable: "Such municipal services as the water supply, street improvements, sewage and garbage disposal, etc., were recognized as being so complex as to require specialists for their administration" (p. 281). Among the "coterie of municipal bureaucrats" was George E. Bailey, a civil engineer originally from Jersey City, who was in large part responsible for the original Passaic waterworks. Bailey was appointed engineer of the Newark Aqueduct Board at its inception in 1861 and remained in that post at least to 1874. Morris Sherrerd served as the engineer of the board of street and water commissioners' water department from the early 1890s until 1905, when he was promoted to chief engineer and city surveyor. Before Sherrerd's appointment the post of city surveyor had been held by Ernest Adam for at least fifteen years. Adam was also the engineer in charge of streets and sewers from at least 1894 to 1903, when sewers were transferred to a separate department. Adam retained control over streets and highways, a post he left in 1905, when Louis C. Dittler took over. The names of departmental personnel are listed in *Newark Annual Reports*.

44. "Annual Report of the Board of Street and Water Commissioners for the Year Ended December 31, 1903," *Newark Annual Reports*, 1905, pp. 80–81.

45. "Mayor's Annual Message to the Common Council," *Newark Annual Reports*, 1894, pp. 16–17; 1897, pp. 8–9. On property owners' complaints regarding

assessments, see "Mayor's Annual Message to the Common Council," *Newark Annual Reports*, 1895, pp. 8–9, and 1896, p. 8. The final quote is from Galishoff, *Newark*, p. 128.

46. *Newark Sunday Call*, January 10, 1897, pt. 1, p. 6. See also "Annexation Squabbles," *Newark Sunday Call*, January 10, 1897, pt. 1, p. 2; Joseph F. Folsom, ed., *The Municipalities of Essex County, New Jersey, 1666–1924*, vol. 2 (New York: Lewis Historical Publishing Company, 1925), pp. 777–778.

47. Stuart Galishoff, *Safeguarding the Public Health: Newark, 1895–1918* (Westport, CT: Greenwood Press, 1975), pp. 49–50. Folsom claims incorrectly that Irvington was dependent on Newark's infrastructure even before the attempts at annexation in 1896, since the Irvington Water Company "bought water from Newark." *Municipalities of Essex County*, vol. 2, pp. 777–778.

48. *Newark Sunday Call*, January 10, 1897, pt. 1, p. 6.

49. Harold I. Effross, *County Governing Bodies in New Jersey: Reorganization and Reform of Boards of Chosen Freeholders, 1798–1974* (New Brunswick, NJ: Rutgers University Press, 1975), p. 70; Newark Board of Trade, *Annual Report*, 1875, p. 13.

50. Popper, "Newark, N.J.," p. 441.

51. Charles G. Hine, *Woodside, the North End of Newark: Its History, Legends, and Ghost Stories, Gathered from the Records and the Older Inhabitants Now Living* (New York: Hine's Annual, 1909), pp. 4–5; "Annexation Squabbles," *Newark Sunday Call*, January 10, 1897, pt. 1, p. 2.

52. Clinton Township Town Committee Minutes, 1872–1888, October 4, 1887, New Jersey Historical Society, Manuscript no. 936; Hine, *Woodside*, p. 136.

53. "Mayor's Annual Message to the Common Council," *Newark Annual Reports*, 1897.

54. "Mayor's Annual Message to the Common Council," *Newark Annual Reports*, 1900 and 1902.

55. *Newark Sunday Call*, March 9, 1902 ("The Town Elections: Voters of Clinton to Decide for or against Annexation," p. 6), and March 16, 1902, pt. 1, p. 6.

56. William P. Sutphen, "Municipal Development," in John F. Folsom, ed., *Bloomfield Old and New: An Historical Symposium* (Bloomfield, NJ: Centennial Historical Committee, 1912), pp. 140–161; quotes on pp. 143, 148. See also Raymond F. Davis, "Incorporation and Subsequent Government," ibid., pp. 69–77, and Stephen Morris Hulin, *Real and Ideal Bloomfield: The Briefly-Told Story of Church-Town, Township, and Incorporated Town of To-day* (Newark: Groebe-McGovern Co., 1902).

57. Hulin, *Real and Ideal Bloomfield*, p. 18; Davis, "Incorporation and Subsequent Government," p. 75; Sutphen, "Municipal Development," p. 151; David Lawrence Pierson, *History of the Oranges: Reviewing the Rise, Development, and Progress of an Influential Community*, 4 vols., vol. 2 (New York: Lewis Historical Publishing Company, 1922), pp. 420–421; Sutphen, "Municipal Development," pp. 143, 151.

58. *Newark Sunday Call*, March 2, 1902, p. 6.

59. "Opposed to Annexation," letter to the editor from "Vox Populi," *Newark Sunday Call*, March 9, 1902, p. 2.

60. *Newark Sunday Call*, March 2 ("The Legislature," p. 3; "Bloomfield in a Ferment," p. 5; "Bloomfield Annexation," p. 2), March 16 ("Newark with Bloomfield Annexed," p. 7), March 23 ("Legislation of Real Importance," pt. 3, p. 3), and March 30 ("End of Legislative Session," pt. 4, p. 1), 1902.

61. Sutphen, "Municipal Development," pp. 154–155. The Bloomfield Board of Trade was officially organized on February 5, approximately one month prior to the movement against annexation.

62. Popper, "Newark, N.J.," p. 441; Newark Board of Trade, *Year Book*, 1899, p. 33. Harrison and Kearny had sought annexation to Essex County again in 1892. The proposal was voted on in the legislature in 1894 and passed in the House, but was voted down in the Senate. State Senate districts were based on counties, and it was thus in the interest of senators not to change county lines. See Henry A. Mutz, *Harrison: The History of a New Jersey Town* (Harrison, NJ: Town of Harrison American Revolution Bicentennial Committee, 1976), p. 59.

63. Newark Board of Trade, *Year Book*, 1902; *Newark Sunday Call*, January 11, 1903, p. 6. According to Popper, various proposals for a Greater Newark had been circulating since at least 1897, initially in response to "the exhaustion of factory sites" in the city ("Newark, N.J.," p. 441).

64. *Newark Sunday Call*, March 1 ("Legislature's Important Work," pt. 2, p. 2) and March 22 (pt. 4, p. 4), 1903. One of the Essex members who opposed the Irvington annexation bill was Boyd, the assemblyman who had previously killed the Bloomfield annexation bill. It is perhaps significant that there was a strong advocate of suburban autonomy from Essex County in the legislature. See also Snyder, "Bounds of Newark," p. 103.

65. Folsom, *Municipalities of Essex County*, vol. 2, pp. 771, 777–778; "Trolley in Irvington," *Newark Sunday Call*, January 26, 1902, pt. 1, p. 2.

66. That the West End Improvement Association supported local home rule for the purposes of infrastructural development is suggested by a meeting of the association at which "the Rev. Adolph Roeder, president of the State Civics Federation, of which the West End Association is one of the most active members . . . argued that it would be best for each town to manage its own affairs. He said that if this was done the local government would be better, as people more acquainted with the needs of the town would be in office." The *Sunday Call* claimed that "Mr. Roeder's talk was practically the basis the association has been working on since its organization." "Irvington's Improvers," *Newark Sunday Call*, January 18, 1903, pt. 2, p. 4.

67. Pierson, *History of the Oranges*, vol. 2, pp. 524–526; "Opposed to Annexation," *Newark Sunday Call*, February 8, 1903, p. 10.

68. "Mayor's Annual Message to the Common Council," *Newark Annual Reports*, 1902. The Newark Board of Trade supported Doremus's position (*Year Book*, 1903, p. 10).

69. There is no record of the size of the majority in Vailsburg that voted in favor of annexation. *Newark Sunday Call*, January 24 ("Annexation the Issue in Vailsburg," pt. 2, p. 3), February 14, 21, and 28 ("Among Our

Neighbors—Vailsburg," pt. 2, p. 6), February 26 ("Among Our Neighbors—
Vailsburg," pt. 2, p. 6), and March 13 ("Vailsburg Annexation," pt. 1, p. 2), 1904.

70. *Newark Sunday Call*, March 8 ("Vailsburg Fight," p. 6), March 15 ("The Taxpayers' Ticket Makes Clean Sweep at Vailsburg," pt. 2, p. 3), and March 22
("Vailsburg Affairs," pt. 4, p. 2), 1903; March 13, 1904 ("Among Our Neighbors—Vailsburg," pt. 2, p. 6).

71. "Let Vailsburg Come into Newark," *Newark Sunday Call*, April 3, 1904, pt. 1, p. 4.

72. Joel Schwartz, "Suburban Progressivism in the 1890s: The Policy of Contain-
ment in Orange, East Orange, and Montclair," in Joel Schwartz and Daniel
Prosser, eds., *Cities of the Garden State: Essays in the Urban and Suburban History of
New Jersey* (Dubuque, IA: Kendall/Hunt Publishing Company, 1977), p. 55.

73. "Vailsburg Will Mark Its 80th Year," *Newark Star-Ledger*, April 5, 1974, from
the "Newark Wards and Sections—Vailsburg" subject folder, Newark Public
Library, New Jersey Room.

74. *Newark Sunday Call*, March 22, 1903 ("Vailsburg Affairs," pt. 4, p. 2); April 3
("Let Vailsburg Come into Newark," pt. 1, p. 4), and April 10 ("Voters Rally for
Annexation," pt. 1, pp. 1–2), 1904.

75. "Mayor's Annual Message to the Common Council," *Newark Annual Reports*, 1904.

76. Davis, "Incorporation and Subsequent Government," p. 76; Sutphen, "Municipal Development," pp. 150–151; "Among Our Neighbors—Bloomfield and
Glen Ridge," *Newark Sunday Call*, January 24, 1904, pt. 2, p. 6.

77. Sutphen, "Municipal Development," p. 151; "Among Our Neighbors—Bloomfield and Glen Ridge," *Newark Sunday Call*, January 24, 1904, pt. 2, p. 6. See
also "Bloomfield Worried by Water Question," *Newark Sunday Call*, February
14, 1904, pt. 1, p. 4.

78. "Annexation for Bloomfield," *Newark Sunday Call*, March 13, 1904, pt. 1, p. 2.

79. Ibid.

80. Ellor's claim was "vehemently denied" by at least one annexationist at the
meeting. "Hot Discussion on Annexation," *Newark Sunday Call*, March 20,
1904, pt. 1, p. 2.

81. Ibid.; "Bloomfield Men in Wordy Battle," *Newark Sunday Call*, April 3, 1904, pt.
1, p. 2.

82. "Bloomfield Men in Wordy Battle," *Newark Sunday Call*, April 3, 1904, pt. 1,
p. 2; 1898 *Sunday Call* article quoted in Galishoff, *Safeguarding the Public Health*,
p. 46. On Gottfried Kruegel and Germans in New Jersey politics, see Rudolph
J. Vecoli, *The People of New Jersey* (Princeton, NJ: D. Van Nostrand Company,
1965), pp. 166–167.

83. "Orange Themes," *Newark Sunday Call*, February 8 (pt. 3, p. 7) and February 15
(pt. 2, p. 2), 1903. The idea of consolidating the Oranges goes back at least to
1873. As Pierson noted, "Prospects of a consolidation of Orange, East and West
Orange were very bright in the autumn of 1873, public meetings in each of
the places having passed resolutions favorable to the movement." The consolidation of the Oranges was ultimately stopped by a negative vote of the East
Orange Township Committee (*History of the Oranges*, vol. 2, p. 379).

84. "Orange Interests," *Newark Sunday Call*, January 4, 1903, p. 10.

85. Newark Board of Trade, *Year Book*, 1905, p. 35; 1908, p. 26.

86. Snyder, "Bounds of Newark," p. 103; Newark Board of Trade, *Year Book*, 1910, p. 21. See also Popper, "Newark, N.J.," p. 443.

87. Galishoff, *Safeguarding the Public Health*, ch. 5.

88. Ibid. The gap of ten years between the establishment of the Passaic Valley Sewerage Commission and construction of the trunk sewer was due to legal difficulties that arose primarily from Paterson's refusal to contribute money to building the sewer (pp. 58–61).

89. Newark Board of Trade, *Year Book*, 1911, p. 44.

90. *Newark Sunday Call*, March 16, 1902 ("Newark with Bloomfield Annexed," p. 7), and April 3, 1904 ("Bloomfield Men in Wordy Battle," pt. 1, p. 2). For connecting roads and railways between Newark and East Orange, see Schwartz, "Suburban Progressivism in the 1890s," p. 59.

91. Schwartz, "Suburban Progressivism in the 1890s," p. 57.

92. East Orange and Bloomfield actually agreed to build a joint outlet sewer as a result of the Bloomfield Board of Health filing "a bill of complaint in the Court of Chancery" of New Jersey "against the Inhabitants of the Township of East Orange, its servants, agents and attorneys" for discharging sewage into the Second River upstream from Bloomfield. "Report of the Sewerage and Drainage Committee," *Report of the Township Committee of the Township of East Orange for the Year Ending February 28, 1894* (East Orange: Gazette Book and Job Print, 1894), pp. 5–7. On the East Orange separated sewerage system, see "Mayor's Introduction," *Annual Report of the City of East Orange, New Jersey, 1899–1900* (East Orange: East Orange Gazette Print, 1900), pp. 9–10. According to Joel Tarr, the first separated sewerage system installed in the United States was in Lenox, Massachusetts, but it was not until the installation of such a system in Memphis in 1880 that separated sewerage systems gained any notice in the United States. Joel A. Tarr, "The Separate vs. Combined Sewer Problem: A Case Study in Urban Technology Design Choice," *Journal of Urban History* 5 (May 1979): 308–339. On sewerage in East Orange, see also Pierson, *History of the Oranges*, vol. 3, pp. 553–555.

93. Schwartz notes the "adoption of a sweeping ordinance in August, 1893, designed to hook the entire town into one sewerage grid and 'drive out' all cesspools and privies" ("Suburban Progressivism in the 1890s," p. 57). In fact, as Figure 13 shows, the number of house connections declined slightly in the mid-1890s, conceivably as a result of the economic slump.

94. At the peak period of sewer construction in the city, from 1894 to 1910, 202 miles of sewers were laid into Newark's streets. During that same period Newark's population increased by approximately 132,500 people. In East Orange at least 39 miles of sewer main—and probably just as many miles of lateral sewers—were constructed between 1890 and 1909 for a municipality of "nearly twenty thousand" in 1896. Thus a conservative estimate is that East Orange built approximately one-fifth as many miles of sewers as did Newark during the turn of the century, but East Orange was far smaller than one-fifth

the size of Newark. Indeed, the entire population of East Orange was approximately one-fifth the size of the population that Newark merely gained over a period of sixteen years. Thus the rate of sewerage construction in East Orange relative to population was probably greater than that in Newark during the peak period of sewerage construction in the central city. Galishoff, *Newark*, p. 129. Galishoff does not distinguish between main and lateral sewers. The population growth figure for Newark comes from assuming linear population growth from 1890 (when the city's population was 181,830) to 1910 (when the city's population was 347,469). U.S. Bureau of the Census, *Thirteenth Census*, vol. 1, *Population 1910: General Report and Analysis* (Washington, DC: Government Printing Office, 1913). The population figure for East Orange in 1896 comes from Henry Whittemore, *The Founders and Builders of the Oranges, Comprising a History of the Outlying District of Newark, Subsequently Known as Orange, and the Later Internal Divisions, Viz.: South Orange, West Orange, and East Orange; Also a History of the Early Settlers or Founders, and of Those Who Have Been Identified with Its Growth and Prosperity, Known as the Builders* (Newark: L. J. Hardham, Printer and Bookbinder, 1896), p. 388. Newark and East Orange actually had connecting sewerage systems. See *Report of the Township Committee of the Township of East Orange for the Year ending February 28, 1894* (East Orange: Gazette Book and Job Print, 1894), pp. 5–9, 17–18; and *February 28, 1895* (East Orange, NJ: Gazette Book and Job Print, 1895), pp. 5–8.

95. Whittemore, *Founders and Builders of the Oranges*, pp. 392–393. See also Pierson, *History of the Oranges*, vol. 3, pp. 549–550.

96. A condemnation commission appointed by the courts valued the water company's property at $425,000, a value that was rejected by the city council. *Third Annual Report of the Superintendent of the Water Department to the Mayor of the City of East Orange, for the Fiscal Year Beginning Jan. 1, 1905, and ending Dec. 31, 1905* (n.p., n.d.), pp. 40, 43–44.

97. On the purchase of the waterworks, an article in the *Sunday Call* commented that $350,000 was "a somewhat large sum, although probably not as excessive as some critics seem to think" (January 4, 1903, p. 6).

98. "Mayor's Introduction," *Annual Report of the City of East Orange, New Jersey, 1899–1900*, p. 4. On the affordability of the separated sewerage system, see "The Waring System of Sewerage," *Paving and Municipal Engineering* 1 (June 1890): 4.

99. For the percentage of streets that were paved in East Orange, see *Annual Report of the City of East Orange, New Jersey, 1899–1900*, p. 5. Speaking of East Orange in 1922, Pierson wrote that "there are about seventy-two miles of streets in the city, all but seven miles of which are paved" (*History of the Oranges*, vol. 3, p. 545).

100. "Mayor's Introduction," *Annual Report of the City of East Orange, New Jersey, 1900–1901* (East Orange: East Orange Gazette Print, 1901), p. 7.

101. "Want Water Supply for East Orange," *Newark Sunday Call*, February 22, 1903, p. 8; Pierson, *History of the Oranges*, vol. 3, pp. 551–554. In 1909, after a new city charter was approved in a referendum vote, control of the water supply system was transferred from the city council to a board of water commissioners. By

1909 the size of the water distribution system was approximately twice what it had been in 1894. *Report of the Township Committee of the Township of East Orange for the Year Ending February 28, 1895*, p. 11; *Annual Report of the City of East Orange, New Jersey, for the Year Ending December 31, 1909* (Orange, NJ: Chronicle Publishing Co., 1910), pp. 42–43, 79–80.

102. *Newark Sunday Call*, January 4, 1903, p. 6.

103. *Third Annual Report of the Superintendent of the Water Department to the Mayor of the City of East Orange, for the Fiscal Year Beginning Jan. 1, 1905, and Ending Dec. 31, 1905*, p. 44.

104. Pierson, *History of the Oranges*, vol. 2, p. 384; vol. 3, pp. 524, 553. See also *Report of the Township Committee of the Township of East Orange for the Year Ending February 28, 1894*, p. 7.

105. Pierson, *History of the Oranges*, vol. 3, pp. 461, 522; see also p. 552; *Third Annual Report of the Superintendent of the Water Department to the Mayor of the City of East Orange, for the Fiscal Year Beginning Jan. 1, 1905, and Ending Dec. 31, 1905*, p. 47.

106. Interestingly, the first charter of the Citizens' Gas-Light Company granted it the power "to lay pipes and furnish gas to any of the townships of Essex County adjoining the city of Newark, except the town of East Orange. By a supplement passed in 1869, the company was further empowered to lay pipes across the bed of the Passaic River to the works of the East Newark Gas-Light Company, and sell gas to that company" (Shaw, *History of Essex and Hudson Counties*, vol. 1, p. 640).

107. Pierson, *History of the Oranges*, vol. 2, p. 322; vol. 3, p. 462. In June 1891 East Orange Township entered into a three-year contract with the Citizens' Gas Company, with which it had previously had a contract. *Report of the Township Committee of the Township of East Orange for the Year Ending February 2, 1892* (East Orange: Gazette Book and Job Print, 1892), p. 23. The contract was renewed in 1894, *Report of the Township Committee of the Township of East Orange for the Year Ending February 28th, 1895*, pp. 10–11. By 1903 gas was no longer being provided by the Citizens' Gas Company, but by the Essex and Hudson Gas Company and the Public Service Corporation. *Annual Report of the City of East Orange, New Jersey, 1903–1904* (East Orange: East Orange Gazette Print, 1904), pp. 10–11. On East Orange Township president Schmidt's research into the electric street lighting of other municipalities, see *Report of the Township Committee of the Township of East Orange for the Year Ending February 28th, 1896* (East Orange: Gazette Book and Job Print, 1896), pp. 6–7.

108. The annual reports of the township and later of the city of East Orange from 1893 to 1902 give the names of eleven contractors who either bid for contracts or were awarded infrastructure contracts in that community. In 1892 George Spotiswoode and Co., Thomas Nevins and Son, and Patrick McCann all bid for a street-improvement contract, with Nevins being awarded the contract. In 1895 Maguire, McKnight and Co., John L. Davis, and P. H. Harrison and Sons worked on sewer projects. In 1896 contracts for sewers were made with Dowd and Co. and William P. Craig. Daniel F. Minihan, James T. Boylan, and the

Harrison Construction Co. worked as contractors in East Orange between 1899 and 1902.

It seems likely that two of the contractors listed in the East Orange annual reports—Philip H. Harrison and the Harrison Construction Company—may actually have been the same contractor under two different names. Similarly, the city of Newark's annual reports from 1894 to 1905 record as many as 165 separate contractors who worked on various infrastructure projects, although the number may be as low as 143 when possible misspellings and duplicate listings are taken into account. In Newark the number of contractors cannot be determined more precisely because it is not clear that last names are spelled consistently, and sometimes only last names are given. For instance, the figure of 165 contractors counts a listing for "Boyd" and another listing for "Boyd, Frank" as two separate contractors.

Given the inaccuracies of the historical record, it is only possible to say that there is evidence of anywhere between one and four contractors having worked in both Newark and East Orange. Two contractors clearly show up on the list of contractors in both Newark and East Orange: the Harrison Construction Company and P. H. (Philip) Harrison. As already noted, however, there may have actually been one contractor. Two other names on the East Orange list of contractors are close enough to names on the Newark list of contractors to suggest that they are the same contractors. One contractor in East Orange was Daniel F. Minihan, while in Newark there is record of a contractor named Daniel P. Minnehan. Finally, the East Orange list of contractors includes Maguire, McKnight and Company. While there is no McKnight on the Newark list of contractors, there is a James Maguire as well as a Maguire with no first name.

109. Pierson, *History of the Oranges*, vol. 1, p. 207; vol. 2, pp. 384–386, 412–414.
110. Mary Corbin Sies, "The City Transformed: Nature, Technology, and the Suburban Ideal, 1877–1917," *Journal of Urban History* 14 (November 1987): 89.
111. On the Ivy Hill section immediately before its annexation to Newark, see E. Robinson, J. M. Lathrop, and Thomas Flynn, *Robinson's Atlas of the City of Newark, New Jersey*, 3 vols., vol. 2 (Newark: Elisha Robinson, 1926), plate 33.
112. Paul A. Stellhorn, "Boom, Bust, and Boosterism: Attitudes, Residency, and the Newark Chamber of Commerce, 1920–1941," in William C. Wright, ed., *Urban New Jersey since 1870* (Trenton: New Jersey Historical Commission, 1975), pp. 47–70, quotes on pp. 48, 54.
113. Ibid., pp. 56–72; quote on p. 66.
114. *Newark Sunday Call*, January 1, 1939, in "Newark Wards and Sections—Vailsburg" subject folder, Newark Public Library, New Jersey Room.
115. Arthur M. Louis, "U.S. Cities: The Worst and the Best," *Washington Post*, January 19, 1975, sec. C, pp. 1, 3, quoted in Susan E. Hirsch, "Newark in Its Prime, 1820–1860: Private Wealth and Public Poverty," in Joel Schwartz and Daniel Prosser, eds., *Cities of the Garden State: Essays in the Urban and Suburban History of New Jersey* (Dubuque, IA: Kendall/Hunt Publishing Company, 1977), p. 1n1.

Conclusion: The Evolution of Urban Politics

1. Kenneth T. Jackson, *Crabgrass Frontier: The Suburbanization of the United States* (New York: Oxford University Press, 1985), pp. 268, 277; Thomas L. MacMahon, Larian Angelo, and John Mollenkopf, *Hollow in the Middle: The Rise and Fall of New York City's Middle Class* (New York: New York City Council, Finance Division, December 1997), pp. 25–26; Martin Shefter, *Political Crisis/Fiscal Crisis* (New York: Basic Books, 1985), p. 107.

2. Robert C. Wood with Vladimir V. Ameringer, *1400 Governments: The Political Economy of the New York Metropolitan Region* (Cambridge, MA: Harvard University Press, 1961), pp. 57, 112–113; Michael N. Danielson and Jameson W. Doig, *New York: The Politics of Urban Regional Development* (Berkeley: University of California Press, 1982), p. 78.

3. David Rusk, *Cities without Suburbs*, 2nd ed. (Washington, DC: Woodrow Wilson Center Press, 1995), chs. 1, 3. See also Gerald E. Frug, *City Making: Building Communities without Building Walls* (Princeton, NJ: Princeton University Press, 1999), p. 4; and Jon Teaford, *The Twentieth-Century American City*, 2nd ed. (Baltimore: Johns Hopkins University Press, 1993), who notes that, after World War II, "As in the 1920s numerous civic leaders and political scientists believed that some form of overarching metropolitan government was necessary to ensure efficient rule and area wide planning" (p. 108). A two-tiered scheme that would include metropolitan consolidation has also recently been suggested by J. Eric Oliver, *Democracy in Suburbia* (Princeton, NJ: Princeton University Press, 2001), pp. 211–213.

4. Ann O'M. Bowman and Richard C. Kearney note, for instance, that "regional government seems so rational, yet it has proven to be quite elusive. Voters typically defeat proposals to consolidate city and county government. To reformers, this lack of success is perplexing." *State and Local Government*, 4th ed. (Boston: Houghton Mifflin, 1999), p. 328. For a good review of the current literature on annexation, see Jered B. Carr and Richard C. Feiock, "State Annexation 'Constraints' and the Frequency of Municipal Annexation," *Political Research Quarterly* 54 (June 2001): 459–470.

5. Geoffrey Brennan and James Buchanan, *The Power to Tax: Analytical Foundations of a Fiscal Constitution* (New York: Cambridge University Press, 1980), p. 180; Keith Dowding, Peter John, and Stephen Briggs, "Tiebout: A Survey of the Empirical Literature," *Urban Studies* 31 (1994): 768–775; Charles M. Tiebout, "A Pure Theory of Local Expenditures," *Journal of Political Economy* 64 (October 1956): 416–424.

6. Jane Jacobs, *The Economy of Cities* (New York: Vintage Books, 1970), chs. 2–3; the quote is on p. 59.

7. Seymour J. Mandelbaum, *Boss Tweed's New York* (New York: John Wiley and Sons, 1965), chs. 3–4, 6; James Buchanan and Gordon Tullock, *The Calculus of Consent: Logical Foundations of Constitutional Democracy* (Ann Arbor: University of Michigan Press, 1962), p. 186.

8. *By-laws of the Hoboken Tax-payers' and Citizens' Association, together with a Statement of Facts and Principles, with Which Every Tax-payer Should Be Familiar* (n.p., 1873), p. 15. Emphasis in original.

9. Margaret Crawford, "The World in a Shopping Mall," in Michael Sorkin, ed., *Variations on a Theme Park: The New American City and the End of Public Space* (New York: Hill and Wang, 1992), p. 22.

10. This phrase come from Bryan D. Jones, *Service Delivery in the City: Citizen Demand and Bureaucratic Rules* (New York: Longman, 1980), p. 2, quoted in Martin V. Melosi, *The Sanitary City: Urban Infrastructure in America from Colonial Times to the Present* (Baltimore: Johns Hopkins University Press, 2000), p. 1.

11. Scott Johnson, discussion of Heywood T. Sanders, "Politics and Urban Public Facilities," in Royce Hanson, ed., *Perspectives on Urban Infrastructure* (Washington, DC: National Academy Press, 1984), p. 172.

12. Melosi, *Sanitary City*, p. x.

13. Michael Barker, ed., *Rebuilding America's Infrastructure: An Agenda for the 1980s* (Durham, NC: Duke University Press, 1984).

14. Mary Corbin Sies, "The City Transformed: Nature, Technology, and the Suburban Ideal, 1877–1917," *Journal of Urban History* 14 (November 1987): 89.

15. John Stuart Mill, *Utilitarianism, On Liberty, Considerations on Representative Government*, ed. Geraint Williams (Rutland, VT: Everyman, 1972), pp. 127–130.

Index